A Reader in Religious and Moral Education

A Reader in Religious & Moral Education

Edited by Eric Lord & Charles Bailey

SCM PRESS LTD

334 01359 3

First published 1973
by SCM Press Ltd
56 Bloomsbury Street London
© *SCM Press Ltd 1973*

Printed in Great Britain by
Northumberland Press Limited
Gateshead

Contents

Preface

Debate on the place and purpose of religious education and moral education in schools (including the relationship between these two activities) has been vigorously pursued in Britain during the past decade and has generated a considerable body of writing. Although there are particular social and educational circumstances in this country which have shaped the terms of the discussion in recent years, the debate itself has a long history and an abundant literature. Discussion about religious education in our schools is at least a century old, while conversation about the nature and content of moral education can justly claim Plato and Aristotle among its earlier and distinguished contributors.

Our intention in the present work is relatively simple to explain if more difficult to fulfil adequately: to provide for the general reader a selection of readings which will serve as an introduction to some of the issues which are to the fore in the present stage of the debate.

This intention has guided our selection and arrangement of material. In seeking to provide examples of differing perspectives on some central topics in the present discussion we have had to exercise a measure of judgment about *which* issues are to be regarded as central. Our criterion here has been to focus upon those topics which relate to matters of principle (such as the grounds upon which religious education might claim, or be disqualified from, a place in the curriculum of county schools), and of basic aims and procedure which would determine the shape of religious or moral education in the future. We have sought to isolate some of the central issues at the time of writing. We make no claim that these will prove to be the central issues for all time. In the space at our disposal we could include extracts from only a small part of the literature on the two fields. We have therefore provided some references to fuller treatments or work on related topics for those readers who may wish to push on into the interior.

We are concerned to provide an introduction to some areas under discussion, not to advocate a position in regard to them. However, since the structure of the book may indicate that we have taken up a particular position on one important issue, that of the relationship between religious education and moral education, it may be as well to confirm the reader's suspicions on this matter. While separate treatment of the two fields might have been justified on grounds of convenience alone we do, in fact, believe that religious education and moral education are not to be regarded as alternative names for the same activity but as referring to distinct and separable realms of discourse. This is not at all to deny that there can be a relationship between the two fields. However, the type of statement characteristic of each field is different in its reference and logical form (in the one case a claim to be describing a state of affairs, in the other value-statements) and we think that there is conceptual confusion as well as educational loss in attempts to assimilate either field completely to the other.

Besides any internal distinctiveness they may have, religious education and moral education as curriculum components are at different stages of development; the one an established (if at times anxiety-prone) subject, the other only now gaining recognition in its own right. The issues with some claim to be central in each are different in kind and in the treatment they demand. We have made no attempt at a symmetry of title in the chapters of the two main parts, judging that diversity will more accurately reflect the facts than an imposed uniformity.

We feel that the debate about religious and moral education is important and hope that this introductory Reader may encourage others to contribute to that debate, whether as teacher, parent, administrator or simply citizen. The realm of ends in education needs and merits the attention of those in whose name the educational task of society is carried on.

ERIC LORD
CHARLES BAILEY

PART ONE

Religious Education

1 · Introduction

The tradition in religious education which was embodied in the first generation of post-war Agreed Syllabuses but drew upon earlier experience,[1] sought to introduce children to the Christian way of life by introducing them to the Bible. Though by no means a spent force in the schools this tradition has been challenged by new views which would centre the subject upon the experience of children and the existential problems they face (and so usually referred to as the 'life-centred' approach), or upon the fact of religion as a cultural phenomenon as well as a dimension of experience. Of these alternative positions the first is particularly associated with Ronald Goldman and Harold Loukes, the second (of more recent appearance) with the Lancaster-based Schools Council project directed by Ninian Smart, and the Shap working party on world religions in education of which Smart is a member.[2]

It would no doubt be possible to interpret these newer movements entirely in terms of response to a changing educational, social and religious climate: the operation of an avoidance-mechanism in religion or stages in a slow cooling-out process. That would be to ignore the strong element of conviction which has accompanied their adoption, the feeling each time (not excluding the first) that new and firmer positions have been reached which do greater justice to the nature of religion and the life-tasks facing the young. Thus it is true that the life-centred approach owed something to evidence of a 'conceptual muddle' (in the phrase of Harold Loukes) about the Bible and religion revealed by the investigations associated with Loukes and Goldman;[3] something to the concern for relevance and an outward-looking curriculum which was voiced by the Newsom Report;[4] and something to similar approaches which had occurred earlier in American programmes of church-based religious education.[5] But the approach owed as much to the belief of its chief advocates that religion (certainly in its Christian form) is not something superimposed upon human experience but rooted there and offering an interpretation and integration of that experience.

Alternatively, each shift could be seen as an attempt to compensate for the errors of its predecessor: the life-centred approach correcting the 'body of knowledge' emphasis of the biblical syllabuses, or the case made for objective religious studies in schools carving out a distinctive place for the subject in exchange for the dangerously diffuse appeal to experience. That, however, obscures the positive achievements each may claim. The concentration upon biblical knowledge has at times led to an obsessive fact-accumulation ('what were the three gifts which the Queen of Sheba brought to Solomon?'), but it brought into the schools the fruits of British middle-of-the-road biblical scholarship in the era of C. H. Dodd, T. W. Manson and Vincent Taylor, splendidly represented in a work such as Alan Dale's *New World*.[6] Similarly, though one peril of a multi-faith religious studies programme may be fact accumulation on a more awesome scale, it at least promises deliverance from the religious and cultural parochialism which has dogged us in the schools.

The chapters which follow in this section attempt to map this process of change in religious education as it has shown itself in discussions on the justification, aims and classroom procedures in the subject, with a final chapter on theological perspectives which may have influenced or been consciously adopted by the participants. In contrast to Part III, with its chapter on empirical investigations, we have not in Part I devoted any space to readings from comparable studies of children's religious development or attitudes. The work of Goldman, Loukes, Hyde, Alves[7] and others on these matters is important and has yielded significant evidence, but we think it true to say that this work now provides some of the presuppositions of the participants in the discussion rather than matters in dispute between them. There is undoubtedly room for further research. It is, however, commonly accepted now by teachers in church and county schools alike that children's capacity for grasping religious concepts is linked with their general intellectual development and may be helped or hindered by the kind of teaching they receive, their contacts with institutional religion and their own or parental attitudes to religion; that many children have only a fugitive grasp of biblical facts after years of teaching devoted to imparting them; that neutral or negative attitudes to religious education are more likely to be found among pupils living in some regions than among those in others and that this regional factor is perhaps more significant than an urban/rural distinction. The matters at issue now are philosophical and theological rather than psychological or sociological, though this last field still has unexplored regions.[8]

Our chief concern is with religious education in county schools because it is there that the issues are at their sharpest. However, many of these same issues affect church schools and one of the interesting features of the past decade has been the increasing attention paid to them in Roman Catholic circles. We have, therefore, included reference to Roman Catholic material at a number of points. Helped by developments in the catechetical movement[9] Roman Catholics have become partners in the dialogue on religious education without masking the significant differences between Roman Catholics and county schools in the character and intentions of the teaching of this subject. Because the term 'religious education' is also quite commonly employed in Roman Catholic schools to describe the subject we have used it throughout, except in a few places where the more technical 'catechetics' (which can have a slightly narrow reference) served a useful purpose when distinguishing in the text between Roman Catholic and other standpoints in religious education.

A new and wider view of religious education has emerged from the discussions of the past three decades, as we hope will be evident from the samples of that discussion which we have reproduced. This wider view is likely to prove equally productive of issues requiring clarification, among them three matters which we take up briefly in conclusion relating to the task of the teacher, the intentions of the subject and the understanding of religion with which it operates.

As the report of the British Council of Churches working party on the supply and training of teachers of religious education recognized,[10] the broader view of the subject which has been taken in recent years in both primary and secondary schools increases the range of skills, knowledge, and qualities which are desirable if the teacher is to move with confidence in this enlarged territory. In addition, this broadening raises new questions about the relevance of the teacher's personal stance in matters of religion. Where once the possibility of the subject being taught by a non-committed teacher was a cause for concern, it is not difficult now to conceive of situations where it is the position of the *committed* teacher which is deemed problematical or seen as introducing a potential distorting factor. This might be the case where religious education is taught with the aim of securing a non-evaluative understanding of a number of representative world-views. However, the personal problem for some committed teachers in such a situation (whether their commitment be to a religious or non-religious view of life), is likely to be less that of accepting neutrality or impartiality as a procedure necessary to the enterprise than of resting content with a non-evaluative understanding as its goal.

Secondly, both Bible-centred and life-centred modes in religious education offer, though in differing fashion, a way of interpreting or de-coding experience. They say to the pupil in effect, 'Your experience has meaning, signifies something beyond the experience itself.' The second mode explicitly encourages the pupil to say how *he* reads the signals and is to that extent 'open', though in practice it has especially commended the Christian reading of experience to his attention.[11] An approach through the study of world religions, by contrast, seeks to describe rather than to interpret. The emphasis there may be upon grasping in a value-free fashion something of the variety of interpretations which are current rather than upon showing their bearing on the pupil's own preoccupations. The one type of approach is primarily concerned with a hermeneutic of experience, the other with a phenomenology of religion. As may be seen in the extract from Working Paper 36 in chapter three, the Lancaster secondary project, accepting Ninian Smart's dictum that 'religious education must transcend the informative', has sought to hold to both the descriptive and 'personal quest' dimensions. Certainly both have a claim, but the problem of operating in the classroom in a way that does justice to both intentions may not be easily solved.

Closely related to that problem is the third, namely whether religious education is to be shaped by reference to an inclusive or exclusive definition of religion.[12] An *inclusive* definition of religion will tend to embrace within religion (and thus within religious education) everything in human life which appears to have an ultimate reference and will reach out to such matters as the adoption of personal values, the choice of a life-style and so on. The life-centred approach plainly makes use of an inclusive definition of this kind. An *exclusive* definition will tend to restrict the label 'religion' to certain phenomena marked off by particular characteristics – as in Ninian Smart's analysis of the dimensions of religion, quoted in chapter five. An objective or descriptive emphasis in religious education (such as that associated with the Shap group) will be likely to employ an exclusive definition of religion, though the Lancaster project seeks freedom to move between the two.

Dangers for religious education lurk in both types of definition: the danger in the inclusive form that it may end up by claiming everything for religion and drown in its own inclusiveness or decline into a form of social engineering trailing vestigial clouds of supernaturalism; the danger in the exclusive definition that in concentrating upon technical religious material it may quite miss the questions which concern the pupil as he searches for his own *gestalt* on life. The problem for an inclusive emphasis in religious education is how to combine inclusiveness with distinctiveness – how to be inclusive without disappearing, and for an exclusive emphasis how to combine academic rigour with relevance.

2 · Justifying the Subject

For more than half a century after the 1870 Education Act the question of what kind of religious education there should be in county schools, and indeed the propriety of including it at all, produced sharp controversy.[1] In view of this background it is striking to notice, in educational writing on the subject in the decade after 1944, the comparative absence of discussion of its justification, beyond reference to what is regarded as the evident need to recall the nation to the faith which it accepted but had come to neglect. Some books of the period have to the contemporary reader the appearance of starting in the middle: addressing themselves to fine details of method or questions of procedure in the subject as though its justification and its character as education into Christianity would be taken for granted among all reasonable men, so rendering any further giving of reasons a needless labour.

At least three factors have changed the situation. First, the appearance of a view, expressed in publications during the 'sixties by secularist and humanist groups but shared also by some Christians, that we now have an open society in Britain and that it is therefore inappropriate for one world-view to have a monopoly in the state schools.

Secondly, changing methods in the schools, beginning with the shift from Bible-centred to problem-centred approaches at the secondary stage and the slightly later parallel movement towards thematic teaching for younger children, have led to a feeling that to regard religious education as the transmission of knowledge about the Bible and Christian faith, with that as its justification, is untrue to practice and inhibiting to further progress. The case for the subject in future, it is felt, can rest upon what Harold Loukes in the first excerpt describes as 'open ground' – the genuinely educational contribution which religious education can make to the development of the young.

Thirdly, the need which Loukes recognized for justifications in educational terms has become more urgent with the application of analytical philosophy to educational discussion. Practitioners in the philosophy of education have subjected to their urbane scrutiny religious education's claim to an admission ticket to the curriculum. In a paper to which we make further reference in chapter six, Paul Hirst has argued that religious statements fall into the realm of beliefs, not 'publicly verifiable knowledge'. Therefore, the subject must content itself in schools with describing those beliefs rather than commending them. This view is reflected in the excerpt from R. F. Dearden. In a scrutiny which is perhaps more abrasive than urbane of the association of religion with values in primary education he seeks to show that without some such restriction religious education is indistinguishable from indoctrination.[2]

The third extract is from those paragraphs of the Durham Report which set out a case for religious education in county schools. The Report shows awareness of all three of the factors mentioned above, and Appendix B of the Report is a consideration by Basil Mitchell of the concept of 'indoctrination'. The section from which the excerpt is taken is headed 'The Educational Argument'. The heading is significant since it follows three other paragraphs in which arguments for retention based upon reference to tradition, to Christianity's part in the formation of western culture, or to religious education as an essential basis for moral education are each considered and found lacking in force. By 1970 the point about justification on open ground had been well taken.

Much of the writing in this country on the place of religious education as an element in general education has been occasioned by the need to meet or anticipate objections to its presence there. This has perhaps limited the freedom of English writers to think in terms of the balance and intention of the curriculum as a whole rather than providing an apologetic for one part of it.

The final excerpt of this section is from the American writer Philip Phenix. It shows an attempt to construct a philosophy of the curriculum on the basis of the fundamental pattern of meanings which (Phenix holds) characterize human existence and of which religion is one. It will be seen that Phenix distinguishes six such realms of meaning. Apart from the self-explanatory *Aesthetics* and *Ethics* he labels the others

Symbolics – which includes mathematics and ordinary language

Empirics – the natural and human sciences

Synnoetics – which he defines as 'personal knowledge', the realm of human relationships in which the emphasis is upon inter-subjectivity and 'I-Thou' relations, and

Synoptics – history, religion and philosophy.

Phenix claims that the synoptic disciplines have an integrative function, bringing together meanings from all the realms into a unified perspective. In the case of religion he says that 'the common element uniting all the realms is ultimacy ... which stands in contrast to concepts of finitude, the relative, limitation, partiality, and the like.'[3]

Though still perhaps less well known in this country than the rather different analysis of the 'forms of knowledge' offered by Paul Hirst[4] the ideas of Phenix have figured in recent writing on curriculum theory.[5] Apart from their intrinsic interest they have the merit, as far as religious education is concerned, of grounding the subject – as Loukes and Durham saw to be necessary – upon something more substantial and convincing than an appeal to a cultural auld lang syne.

Harold Loukes · *Teenage Religion*

Harold Loukes, *Teenage Religion*, SCM Press 1961, pp.96-99

The defence of Christian education must be made to rest on the same open ground as that of all our education: it must seek to perform some task which would be accepted as *healthy*, contributing to wholeness of the personality, and would not be judged by the conscientious agnostic to be limiting or hampering. Education offers an enlargement of personal horizons, in the understanding that there is more to the world than the untutored eye perceives, and in the learning of skills by which men and women respond in greatness. Religious education, too, must be concerned with the enlargement of personal horizons, with what there is to be seen beyond the obvious, and with the power of the seeing eye. Faith, wrote the schoolboy, means believing what you know isn't true. Faith, wrote Dean Inge, is the resolution to stand or fall by the noblest hypothesis. Our religious education must side with the

Dean rather than the schoolboy; for none, even in a secular society, will cavil at the presentation of a creative vision.

The 'open' defence of the presentation of the Christian world view is not that it is 'true' (which merely means that Christians say it is true, and is therefore, in an open society, tautological) but that it is 'larger' than any other view. We are all materialists in the sense that the obvious realities seem both obvious and real. But then we are all pre-copernican in the sense that as far as we are concerned the sun goes round the earth. And as the scientist has enlarged our pre-copernican assumptions, so the Christian seeks to enlarge our material assumptions. Merely to ask the question 'Did God create the world?' is to push out horizons, for it raises at once the other question: 'Or did the world just happen?' To ask, 'Is Jesus divine, and does he represent an intention of God for humanity?' is to raise the other question: 'Or may man be just what he pleases?' And to consider the doctrine of the Holy Spirit is to ask: 'In the apparent hopelessness of the human predicament is there really hope or is there really no hope.'

No theory of education can stand which rules out the possibility of these questions being raised; no one can believe that a man is the worse for having faced them; and no one can object to the search for nobility among the grand hypotheses of the human mind. What *can* be objected, by the conscientious agnostic, is that while children are too young to judge, they should not be indoctrinated in such a way as to reduce their powers of judgement in the years to come. But this is no argument against including in the school curriculum the Christian view of man and his meaning. No one can be the worse for having met it: to meet it squarely is an exercise in freedom. Even on the narrowest libertarian grounds, a man is free to choose only if he knows what he chooses between.

This argument does not constitute an attempt to find a highest common factor among all shades of opinion in the community, by way of producing a harmless, universal syllabus of religious instruction that no one can object to. It is an attempt to clear the grounds on which a Christian must stand if he is to be honest in his acceptance of the charge laid upon him. This he must do, not merely because he lives in an open society, with no more authority than that society confers upon him, but because his duty as a teacher is first to the children under his care. These children are soon to be men and women, out in the open society; and if when they arrive there, they find themselves on totally different ground from where they stood in school, they will abandon everything they stood by.

The common ground between the two worlds, of school and life, is to be found in the continuing growth of the child's personality. In the adult world it is a man's business to be a person; in school it is the child's business to mature. The secondary school child is well aware of this, and seizes eagerly on any opportunities of acquiring such knowledge and skill as demonstrably add to his personal stature and give promise of adult effectiveness. Vocational interest runs high because the boy sees himself as a worker instead of a dependant, or the girl sees herself in her home. Problems of etiquette and personal relations assume importance because the youngster is about to be responsible for his own effectiveness. And as any sixth form teacher knows, there is an interest ready to be awakened in the ideas of adult life, often appearing as a snobbish interest in the U and non-U of the intellectual world, but yet to be recognized as important, a uniform to be worn even if not yet a true garment of the soul.

What the adolescent is asking is to be brought up against the kind of thought that will help him to maturity, to know the kind of question that men ask, to practise thinking as men think, and to gain the insight into his own condition and the human condition at large, that a man must have if he is to stand without fear. It is this that lies beneath the desire of our commentators for a more 'adultish' treatment of religion and their satisfaction when they get it. 'We don't always learn about the Bible, but other things which grown-ups discuss.' They are right to want it, and it is the school's business to provide it.

But this particular commentator was wrong in implying that the Bible is not a 'thing which grown-ups discuss'. The case for scripture teaching rests on the fact that the Bible treats of the great themes that truly mature adults must discuss. There are three fields of thought and experience which a mature person must enter with his eyes open, which as a child he could afford to ignore. He must understand something of the nature of other human beings, their needs and dreams, so that he can act responsibly towards them, and win response from them to himself; he must understand something of his own nature, because he can no longer leave the control of it to others; and he must find some sort of meaning in the chaos of experience, for he can no longer live at second hand with the selection of experience provided by his parents and teachers.

In other terms, the mature person must deal for himself with problems of human relationships and ideals, problems of personal responsibility, and problems of meaning.

This is substantially the picture that emerges from G. W. Allport's study of personality[6] in which he describes three 'marks of maturity'. 'First,' he says, 'a variety of interests which concern themselves with ideals, objects and values ... Second, the ability to objectify oneself, to be effective and insightful about one's own life ... Finally, some unifying philosophy of life, not necessarily religious in type, nor articulated in words, nor entirely complete. But without the direction and coherence supplied by some dominant integrative pattern any life seems fragmented and aimless.'

If we accept these 'marks of maturity' as broadly valid, they enable us to see more clearly the significance of religious education, which becomes a means of promoting a mature religion. In so far as the Bible and the witness of the Church are concerned with the human condition, in its loneliness and its community, and are presented in such a way as to contribute to maturity, they can be defended with confidence as a direct meeting of the needs of adolescence.

The special task of the secondary school may be defined as an examination of religious concepts, directed towards the shedding of infantile forms and the acceptance of adult ones. This would at once cut through most of the difficulties aired by our young critics, as it does the more searching objections of older critics. For as Allport later observes, 'Most of the criticism of religion is directed to its immature forms.'[7] This is certainly true of Freud's attack upon it. Religion, he argues, is an infantile fixation. It is a means whereby men and women dream out their unfulfilled desires, escape from their own conflicts, and shirk the realities of the world. It is true that the immature will use their religion in this way, as they will use anything else, from film stars to sex; but this does not mean that religion is itself an illusion, any more than film-stars or sex are illusions. The business of the school is to encourage growing-up, in religion as in everything else: to face in a mature manner the ultimate issues of an adult life.

R. F. Dearden · *The Philosophy of Primary Education*

R. F. Dearden, *The Philosophy of Primary Education*, Routledge & Kegan Paul 1968, pp.55-59

The status of religion in schools is becoming increasingly problematic as the meaning and truth of religious doctrines come to be questioned, inside the churches as well as among those who have dissociated themselves from anything to do with religion. Whether contemporary theology will be able to reconstruct from this a set of doctrines which is both intelligible and convincing remains for the future to show, though there are many who would argue that the attempt at such a reconstruction must be misconceived. Some of the views presented by modern theologians are certainly attractive, but on the other hand it is often hard to see why they should be thought to be religious, at least in any sense of that word which implies God, the divinity of Christ and immortality. This problem of meaning and truth in religion is one which we shall take up again later.

One thing, however, is very clear. It is indisputable that the doctrines of religion have been brought into serious question by many who have gone to the trouble to reflect on them carefully and critically, and whose views are therefore worth rather more than are those of people who, on this matter at least, are no more than the echoing repositories of what they have been told to believe in childhood. And if, as is indisputable, the truth of the doctrines of religion is seriously doubted, on excellent grounds, then it is an objectionable form of indoctrination to propagate these doctrines in common, public schools as if they were unquestionably true. One might also add that it would be equally unjustified to refer to them as if they were unquestionably false.

It may be argued that 'indoctrination' is, essentially, not so much a matter of doctrines and of doubts about their truth, as of getting people to believe things in such a way that nothing, not even good counter arguments, will shake those beliefs. This may well be so, but if it is so, then it is very natural that 'indoctrination' should have its main application in teaching such beliefs as those of religion. It is especially here that groups of people have an interest in establishing beliefs which will then be held with a conviction which the doubts and open disbelief of others will not shake.

'Catching them young' will obviously be a highly expedient policy for the indoctrinator. Nor, it may be added, is there any substance in the reply sometimes made to this that *everybody* indoctrinates, even the mathematics teacher. For first, whatever other sorts of teaching are *called*, important differences from the teaching of religion remain, and secondly, it does not in any case meet a charge to plead that someone else is up to the same thing.

This is not, of course, any objection at all to teaching *about* religion, which need imply only a belief on one's own part that certain things are the beliefs of others. This could be done by an atheist without any loss of intellectual integrity, just as a religious person could teach about Marxism. Moreover, there are good cultural and historical grounds for teaching *about* religion. But the schools do more than this. 'Many teachers openly admit that they attempt to attach their pupils to some worshipping community'.[8] But prayer and worship are hollow, meaningless activities unless certain beliefs are held about the object to which they are addressed, namely God. One cannot pray or worship *about* religion; such activities are logically impossible apart from the presupposition of an actual belief in God. The external forms of prayer and worship can, of course, be compelled, and recalcitrant children can, individually or collectively, rebel with a 'prayer strike', or be punished for not praying, as sometimes happens in secondary schools, but this could be regarded as valuable only by one who esteemed cynicism a virtue.

The objectionable character of religious indoctrination, which derives from inducing conviction in the truth of beliefs which are in fact highly questionable, has certain further consequences. First, it puts an aspect of education in a liberal democracy exactly on the same footing as a corresponding aspect of education in totalitarian states, and hence removes the ground of objection to these totalitarian practices. Yet the attempt to deform the growth of rationality by appropriating an area of belief for the indoctrinator is as objectionable when the indoctrination is religious as when it is political. For example, one cannot view without misgivings a situation which leads Plowden to recommend that the 'teacher should not try to conceal from his pupils the fact that others take a different view' (Plowden Report, para. 572).

Secondly, religious indoctrination is incompatible with respect for personal autonomy, in that it positively encourages dependence on authority for what one is to believe. It is a characteristic but shameless inconsistency on the part of some child-centred theorists that they encourage questioning, testing truth for oneself, and critical acceptance of beliefs in all fields except that of religion. Here they capitulate, and even gladly, to authoritarianism. Thus children 'should not be confused by being taught to doubt before faith is established' (Plowden Report, para. 572). But if they do ask questions, how should one reply? 'They should be given an honest answer' (loc. cit.). What are the actual alternatives that render this particular recommendation necessary?

A third possible consequence of indoctrination, and of its violation of autonomy by 'getting faith established first', is that it runs the risk of unfortunate collapse should those in whom faith has been so established later come to doubt. The subsequent collapse would be highly unfortunate, in the first place because of the general distress attendant on such a disorientation, with its sense that 'everything has become meaningless', and in the second place because morality will have been bound up with the now disavowed beliefs. The indoctrinator cannot dissociate himself from some responsibility for this state of affairs. In part, at least, he has himself been the cause of this distress, a reflection which ought to give him pause in his view of himself as a distributor of unqualified benefits.

The consequences for the teachers themselves are hardly less disagreeable, since the present unsatisfactory arrangements breed frustration, hypocrisy, timidity and a loss of intellectual integrity. Teachers who dislike giving religious instruction, or leading prayer and worship, are presented with unfair choices. In the classroom, they have to choose between either doing something that they detest, or loading colleagues with extra work and causing a general disturbance of arrangements. In respect of their legitimate ambitions, teachers lacking religious convictions must in practice choose between furtive concealment of this fact and an honesty that may well block promotion (see Plowden Report, 491, section 4, and para. 563).

Before blaming those who choose furtive concealment, one should look at the unjust institutional pressures which make this a condition of their advancement, just as when children are cheating a great deal one should look at the classroom régime as well as at the individual child's morals. Finally, a teacher who lacks religious conviction but who does achieve a headship must then either exercise his ingenuity in evading the legal requirements for the daily act of worship, or succumb to all sorts of rationalization in order to preserve his self-respect.

An apparent counter to these arguments for ceasing to indoctrinate or initiate into religious practices, and so do no more than teach *about* religion, is provided in the Plowden Report. It cites some opinion surveys which show there still to be a majority of teachers and public in favour of religious teaching, though only about one-fifth of them are also in favour of their own active church membership. But the Plowden Report's reasoning here looks less like reliance on a principle of argument than picking up a handy stick which has a certain usefulness. For elsewhere in the Report, in connection with corporal punishment, the *same* conditions hold (in fact, absolutely overwhelmingly and convinced majorities in this case) but the *contrary* conclusion is drawn, namely to go counter to majority opinion and lead the way to change. 'We believe ... that the primary schools, as in so much else, should lead public opinion, rather than follow it' (Plowden Report, para. 750).

But if there is one thing that a principle of argument will not allow, it is having the conclusion whichever way it currently happens to suit. Unfortunately, one cannot, as D. J. O'Connor justly observes, 'claim the benefits of reason without acknowledging its risks'.[9] Our own view is that the primary schools should, for the epistemological and moral reasons already given, lead the way on religion, for which a sufficient legal change at the present juncture would probably be that what is at present an obligation be reduced to permission.

Questions of what is true and right are never settled by an appeal to the fact of a majority opinion. That is to appeal to who says so rather than to what makes it so. This is not to deny that determining what is true and right is often very difficult, and that it may sometimes be preferable to abide by the majority's wishes rather than run the dangers of riding roughshod over those with whom one disagrees. Even those whose views one takes to be unconsidered or in error are still persons, and hence deserving of respect. But since the present discussion is an attempt to change opinion by argument, and not an actual political attempt to change practice by coercive legislative acts, it stands in no need of respecting existing majority wishes but can simply urge what seem to be highly relevant considerations in this matter. The indoctrination of religious beliefs and the initiation of children into religious practices will therefore be assumed to be no proper part of the primary school curriculum.

It will also be assumed that they ought to be separated from such proper devices for getting institutional cohesion at the school assembly.

Durham Report · *The Fourth R*

The Fourth R, The Durham Report on Religious Education, National Society/SPCK 1970, pp.98-103

The Educational Argument

201 All major educational reports in recent years have made it plain that the principal argument for religious education in county schools is that it is a subject with its own inherent educational value and must have its place on the curriculum for educational reasons. We entirely agree.

202 As has already been stated in ch. 1, this view found expression in the Spens Report of 1938 on Secondary Education, where the affirmation was made that 'no boy or girl can be counted as properly educated unless he or she has been made aware of the fact of the existence of a religious interpretation of life'. This essentially educational approach is developed by the Crowther and Newsom Reports.

The teenagers with whom we are concerned need, perhaps before all else, to find a faith to live by. They will not all find the same faith and some will not find any. Education can and should play some part in their search. It can assure them that there is something to search for and it can show them where to look and what other men have found (Crowther, p. 44).

The best schools give their pupils something which they do not get elsewhere, something which they know they need when they receive it, though they had not realised the lack before. We believe that this can be, and usually is, given in a way which does justice to the mixed society in which we live, recognising the range and degrees of religious belief and practice to be found in it, and respecting the right of the individual conscience to be provided with the material on which freely to decide its path (Newsom, pp. 55–6).

203 Very broadly, what lies behind these statements are certain assumptions about the nature of man, about religion, and about the educational process. In former ages man was thought of as body and soul. Nowadays it is a good deal more difficult to find a generally acceptable formula. To the behaviourist, man is a complicated piece of social patterning; others see him as a piece of mobile biochemistry, wholly part of the natural order and subject to control by external stimuli. Very many people, and all Christians, would see this as inadequate, untrue to the richness and depth of human experience. Man is a phenomenon, a complex structure of physical, emotional, and psychical characteristics and there are aspects of his being which are not adequately explained by any reductionist theories, whether in science or psychology.

204 Man is a creature who finds himself perplexed with the mystery of his existence. He knows that he is, and ponders why he is, what he is, and what he is for. From the start of recorded history he has sought to find answers to the enigma of his origin and destiny, he has puzzled about the meaning and purpose of his life. He has sought explanations for his pain, his suffering, and the fact of his finitude. He has sought value systems to provide dignity and direction to his life. The great religions of the world find their frame of reference within these ultimate questions which man has asked and continues to ask – questions which are part of the human condition.

205 The existence of a religious interpretation of life is a fact of history and of present human experience. There are many millions of men and women throughout the world who find through their religious beliefs a deep meaning and purpose for their lives and a system of values by which their lives can be lived. There appears to be a 'spiritual dimension' in man's nature which requires to be expressed by 'religion' of one kind or another. By religion we mean some pattern of belief and behaviour related to the questions of man's ultimate concern. For some, it is an Eastern religion; for some it is Christianity; for others it is one of the secular creeds of the West, for example Marxism; for others it is agnostic humanism; for many it may be little more than moral stoicism. Man seems to have to find 'a faith to live by', however noble, or simple, or debased. Young people share in the human condition. They should have some opportunity to learn that religion is a feature of this condition, and for some men a deeply significant area of human knowledge and experience.

206   But is it right that this opportunity should be provided within the processes of formal education? Should this not be wholly the responsibility of the religious organizations and the home? One of the more obvious truisms to be culled from the writings of the educational philosophers is that a distinction has to be observed between training and education. An 'educated' person is one who has achieved something more than mastery of a craft or skill, or the assimilation of a body of knowledge. In recent years many descriptions of the purposes of education in western society have been advanced. 'The education of the whole man', 'education for growth', 'education for self-fulfilment', and so on. It would be possible to embark on extended arguments to show that the teaching of religion could be given a place in the educational processes envisaged by these descriptions. But it would be more profitable to limit the discussion to a concept of education which is influential at the present time.

207   By reaction from philosophies of education which were influenced by metaphysical thinking, a recent description of the educational process sees education as initiation. It is the task of the teacher to initiate the young into bodies of knowledge, activities, modes of thought and conduct, which are believed by society to have 'worthwhileness'. 'Education implies standards, not necessarily aims ... it consists of initiating others into activities, modes of conduct and thought which have standards written into them by reference to which it is possible to act, think and feel with varying degrees of skill, reverence and taste.'[10]

208   If education is to be conceived in this way – as initiation into public traditions – it can be reasonably argued that public religious traditions are candidates for inclusion if such religious traditions are thought by society to possess the required criteria of 'worthwhileness'. This process will involve rigorous thought and study, for the only way of mastering the 'language' of any form of thought or activity is by being first initiated into its 'literature'. Thus the development of religious appreciation and understanding will involve the close study of texts and beliefs, forms of worship, social and ethical teaching.

209   R. S. Peters has suggested that 'to be educated is not to have arrived at a destination: it is to travel with a different view'.[11] We think that an understanding of the religious interpretation of life should be a feature of this view.

210 The argument so far has been that the nature of man, the fact of the existence of a religious interpretation of life, and the nature and purpose of the educational process, point to the need for some form of religious education. The term 'religious education' has been given, so far, very wide and general meaning. Does it follow from this that religious education should take the form it does in schools in England and Wales at present? The argument thus far might be taken to imply that, while religious education should take place, it should be a generalized study of all world religions and belief systems. In short, why should it take place in schools, and why should it be mainly the study of Christianity?

211 Religious education has its place on the school curriculum because it draws attention to a significant area of human thought and activity. A curriculum which excluded religion would seem to proclaim that religion has not been as real in men's lives as science, or politics, or economics. By omission it would appear to deny that religion has been and still is important in man's history. To the question, would something be lost if religious education were excluded from the school curriculum, we must answer, definitely yes.

212 If then religious education should continue to have its place on the curricula of English schools because a curriculum without it would be seriously deficient, why should it remain as specifically Christian? The comparative study of religions and other belief systems will certainly have an important place in the religious education of many pupils. More will be said of this later, when the content of the religious education curriculum is being examined. Nevertheless, it must be recognized that the kind of understanding which is involved in religious education, as we shall later show, can be achieved only if pupils study the religious tradition or traditions of their own particular culture. For the great majority of pupils in England and Wales this is the Christian faith.*

213 The claims of religions differ profoundly in certain respects

---

* We fully recognize that Jewish parents will wish their children to be educated in the Jewish faith. We further recognize that the parents of some immigrant children will wish them to be taught their particular faith.

and so do the cultures which they have influenced. All serious religious thought and experience has arisen within a tradition and cannot be understood apart from it. Hence there cannot be a religious education which is concerned simply with religion as such. It would be educationally unrealistic to propose that all pupils in the schools of England and Wales should study the Bible and, *as well*, the *Qur'ān*, the *Bhagavadgītā*, the *Upaniṣads*, and the Buddhist scriptures. This would inevitably lead to extreme superficiality, even if there were enough teachers possessing the relevant qualifications. Religious education, to be of any value, must involve the thorough study of some particular religion. In the final analysis, the decision as to which particular religion will be studied will depend not only on what religion is prevalent in the culture, but on the extent to which that religion is believed to be true.

214   The argument has thus been that religious education, in one form or another, contributes something of value to the education of children and young persons and that the content of the curriculum in this country should consist mainly of the exploration of the literature and beliefs of the Christian faith. This, in the very broadest terms, is the educational argument for religious education which finds expression in the various official reports of recent years. What has been said so far in this chapter is only the barest outline of an argument which could be given a great deal of detailed expansion.

215   If religious education is placed in this general educational context, what should be its aim? The aim of religious education should be to explore the place and significance of religion in human life and so to make a distinctive contribution to each pupil's search for a faith by which to live.

Philip H. Phenix · *Realms of Meaning*

Philip H. Phenix, *Realms of Meaning*, pp.267-271. Copyright © 1964 by Philip Phenix. Used with permission of McGraw-Hill Book Company

In Part One it was argued that human beings are distinguished by their capacity for meanings and that there are six basic realms of meaning that are characteristically human. In Part Two the fundamental patterns of meaning in these six realms were set forth. In

Part Three an attempt will be made to draw some conclusions regarding curriculum on the basis of these considerations about human nature and the patterns of meaning.

We begin by asking: What does a person need to know? What is the appropriate scope of the course of study that ought to be provided? The answers to such questions depend upon many factors, including the unique personality of the student, the social and cultural context in which he lives, and the available resources for teaching and learning. More important than all of these, however, is the end to which education is directed. For example, the recommended curriculum aimed at technical efficiency differs from one that considers the delights of contemplation to be the highest good.

The premise of the present argument is that the highest good to be served by education is the fullest possible realization of the distinctively human capacities and that these capacities consist in the life of meaning. Hence, the course of study should be such as to maximize meanings.

Then the question becomes: What should be taught in order to maximize meanings? What provides for the fulfillment of the life of meaning? There are five principal answers to such questions, and each has certain merits. The first answer is that fulfillment consists in *mastery*. The meaningful life is that in which the person finds *one thing* to do and learns to do it very well. The realization of existence lies in *depth* of understanding. The wealth of possible meanings is so great that a person has to choose the one channel into which he can pour his energies with maximum effect. People who scatter themselves in many directions dissipate their powers and never transcend superficiality. Most of the outstanding achievements of mankind have been made by people who have developed a single line of competence to a point sufficient to yield something really new. The all-round person can only follow the paths laid out by the single-minded pioneers.

According to this view, the scope of the curriculum for any given person should be narrow rather than broad. Each person should be highly trained in a specialty instead of comprehensively as a generalist. Depth of knowledge and skill should be the goal, rather than superficial acquaintance with a variety of fields.

A second position is that fulfillment consists in *belonging to a community* in which the various meanings are realized. The significance of each person's life results from participation in the meaning of the social whole. The good life is not conceived as depth of mastery, as in the first view, but in loyal membership in the social body.

From this standpoint the course of study to be followed depends upon a person's place within the social complex. Each individual plays his part and is required to develop competences that best equip him to contribute to the whole. Unless his function is that of comprehensive social planning, he does not need to cultivate meanings in other than the special sphere in which he serves the community. Nor does he need to plumb more deeply in any given field than his social position requires. This view results in specialized curricula for most students, usually with less depth than the first position entails and with particular provision for understanding the nature of the social enterprise as a whole.

A third answer to the question about fulfillment is that it consists in *many-sidedness*. The desirable goal is well-roundedness and variety of interests, and the curriculum should be correspondingly broad and diverse. Instead of specializing in one field, it is said, the student should gain some understanding of many different fields. Rather than developing one skill to a high degree, he should be encouraged to gain some competence in a number of different types of activity.

A fourth position is that the fulfillment of meaning consists in the *integrity* of the person. The main objective is to secure a coordination of whatever meanings are acquired into a coherent whole. The evil to be avoided is inner division and partiality. Each person should possess a sufficient range of meanings in his own self without depending for the significance of his life upon his position in the social whole. That is, he should become relatively independent, with rich inner resources for meeting a variety of situations and exigencies. From this standpoint the most important consideration in the curriculum is that the studies form an interrelated whole and not a collection of unrelated pieces. The materials of learning also need to be capable of assimilation by the particular person so that they may contribute to his integral selfhood.

A fifth and final view is that fulfillment consists in gaining a certain *quality* of understanding, that the ideal of life has to do with quality rather than with depth, participation, extensiveness, or coherence. According to this position, there are certain essentials which need to be learned, and beyond them everything else is unimportant. In this case the breadth of the curriculum depends upon what it is deemed essential to know, whether a few things or many.

Fortunately, the foregoing positions are not mutually exclusive. It is not necessary to choose one and reject the others. Since in modern civilization study extends over many years, sometimes for the greater part of a lifetime, it is possible to achieve fulfillment of meaning in more than one way. Indeed, in the long run it is possible to achieve fulfillment in all the ways suggested above. A person can attain high mastery of one field and good understanding of many other fields. He can achieve both inner integrity and satisfaction in belonging to a larger whole. He can pursue essential understandings without minimizing the significance of less than essential ones.

The analysis in Part One suggests that human nature itself supplies the clue to the minimal scope of the curriculum. Human beings are characterized by a few basic types of functioning. They use symbols, they abstract and generalize, they create and perceive interesting objects, they relate to each other personally, they make judgments of good and evil, they reenact the past, they seek the ultimate, and they comprehensively analyze, evaluate, and synthesize. These are the universal, pervasive, and perennial forms of distinctively human behavior. They are the foundation for all civilized existence. All of them are deeply woven into the texture of life whenever it transcends the level of biological and social survival.

Furthermore, the analysis of Part Two shows that these fundamental types of human understanding are interdependent. No one realm of meaning can be perfected without the aid of the others. All six realms form a complex unity of interrelated yet relatively autonomous domains.

It follows that the curriculum should at least provide for learnings in all six of the realms of meaning: symbolics, empirics, esthetics, synnoetics, ethics, and synoptics. Without these a person cannot realize his essential humanness. If any one of the six is missing, the person lacks a basic ingredient in experience. They are to the fulfillment of human meanings something like what basic nutrients are to the health of an organism. Each makes possible a particular mode of functioning without which the person cannot live according to his own true nature.

This sixfold curriculum answers to the fifth or qualitative criterion of fulfillment. Since the six realms form a whole integrated by the synoptic meanings, it also satisfies the fourth criterion, of wholeness. Similarly, it indicates the need for a varied curriculum with at least the six fundamental components. What of the other two criteria – of mastery and belonging? Is the six-realm curriculum consistent with them? It might seem at first that concentration on mastering one field would exclude concern for anything else. Such is not the case, because *the basic realms are such that all of them are required if a person is to achieve the highest excellence in anything at all.* They are essential in the sense that a person cannot do his best in any human undertaking without some understanding of all the realms.

For example, a person cannot attain maximum mastery in any scientific field without having some competence in language, the arts, personal relations, morals, and synoptics, since scientific activity in its own structure includes symbolic, esthetic, personal, ethical, and integrative factors. Again, a person cannot attain the highest mastery in the arts unless he knows how to communicate, understands facts and generalizations, relates insightfully with others and with himself, has a sensitive conscience, and has achieved a certain perspective on the whole. Similar conclusions hold for the mastery of any of the other departments of human activity.

It follows that learning in the six realms is necessary even when the goal of specialized mastery guides the construction of the curriculum. Concentration should not proceed to the point of neglecting any of the essential human capacities, since the fullest mastery itself requires all these abilities. The same is true of the curriculum based on fulfillment through communal participation. A person cannot understand his place in the whole and behave accordingly unless he is aware of the basic functions of civilized man. He must possess the powers of speech, description, creation, relation, choice, and integration if he is to play a significant part in the human commonwealth. In other words, he has to become essentially human himself if he is to participate in a meaningful civilized order.

The foregoing concept of the six essential domains in which every person needs to develop understanding and skill is the basis for the idea of *general education*. The curriculum of general education contains those provisions for learning that are necessary for the development of the person in his essential humanity.

3 · Formulating Aims

The 1944 Education Act and the discussions surrounding its religious provisions seemed, especially to those in the churches, to yield a clear and large aim for religious education: the communication of the Christian faith in schools as preparation for citizenship in a Christian society. True, many things had helped to prepare the ground for this position, not least the experiences of the war which were read as confirming the need to retain and strengthen the Christian basis of society for which T. S. Eliot had argued in 1938.[1]

Nevertheless, that such a view of Britain as a Christian nation could be taken as agreed, and such an undertaking in securing its future be embarked upon in the schools was remarkable, as those who had pressed the case for religious education recognized. In his 1944 Bampton Lectures on 'Christian Education' Spencer Leeson, who had been close to the discussions, acknowledged that the aim was clearer and larger than might have been expected, going well beyond the passage from the Spens Report of 1938 which had spoken of the need to make pupils 'aware of the fact of the existence of a religious interpretation of life'. As Spencer Leeson saw it, speaking of the provision in the Act for religious education and the daily act of worship:

> It is not now a question of saying that every educated person ought to know the Christian interpretation of life. That stage has been passed. Parliament has declared by and through this requirement the will of the nation that it shall be a Christian nation.[2]

This ambitiously simple aim, to which it was assumed the Christian character of the school as a whole and not only the overt religious education and daily assembly would contribute, ran into sizeable difficulties of practice and principle. It became apparent especially in urban schools that many pupils represented groups in the population where, though residual religion persisted, there had long been no live connection with institutional religion. Neither they nor their parents acted as though they accepted the Christian faith as regulative for life and conduct. Moreover, they showed a marked lack of interest in having any deficiency in these matters filled out. The school leavers of 1950 were inclined, like their successors sampled in a government social survey in 1968, to assign religious education to that capacious category of subject labelled 'useless and boring'.[3]

It was hard, and some argued it was downright wrong (their argument given added force by the arrival of immigrants of other faiths), to view the task of religious education as training for Christian citizenship. If at first it was supposed that the difficulties for religious education were chiefly confined to the secondary school, that notion was shown to be too simple with Ronald Goldman's empirical investigation of children's religious thinking – though warning of the dangers attending the attempt to do 'too much too soon' in the subject had been given by J. W. D. Smith as far back as 1936.[4] Ideas of what children *ought* to know in matters of religion had now to reckon with what they *could* know. Religious education in the county school was obliged to think again about its aims and to bring them into closer touch with educational and social reality. The readings in this chapter provide examples of this process of revision and adjustment.

In the excerpt from his *Readiness for Religion* Ronald Goldman sees the personal needs of children providing the basis for religious education as also, he believes for the rest of education. The general thesis of education as a needs-satisfaction process has since been subjected to some damaging criticism.[5] However, the idea of children's needs as dictating the aims of religious education found wide support and was made the organizing principle of the revised West Riding Agreed Syllabus of 1966. The attractions are not difficult to see. Religious education in being allied more closely with general education can be seen as a natural component of that education rather than as an intruder grudgingly given a place there, and the psychological base for the subject appears to provide a refreshingly objective criterion by which the suitablity of material may be judged.

Goldman had asked, as had other writers,[6] that religious education should remain close to the needs and experience of children. The second extract, from Harold Loukes' *New Ground in Christian Education*, expresses a similar view. Reviewing the results of his investigation of practice in secondary schools Loukes suggests that whatever else it might involve 'good' religious education in the schools surveyed had something to do with situations in which the experience and concerns of adolescents were taken seriously and the subject offered encouragement to the adolescent's 'personal quest' – the search for significance in one's own life and for some understanding of the mysteries surrounding existence.

Loukes and Goldman sought to articulate aims in religious education which were consonant with contemporary *educational* thought and thus of a sort which would gain assent from those who did not share a Christian commitment. In the third reading Edwin Cox, writing six years later, is plainly concerned to express the aims in a way that takes account also of a changed *social* situation. He believes that Britain is now a pluralist society and therefore feels that one important aim should be to give young people sufficient understanding of religion to decide what their own position is to be.

All three writers agree in wanting a religious education that is experiental in approach and 'open' – in the sense of neither assuming in advance the truth of the Christian claims nor counting the work lost if that territory is not reached in conclusion. These two emphases have been influential in shaping practice in the schools. However, they do not represent the end of the debate. Thus, in the fourth extract the philosopher John Wilson (who in his *Introduction to Moral Education* had spoken with approval of Loukes' view) argues that in large part the aim of religious education should be seen as the education of the emotions. In particular it should aim at the development of those emotions and attitudes, such as empathy (EMP) and the capacity for acting in accordance with one's principles (KRAT) which figure largely in religion and which are also qualities of the morally educated person (see chapter nine).

A more direct critique of Goldman and Loukes is made in the Schools Council Working Paper 36. It is suggested that Goldman's experiential basis proves on examination to be 'neo-confessional-ist' in aim, while the 'implicit religion' approach of Loukes, in its wish to include within religious education virtually all reflection upon the human condition, claims too much. The working paper then goes on in the excerpt quoted to suggest more appropriate aims and objectives. It considers that in our multi-racial society religious education should be seen as embracing both an objective study of religion and the fostering of the 'personal quest' advocated by Loukes, and then outlines some objectives intended to secure this.

For all their differences these writers on aims seem united by a common wish to reduce any discontinuity between the aims of religious education and the goals sought in general education. So, by unexpected paths, something like the Spens position of religious education as aiming at making pupils 'aware ... of a religious interpretation of life' has been returned to again. This time not as that reduced or second-best solution which Spencer Leeson saw, but as the proper educational task of the subject in a multi-racial society.

Ronald Goldman · *Readiness for Religion*

Ronald Goldman, *Readiness for Religion*, Routledge & Kegan Paul 1965, pp.65-70

The Basis of Children's Needs

What I have called the social aims of religious education are only partially suitable, as I have tried to indicate when discussing the moral, cultural and missionary arguments. They are only valid in so far as they coincide with the personal needs of children and young people. To me, the basis of children's needs must be the starting point and the ultimate purpose of Christian education. Religion is eminently a personal search, a personal experience and a personal challenge. It is first and foremost a personal encounter with the divine. The aims of Christian education should therefore be directed towards the fulfilment of a child's personal needs as they are felt at the various stages of his development.

It follows from this that all really effective religious education stems, wherever possible, from the natural interests and activities of children, for these are the expression of their basic needs. Religion, therefore, as an interpretation of all that the child does, is bound up with every subject taught in school and cannot be segregated into one particular series of lessons on the timetable. The holding of 'religious' lessons, as something introduced from outside the child, is unnatural and contrary to the child's needs.

Ideally, then, we should follow and extend children's interests so that they come to see their experiences in depth. In such a setting religious truth as an interpretation of all experience is known not artificially but at a truly personal level. In this way religion and life are experienced as inseparable.

More and more teachers of the young are beginning to recognise this as a basic principle. But many are puzzled to know how it can be applied in the school and classroom situation. The suggestions I make in Part II are designed to help teachers towards the principle, summarised in what I call 'developmental religious education', based upon the needs of the growing child. I regard my suggestions, however, as merely a bridge across the gap between traditional Bible-centred aims and the emerging ideas of a more child-centred method.

When we talk about a child's basic needs, let me first of all dismiss the idea that a child has specifically religious needs. He needs religion, in its widest meaning, but he has no specific religious needs. That is, a child has physical needs, emotional and intellectual needs, he needs security and he needs standards of behaviour, but they are not religious in a narrow sense. Yet in a broader sense they are religious, since they are all expressions of a human being's desire to fulfil himself, and achieve his highest purposes, which for the Christian is 'to glorify God and enjoy him forever'. To impose upon a child something which is alien to his needs is quite contradictory to educational endeavour; to impose a Religion, with a capital R, which does not evoke any echo in the child's experience and which cannot satisfy his needs, is not only a wasted effort but may also destroy a child's true spiritual potential.

Emotionally, a child needs to be secure, and the roots of this need lie in the experience of love. A child therefore needs to feel that he belongs, first of all, to an intimate family, then to a community which cares for him. The aim, therefore, of Christian education is to build up a confidence in life and in people from the earliest years. This is done by persons reacting upon each other, and we know that Christian parents and Christian teachers and clergy, who really express this love and help the young to feel that they belong, are those who have the most lasting influence upon them. The home, the church, the school, are all communities in which children must be made to feel secure, so that they learn to trust and eventually themselves learn to love.

This is probably more true of the adolescent, who passes through a crisis of trust in his personal development. We tend to be much less permissive of adolescents than of children – there is far more freedom in an infant school than in a secondary school – and our most natural tendency with young people seems to be to criticise and condemn. There are many deep-seated reasons for this, the principal one being our reluctance to let them grow up, beyond our control. But the need for young people to experiment with their lives, within the context of security, is a need any religious community, church or school, must satisfy. This has implications for the methods by which we try to teach religion to adolescents.

The greater freedom of growing up also focuses upon a need of the young to be someone of significance, to have a personal identity of his own, an area in which personal integrity, personal values and personal choice are exercised. Some religious communities have difficulties in building up the young in this positive manner, because of a negative and repressive obsession with guilt. Many a young person's self-confidence and sense of significance has been destroyed by a morbid sense of sin. There is a normal sense of guilt to be encouraged in all children, a warning function as pain is a warning to the physical body, but it must be used to build up rather than to break down personality.

The need for moral standards are in part emotional as well as intellectual. They are emotional in that most children wait to be told what to do, only slowly learning to act responsibly and to behave at a genuinely personal level. Children, as indeed all of us, want an authority upon which to lean and where behaviour is concerned this authority has to be more and more convincing an authority as children grow forward into their adolescence. Intellectually, it is a growing sensitivity to the needs of others and a rigorous search for values which are sound and defensible in the light of experience.

These emotional needs are largely satisfied through individuals, and through individuals in communities. The school is one such community and teachers, as powerful individuals within it, exercise their major influence upon their pupils more by what they are than by what they teach. In this sense many are religious teachers rather than teachers of religion. A staff, even those not committed to a religious allegiance, can create a community of trust, of belonging, of standards and of an acceptable authority and so contribute richly to their pupils' religious education. On the other hand, negative responses of suspicion, condemnation or rejection, of poor standards and little authority of a school staff will undermine much that is taught of religion in the classroom or assembly.

The intellectual needs of the young can be summed up in their increasing desire to make sense of their total experience and their search for a meaning in life. Christian teaching should aim at satisfying their desire to make sense of life, within the context of a divine creation. The Christian faith is a frame of reference through which everything can be experienced, related and interpreted. As such it has an outstanding contribution to make to the intellectual development of children.

Until recently it seemed to be implied that understanding was of minor importance in religious teaching. We now know better, since thinking of a demanding kind at a high level of insight is necessary. The old conditioning question, What does the Bible say? must give way to the more insightful demand, What does the Bible mean? For this reason critical thinking about the Bible and religious belief must be encouraged in the late junior years in preparation for the critical years of early to middle adolescence. As we have noted previously, if the fruits of critical research into the Bible are not shared from an early age, childish views of the Bible linger on too long and retard the religious thinking of adolescents.

A major contribution to the intellectual needs of our pupils is the bridging of the two worlds, religious and scientific, which are beginning to grow apart by the end of the junior school. If a unified frame of reference is seen in religion, children should be encouraged to relate all that they learn, in all subjects, to this assumption. In this way they see that religion is not something separate, alien and imposed upon life, and they begin to comprehend, however dimly at first, that religion must be identified with life itself. Much of this can be achieved by across-subject teaching in the junior school, which I shall outline in greater detail later.

In addition, allowance must be made for the gradual development of a sense of time, concepts of the nature of God, of his activities in the natural world, of divine love, justice and righteousness and many other related concepts. Premature concepts can only be misinterpreted or distorted by children and the content of religious education must be radically revised.

Harold Loukes · *New Ground in Christian Education*

From Harold Loukes, *New Ground in Christian Education*, SCM Press 1965, pp.96-99, 101-4

We are driven then to make two fundamental demands of the 'something' that we are asked to teach: first, that it should be concerned with what ordinary men and women feel are living issues and give what they would recognize as insight into what they feel to be the realities of the human situation; and second, that it should be, in essentials, within the range of understanding open to immature minds. For if the parents do not in general support it, the children's minds will be closed against it; and if the children's minds cannot grasp it, they will be muddled by it.

At first glance, these two principles may seem to rule out the possibility of religious education altogether. Most parents, it will be objected, are pagans; and you are telling us that we cannot 'teach Christianity' to the children of pagans. And furthermore, Christianity is concerned with ultimate, general propositions about the universe, and the meaning of life. You are telling us children under 13 cannot cope with general statements: therefore we cannot 'teach Christianity' to children.

From this dilemma we can escape by applying to religious education the fundamental concepts of all education. In other subjects we have learnt how to overcome both these difficulties. Most parents are both illiterate and innumerate, in the full 'Crowther' sense of those words, and young children cannot grasp the ultimate concepts of literature and mathematics. In all these areas, we succeed by a process of generalizing from experience: we begin with raw, concrete experience, and proceed by means of rational discourse, to the understanding of it. It is the principle established by the scientific revolution of the seventeenth century, with its attack on traditional 'words' and attention to the stark reality of 'things'; by Locke and Rousseau and Pestalozzi and Froebel ... In all subjects now, except religion, we look round first for the concrete material with which the abstraction that we call a subject is concerned: the hill that may be adumbrated in contours, the old building or the documents that combine into history, the boiling water that gives rise to the concept of convection. To our children we say, Look here, watch this:

and then, as their wonder dawns, we ask, What do you see in it? Why do you think this happens? What else ought we to look at if we want to understand it fully? And only when they have savoured and argued and sought for themselves do we nurse them into explanations and meanings, and provide them with the formulae and technical terms that serve as pigeon-holes and filing-systems. Of course, no teacher does this all the time, and with all his material, for there is too much to learn, and some of the useful principles a pupil needs, if he is to make progress, must be taken on trust. But the law is still a law: that *unless* a subject proceeds from the concrete to the abstract, unless the whole process is set about with sense-experience, returning perpetually to the questions 'What are we talking about? What do you see? And what do you think about it?' then it will not be educative.

As a corollary of this 'law of experience' we now insist on a 'law of activity', and claim that insight into experience comes best, and reaches deepest, as the learner is able to do something ...

We go further, and argue that if a pupil is to be active about his experience, he must be interested in it: he must be able to recognize it as in some way important to him, something in which he can be personally involved, not dimly in the distant future, but vividly in the urgent present. This is why training in literacy is now achieved not by primers but by personal messages, why early mathematics turns to playing shops, why history makes use of drama, and science is directed, wherever possible, to the things children can collect or manipulate for themselves.

This cardinal principle, that pupils should be personally and actively concerned with reality, makes certain consequent demands on the teacher, which, even in other subjects than religion, we are only today beginning to explore. He has to understand how a child's mind works: what is the meaning, at the age of 7 or 12 or 15, of 'experience', and what degree of meaning the young mind can grasp. He has to understand himself the raw experiences on which his abstractions are based, and to select from the whole field such items as are both fundamental to the subject and comprehensible to the child. He has to devise means of disposing the raw material so that his little explorers will look for essentials and not extraneous accidents. He has to learn how to use language about it all so that the deceptive word does not lead his children away from the ever-truthful thing. And he has to know all the time the direction of the quest, whether or not he knows exactly where his children will one day arrive.

Good teaching is thus a process of dialogue about experience: the teacher selecting from the chaos of 'things' those items to be attended to, the child looking and touching and smelling and pushing about until he 'sees into' the experience; the teacher challenging and helping to the framing of statements or the expression of feeling, the child practising these skills of thought and expression to the point where he has mastered the experience, made it part of his own growing life; the teacher tempting him on to ever more complex skills and general statements until the pupil is a 'geographer' or a 'historian' or a 'mathematician'.

The teacher seeking to demonstrate the concept that two and two make four turns first to things. When we begin the infinitely longer journey towards the concept of God, we need to obey the same law. From what 'things' – concrete objects, direct personal relationships, felt hopes and longings – do we infer 'God'? Just what are we talking about when we say 'God'? To what sense-experience, to what moment of insight are we referring? What evidence, genuine sensed-evidence, with hearsay evidence excluded, can we call in witness to what we are saying?

I am not implying here a judgement on the doctrine of revelation, or claiming finality for natural religion. I simply ask, What is the revelation revealed in? What *is* the 'experience of God'? And where, in a child's experience, is God to be seen? If anywhere, we must begin our teaching by pointing to it. If nowhere, then we ought not to talk about it.

God in Experience

The crux of the problem of religious education thus becomes the problem with which the contemporary theological debate is concerned. How can we talk about God in natural or secular terms? This does not mean that the teacher is compelled to abandon, for himself, his traditional concepts, and become a 'new theologian'. It does mean that he must perform for himself the task of translation and explanation, in his own personal language, of the terms he uses. He must do his own de-mythologizing, making no judgement, perhaps, on what super-naturalist imagery an adult Christian may make use of, but for the time being, in the teaching situation, perpetually and rigorously subjecting his statements to the test of concrete illustration, from events and experiences, sensations and judgements that are open to description and identification somewhere between the limiting events of birth and death.

Then what is religious education to be about? Ultimately it may be 'about' different things for different people:

> The Vision of Christ that thou dost see
> Is my Vision's Greatest Enemy:
> Thine has a great hook nose like thine,
> Mine has a snub nose like to mine.[7]

But if we suspend judgement on the abstraction and turn to the realities we may find ourselves nearer to common ground in which not only Christians of various traditions but men and women who describe themselves as agnostic or humanist would be able to share a common outlook. We may begin with Julian Huxley's statement[8] that

> In any intellectual organization of religious thought there appear ... to be three main categories to be considered. The first is constituted by the powers of nature; the second by the ideal goals of the human mind; the third by actual living beings ... in so far as they embody such ideals ... The personification and glorification of these would give us an approximation to the theological doctrine of the Trinity.

Huxley here talks of the 'intellectual organization' of religious thought. We are concerned with the stage before its organization: with the experiences which are later to be organized. Are these not the areas in which children may meet God for themselves, in the mystery of the world around them, in the dreams men have had of the possibilities before the race, in the men and women whose lives give witness to the dreams? Children still bear out Wordsworth in their vivid sense of wonder in nature, until we tame it for them in academic science. They hope passionately for the good life, until the compromises of society wear them down. They respond to warmth and outgoing affection and integrity and courage. Is it not, then, the business of religious education to show them these things? And having shown them to engage in 'intellectual organization' to the point where they encounter the issues of faith? And is not this what the 'public voice' was talking about? Was it not saying, in the end, 'Awaken our children to a sense of the largeness of the world they live in, give them a dream of human achievement and an active concern about the human predicament here and now. And if you must call them God and Christ and Spirit, well and good, but it is the awakening we ask for, not the terminology.'

It may seem that I am advocating a purely pragmatic religious education, centred in and bounded by sense-experience, guided by no more ultimate concepts than 'life-adjustment', no values save such as can be derived from or evolved out of the actual working of human society. But to do this would be to *deny* a part of human, and child-human, experience; and when the public voice decided against the American prescription it decided against this too. The child's wonder is a cosmic wonder, and requires myth for its evocation and expression: the dream of human achievement is, at its centre, an ultimate dream, and is shot through with perfection. The 'actual living beings' are those who will be found to have held a dream more golden than they succeed in realizing. The experience itself, of men and things, involves its own transcending.

Again, I make no theological judgement about this. I speak simply of the actual experience of the child who lives with mystery and hope and love at every turn of his life. These are the air he breathes, as he presses up against the close frontiers of his ignorance, as he counts the time on the way to maturity and grows by the affection and assurance he receives from parents and friends. His experiences are always leading outwards into mystery, onwards into the future.

Starting in the real, and the concrete, and the present, does not mean stopping in it. That would be to deny the other half of our grand educational principle, that we progress from the particular to the general, the concrete to the abstract. This *is* education: the move from the narrow circle of first-hand experience to the point of vantage from which all experience may be viewed: the shift from chaos to an intellectual order, from 'what I see' to 'what the race can see'. Education, it has been said, is nothing more than making a child aware of his history. It is his entrance upon his cultural inheritance. And provided that we use these words 'history' and 'culture' broadly enough, to embrace the skills men have learnt, the feelings they have grown by and the dreams by which they have been able to press on beyond both history and culture, the definition will serve.

An experiential religious education is not an existentialist education, concerned only with the significance of the present moment, historically ungrateful. It is one that begins in a moment of history, the present moment, and explores its significance by all the means man has at his disposal. The religious tradition is one of those means: the racial memory of other experiences by which men and women in other times saw that they were driven to speak of 'God', and the experiences of men and women who followed them and came to see for themselves.

Equally, a religious education is not a 'humanist' or 'atheist' education, if by these terms is meant a settled system of dogma: that man is the measure of all things, or that the cosmos is an accidental collision of blind, meaningless force. These are dogmas as inaccessible – and if accessible, dangerous – to a child as any celestial structure 'up there'.

In seeking to discover the ground of our departure we must look for experience open to all children simply because they are children: wonder and hope and love. This we must explore and deepen and make available, with all the means we inherit. What we must avoid is sealing off the mystery, canalizing the hope into dead water, chaining the love in taboo, with no prescriptions of any dogma whatever.

Edwin Cox · *Educational Religious Education*

Edwin Cox, 'Educational Religious Education', *Learning for Living*, March 1971, pp.3-5

A Secular and Pluralistic Society

When we speak of our present age as secular we do not necessarily mean it is irreligious. The antonym of secular is perhaps not religious but ecclesiastical. There have been ages in the past which might have been described with some accuracy as ecclesiastical irreligious, ages much dominated by church politics and administration, but with a cast of thought that lacked truly religious sensitivity. Our age is one that has found the ideas that the church deals with not altogether relevant to the experiences of a scientific and technological age, and so has repudiated both those ideas and the authority of church leaders, while still retaining religious sensitivity in a changed form. Having repudiated the existing religious formulations there are no generally agreed patterns of thought by which this present religious sensitivity can be expressed. Each man has to think out his own pattern for himself. So some remain orthodox, others are agnostic in various ways, some of the young look to Indian religions and gurus and maharishis, some are materialistic. Scientology, existentialism, Becketian fatalism, Mormonism, and many others have their followers. Whatever religious stance you care to mention, you name it we have it, in our present world. The sensitivity is there, but there is no publicly agreed method of describing or expressing it, and every man's ideas are as good as the next. That is what I mean by a secular and pluralistic society.

In What Way is That Society Religiously Sensitive?

If we define religion, and there is some justification for doing so, as man's attempts to find answers to his deepest problems, and examine those problems, we find that they have changed significantly in the last hundred years, and this may explain the shift in religious sensitivity. Formerly the deepest problems facing man were:

> How was the world created and why does created matter behave as it does?
> Why is life so precarious, with death coming as frequently to the young and middle-aged as to the old?
> Why is life so unfair, with many better endowed than others with strength, acumen, wealth and opportunity?

These problems were swept aside in the East by a denial of the reality of experience, but in the West they were generally answered by postulating a creator God, who had made the world in a particular way (which is why it is here and behaves as it does), who was omnipotent and just and would therefore compensate for the precariousness and unfairness of life by redressing the balance after death. Western religion has fitted into that framework, and seemed reasonable and acceptable as long as the mythology behind it appeared consonant with experience. In the past hundred years, however, those problems have largely ceased to trouble, and when they do, we look for answers in other terms.

Creation and the interaction of matter we now try to explain in terms of astronomy, physics, anthropology and biology. Even when the very young ask 'How was the world made?', the religious answer of 'God made it' seems to them unconvincing and skipping too many intermediate steps. The problem of the precariousness of life has been largely solved by medical science. Tuberculosis, diphtheria and diabetes have within my own memory ceased to be inevitable killers. As for the unfairness of life, we hope to remedy that, not by pie in the sky, but by political and social action. So the problems that traditional religion deals with begin to look irrelevant and religion is, to many, answering problems that no longer puzzle, in terms that don't seem very practical.

Even if that is so, it does not mean that the human race has no longer any deep problems. It seems to have found itself a new crop of them which can briefly be summarized in the term living together. The population explosion means there are so many of us crowded together in a small space; the complex nature of the industrial and commercial system, which many feel controls their life and from which they can't break loose, and the pollution of environment by industry in order to provide for the crowded population (almost to the extent of endangering the continuance of the species) have brought this new set of problems. The solution of them may not be entirely in social and mechanistic terms. It involves consideration of the nature of people, the purpose of life, our responsibility for natural wealth, all of which are at bottom religious considerations. So our new problems may make us approach religion from a different angle. It may be encouraging that the young seem more alive to these problems than the older folk, as their zeal for social righteousness expressed in protests and marches, and some of the involved words of their pop songs bears witness. But this is the way in which our secular society can be called religiously sensitive.

What Sort of Aims Can a Teacher of Religious Education Use in This Situation?

If what has been already said describes accurately the existing climate of thought, what criteria can a religious education teacher use in selecting between the various aims he sets himself?

The aims should be realistic and attainable. He can set himself the aim of making all pupils believe in the complete historical veracity of all the Bible, and go to church twice on Sundays. Such an aim is possible, but I doubt if it is realizable. It seems more sensible to take notice of the situation and choose aims more likely to succeed.

They should be acceptable to the community. If the community has an agreed religious position this is easy, but in the present pluralistic society it is difficult to know what it will accept – hence the active debate about what may be taught of religion in schools.

They should seem worthwhile to the teacher, otherwise his lessons will lack conviction. One has seen lessons where one suspected the aim was to keep the beggars quiet until the bell went. The educational temperature in them was low.

They should also seem worthwhile to the pupils. If the teaching is assuming a situation that no longer exists outside the school, and dealing with ideas that are unlikely to have any practical relevance, the academically inclined may still find them interesting as an intellectual exercise, but other pupils are not likely to give them serious attention or remember much that is taught.

They should above all be justifiable on educational grounds and no other. Even in church schools religious education must be seen to do something more than recruit members of a church. It has to be shown contributing to the growth of the pupils' understanding and their ability to think about and deal with the secular pluralistic setting of their lives.

What Aims Satisfy These Criteria?

What precise aims any one teacher sets himself will depend to a large extent on what sort of person he is, and how he sees religion. If he has derived personal help and peace of mind from a traditional religion he may charitably hope that he can share this with his pupils. And he will succeed with a few. If he thinks the present empirical modes of thinking and the present pre-occupation with the problems of personal relationships are a passing phase in the history of thought, and that we shall eventually return to the older religious expressions, he will try to perpetuate belief in those expressions in some of his pupils. And he will succeed with a few. He will make his faithful remnant. If he teaches in a church school he may, with some plausibility, maintain that his job is to teach the doctrines of that church, and if the customers don't like it they can go to another school. And he will succeed with some. But is there not some deeper purpose that may apply to all? I suggest there is, and that it is to help pupils to understand the nature of our present secular, pluralistic society, to help them to think rationally about the state and place of religion in it, to enable them to choose objectively and on sound criteria between the many conflicting religious statements that are made in a pluralist society, and to work out for themselves, and to be able cogently to defend, their own religious position or their rejection of the possibility of having one. This seems on examination to come down to four main aims, which seem to fit the criteria described and to be practicable.

1. To enable pupils to understand what religion has contributed to our culture. It has greatly influenced music, art, architecture, drama and literature. To understand much of these and to appreciate their effect on our lives one needs to know something of their religious inspiration and origin. And this has the advantage of being an objective study. Religion has had this influence on our culture and it is difficult to object to studying it on ideological grounds. It is therefore something all can do irrespective of their religious backgrounds.

2. The second aim is to help pupils understand what people believe and how their beliefs influence their lives. This has become all the more urgent and accessible by the extension of travel and by immigration. We come across a far more varied section of religions nowadays, often we have to live in proximity to their adherents. Learning to understand neighbours and their motivations is a part of education and this is a contribution that religious education can make to it. Admittedly in Britain this will include a large element of study of Christianity since this is still the major religion here, but it will also include other world religions and certain religious, if non-theistic, philosophies.

3. The third aim will be helping the pupils to understand that a rational attitude to life includes making up one's mind on certain fundamental or ultimate questions of the nature of life and of human personality. This will spring to some extent from the previous aim of studying religious phenomenology, but it can also be evoked by much of modern literature, the words of protest and pop songs, and by the practical necessities of choosing a career, and so on. The way to deal with it is probably not to pose the questions directly and starkly, but by this indirect approach, and, if it is achieved, this aim will involve showing how these ultimate questions do not permit of an empirical solution, but involve, in the last resort, making a working hypothesis or an act of faith.

4. Fourthly there is the aim of helping the pupils to decide for themselves what their working hypotheses or acts of faith are going to be; that is, deciding their own religious stance. This is where RE can so easily go wrong by appearing at this stage to produce the answers out of a hat and dictating what that stance must be, so that

the pupils accept it without referring to their experience, and the decision is not a genuine one and breaks down under stress. In the present pluralistic confusion it is all the more important that RE should let the pupils know what choices are available and help them to realise the implications of making any one of them, but not deprive them of their right and duty to make up their minds honestly in a decision that is all the more committing for being a genuine personal decision. These then are the aims that seem worth attempting. They may not be all that a strongly religious person of the older type would think adequate. But it can be argued that they are morally permissible in the present situation, because they lead to a type of teaching that increases pupils' awareness and understanding. And an activity that does that can justify itself as a contribution to the educational process.

John Wilson · *Education in Religion and the Emotions*

John Wilson, *Education in Religion and the Emotions*, Heinemann 1971, pp.161-166

TEACHING 'R.E.' AND EDUCATING THE EMOTIONS

The Logical Connection

The reader who has followed us so far should now be able to see more clearly the points made in Chapter 1, about the connection between religious education and the education of the emotions. Above all, he should now be able to see that we do not have to choose between (a) teaching children some facts *about* religion, which saves us from indoctrination but fails to get to the emotional heart of the matter, and (b) persuading children *into* religion, which is more likely to involve the emotions but is indoctrinatory and not a satisfactory educational aim. We have a third choice, (c) that of educating them *in* religion – that is, of helping them to become more reasonable in respect of those emotions and attitudes that are central to religion, so that they may more reasonably make or not make their own religious commitments, and assess those of other people. In other words, we can make 'religious education' into a *respectable subject*, by recognizing that the criteria of rationality appropriate to it are similar to those appropriate to the education of the emotions, and by devising teaching-methods to fit those criteria.

It should also now be clear that 'religious education' and 'the education of the emotions' are not on all fours. For a large *part of* 'religious education' will precisely *be* 'education of the emotions' – that is, of those many emotions which are characteristic of religion: and conversely, a part of the 'education of the emotions' can take place *under the heading of* 'religious education'. Religion, we might say, provides us with an *arena* or a topic-area in which we may try to educate our pupils' emotions: although there may be other things we want to do also. In the same way, topic-areas like 'sex', 'money', 'war', or 'the family' may include logically distinct types of education, including the education of the emotions, as well as other matters: thus in 'sex education' we should be partly (perhaps primarily) concerned with how our pupils *felt*, though also with whether they knew some elementary biology.

In order to get quite clear about this, I should like to refer the reader to Appendix VII (on the meaning of 'moral'). I there explain why I thought it sensible to take 'moral education' in a very wide sense: that is, education about what a person ought over-ridingly to *do*, and about what he ought to *feel*. Now during the course of the book we have seen that not only religious beliefs but all other ideals and 'outlooks' come into this area: for they are all ultimately based on the emotions. Hence we were forced to turn to the topic of the education of the emotions in general, in order to make sense of religious education. When we considered this topic, we found that the best way to proceed was to list and clarify a number of 'components' or qualities which we needed to develop in our pupils – EMP, GIG and KRAT. And these components are among those which we have outlined elsewhere as forming the objectives of moral education. We have, indeed, concentrated on certain components (especially, EMP and KRAT) as *particularly* rele-vant to the emotions, and hence to religious and other 'outlooks': but we have, nevertheless, remained within the area of moral education all the time.

In our terms, then – and it does not perhaps matter very much if the reader prefers other terms, so long as the logic is clear – we begin with the concept of moral education, which we might divide into (a) education of behaviour (what to do) and (b) education of the emotions (what we feel). We have been chiefly concerned with the latter. 'Moral education', in this sense, is *defined* as education which develops or is intended to develop the moral components (EMP, GIG and so on). To this form of education a large number of curricular subjects and topics, as well as many of the social and psychological features of the school, will contribute. Among these topics, as we have seen, will be 'religious education', 'sex education', and many others – perhaps 'health education', 'social education', and so on. Education in these topics will be chiefly a matter of developing the moral components, each topic being particularly concerned with those components most relevant to it (religious education with EMP and KRAT, 'social education' perhaps with GIG, and so forth): though, of course, in so far as any topic is taught without any particular concern with what the pupils ought over-ridingly to do or to feel, the topic may include other things that would not come under moral education at all.

We may represent this logic in schematic form, thus:

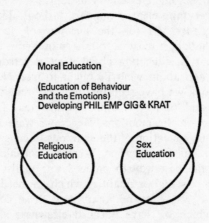

Here the topic-areas 'religious education', 'sex education', etc. are chiefly concerned with developing at least some of the moral components: but there is room also in each, outside the 'moral education' circle, for education that is not concerned with the pupil's behaviour or emotions. Thus one might want to discuss certain heresies, or certain aspects of church history, without this in any way bearing upon the pupil's own feelings, behaviour or religious awareness: and similarly one might want to discuss the sex practices of the Polynesians for the subject's own sake, and not with a view to educating the pupil's own sexual behaviour or emotions.

Such discussions could still, in a loose sense, count as 'religious education' or 'sex education'.

But only in a very loose sense. For as soon as we step outside the circle of moral education, as defined by the moral components, we immediately find ourselves confronted by the question of what *other* aims, if not those of moral education, we are trying to satisfy. Any answer we give to this question will have to be in terms of particular disciplines, or what Professor Hirst has taught us to call 'forms of knowledge'. Thus we can, of course, use the topics of 'religion' or 'sex' to make our children better at history, or science, or the appreciation of literature, or sociology. Somebody who thought (as we do not) that there was no form of thought and feeling peculiar to religion outside these other disciplines (history, etc.) could, I suppose, use the title 'religious education' to name a topic-area in which these disciplines or forms of knowledge were taught. In the case of some topic-areas, of which perhaps 'sex' may be one, this move might be plausible: but we have tried to argue that religion is *centrally* concerned with questions about the appropriate-ness of various objects of awe and worship, and with other human emotions. Hence the larger and more important part of anything we could sensibly call 'religious education' would fall within the sphere of the education of the emotions, and hence of moral educa-tion. Indeed I should argue that other forms of knowledge that are not peculiar to religion – history, sociology, etc. – should only be brought into the area of 'religious education' in so far as they contribute to this larger and more important part and relate to the education of the emotions.

We cannot discuss at length here the merits or demerits of the topic-area 'religion', as against other topic-areas, for the education of the emotions; but there are good prima facie reasons for believing that it forms an excellent arena in which the educator can work. Nearly all the important emotions – love, hate, fear, guilt, anger, etc. – find a place in most religions: indeed one might almost say that a religion can be regarded from one viewpoint as an institution-alization of these emotions. Secondly, there are two areas that religious education seems peculiarly well adopted to cover: (a) the area of the specifically religious emotions and attitudes (awe and worship), and (b) the area concerned with this whole process of institutionalization itself – the whole business of 'finding a meaning to life', or 'making sense of the world', which we have mentioned earlier.

Now it is of course obvious that the moral components (EMP, GIG, etc.), which define the aims of religious education and the education of the emotions, are not likely to be developed *only* – perhaps not even chiefly – in R.E. lessons, religious assemblies, or anything else that might go on under the official title of 'R.E.' For the components are not to be represented as constituting a particular 'form of thought' or 'form of discourse' which can be, as it were, insulated from other forms, and taught separately (in the way that, perhaps, mathematics may be). They represent qualities which can be, and no doubt are being, developed in many other contexts – in the teaching of other curricular subjects, in the social organization of the school, the day-to-day contact with teachers, and so forth. What attitude is the R.E. teacher to adopt towards this?

The R.E. teacher will first *recognize* that this is so: that he must rely, at least to some extent, on other teachers and other factors beyond his immediate control for the development of the moral components. But he must also appreciate that the components represent *his* particular aims as an R.E. teacher. Other teachers concerned with moral education and the education of the emotions may specifically adopt these aims: but it is likely that most will be concerned with teaching subjects – mathematics, history, French, etc. – with more specialized aims that have little relation to the moral components. So the responsibility for developing the components is his, *qua* R.E. teacher: and he should be concerned to do what he can to make such changes in the school generally as he believes will contribute to this end. (Most R.E. teachers and chaplains have long recognized this, even though they may not have associated the point specifically with our own aims.)

What the R.E. teacher will actually do in his lessons, or in whatever contexts he has under his immediate control, will thus depend on what he thinks is being done, or not being done, elsewhere in the school. For instance, if he thinks that (say) the children learn enough 'hard' facts (GIG(I)) elsewhere, he will be more inclined to concentrate on whatever methods he believes will assist the development of emotional awareness and insight (EMP). Or if he thinks that EMP is adequately taken care of by English teachers, perhaps in the form of impromptu acting or group discussion, he will make some attempt on the area of KRAT(1) or (2). He will, in fact, have to fill the crucial gaps: and since this whole topic is still very much under-researched and obscure, there will be plenty of gaps to be filled in. He might profitably begin by looking critically at the curriculum and social organization of his school, to see how they stand with references to the moral components.

Further, it is very much to be hoped – and this should be borne in mind during what follows – that the teacher of R.E. will not confine his attention solely to those emotions, ideals or 'outlooks' that may properly be called 'religious'. As we have seen in Chapter 5, religious outlooks are only one sub-class of emotion-based outlooks in general. We must include not only near-religions, like Communism or the Nazi movement, but (for instance) ideals like the ideal of 'honour' (not losing face), or 'Stoic' ideals of nobility and self-sacrifice, or 'Epicurean' ideals concerned with pleasure and a quiet life. So what we shall now go on to say about R.E. will apply to this wider area of 'outlooks' also.

Schools Council · *Religious Education in Secondary Schools*

From Schools Council Working Paper 36, *Religious Education in Secondary Schools*, Evans/Methuen 1971, pp.43-45

The foregoing discussion of three interpretations of the term 'religious education' also indicates three general aims, the 'confessional', the 'personal quest', and the objective or 'phenomenological'.

We take the view that the 'confessionalist' aim, though perfectly proper within a community of faith, is not appropriate within schools serving a multi-belief society. Moreover, it conflicts at several points with the principles on which education is based ...

We incline to the view that religious education must include both the personal search for meaning and the objective study of the phenomena of religion. It should be both a dialogue with experience and a dialogue with living religions, so that the one can interpret and reinforce the other. Within this wider context 'confessional' teaching should sometimes be heard, both as part of the evidence in the study of a given religion (for example, Protestant Christianity) and as part of the dialogue between the pupils and the world in which they live.

It is not right that controversial religious material should be kept outside school. Teaching must be meaningful and existential, not dull and harmless, and this means bringing in even what is controversial. But religious material is difficult to handle and needs special training of the teachers. A teacher of history dealing mainly with political and economic history is not the right man to deal with the history of religions. A teacher of literature, skilled in novels and lyrics, may not be the right man to teach about the basic religious texts. And moral abstracts from religion do not give a true description of what religion is. Teaching of religion has to be a separate subject, because the teachers need special training.[9]

Such training should equip them, not only to handle religious matters sensitively and with perception, but also to handle the classroom situation in such a way that, although 'confessionalist' views are given a proper hearing they are not allowed to override or inhibit the pupils' free spirit of inquiry.

... the recognition of alternative possibilities of belief and practice is essential. This is not to affirm that all such possibilities are true, or valid, or equally desirable. It is not inconsistent even with some existing historic religion being the one true and ultimate faith. If there is such a faith, it should be able to win its way among the other possibilities in a fair show of evidence. The devoted study of alternative orientations, from a variety of disciplined perspectives, should only serve to vindicate the true faith in competition with its false rivals.[10]

In any attempt to frame an adequate curriculum it is logically and educationally wrong to begin the process by considering the lesson content. Before it is possible to decide on content and method the general aims of the exercise must be analysed and sub-divided into a series of specific objectives. On pages 16 to 19 of this working paper we listed the general aims of religious education as conceived by a number of important commissions and committees concerned with this aspect of education. Although these statements represent many religious viewpoints and a variety of academic interests there is a remarkable harmony between them. This consensus as to the aims of religious education is impressive. We would not presume to summarize, but it is helpful in the present discussion to list some of the main strands: religious education seeks to promote awareness of religious issues, and of the contribution of religion to human culture in general; it seeks to promote understanding of religious beliefs and practices, it also aims to awaken recognition of the challenge and practical consequences of religious belief. Like all liberal education it is concerned that such awareness and under-standing should be founded on accurate information, rationally understood and considered in the light of all relevant facts.

These general aims can be broken down further and more par-ticularly as follows (and here we also give *examples* – instances of the kind of objectives the teacher may have when devising a course of study).

1 *Awareness of religious issues*
  (*a*) *explicit* issues – e.g. the capacity to understand the reasons for differences of religious belief, for instance within the Chris-tian tradition.
  (*b*) *implicit* issues – e.g. the capacity to explore music with a view to seeing whether it can give one new insights into the nature of the world; and, if so, the connexion of these with questions about the 'purpose' of life.

2 *Awareness of the contribution of religion to human culture*
  e.g. acquiring knowledge of the ways in which the Christian heritage has influenced social life in different parts of the UK.

3 *Capacity to understand beliefs*
  e.g. understanding the Muslim conception of Allah, and the type of language employed to express this.

4 *Capacity to understand practices*
  e.g. understanding what worshipping is intended to do, and the use of symbolism in it.

5 *Awareness of the challenge of religious belief*
  e.g. the capacity to form a well-informed judgement about Christian or atheistic belief.

6 *Awareness of the practical consequences of religious belief*
  e.g. capacity to understand issues raised by pacifist elements in, for instance, the Christian and Buddhist traditions.

Educational objectives have been defined as 'changes in pupil behaviour which it is intended to bring about by learning'. Al-though they are concerned with the development of certain cogni-tive skills, attitudes, and interests, it is evident from the examples given that this involves the acquisition of accurate, factual information.

These general objectives need to be broken down even further before a particular teaching unit can be devised. Such 'specific educational objectives' will vary from one teaching situation to another – and they must be worked out by the teachers concerned; but they must be arrived at by considering three main factors:

Information about the level of development of the pupils, their needs and interests, must be taken into account. The social conditions and problems which the children are likely to encounter provide a second source of data. And thirdly, there is the nature of the subject-matter and the types of learning that can arise from study of the subject-matter.[11]

The important thing to realize is that specific objectives provide the real starting-points for syllabus planning. They begin to suggest methods and contents – the kind of behaviour and the activities in which the pupil must engage if the required development is to take place. They also provide the real basis for any attempts to assess the teaching's effectiveness.

4 · Questions of Procedure

It will have been noticed in the two preceding sections that the issues of the justification and the aims of religious education tend to overlap. 'Should it be done at all?' is a close relative of questions about what the subject is *for*, and that in turn of how it should best be done – considerations of method and procedure which we take up in this section.

Changes in styles of learning pressed hard upon the didactic mode and class-lesson technique once characteristic of religious education. Though that method is still to be found it has increasingly given place to an approach which starts from the child's experience and accepts him as a full partner in the learning process in religious education as he is in other aspects of the curriculum. In the first extract J. W. D. Smith, one of the patriarchs of developmental religious education, suggests ways of building upon and enriching young children's experience. As the title of his book makes clear, Dr Smith is concerned that the teaching should fit the organizational pattern of the modern primary school and equally the secular setting in which the county school operates. He approves of Ronald Goldman's efforts to secure the first but finds Goldman deficient in recognition of the second. His own suggestions include plentiful biblical material intended, alongside of similar material from other faiths, to serve the larger objectives of evoking a sense of the numinous and preparing for a later understanding of religious concepts.[1]

The adoption of discovery methods and individual styles of learning in general education has been no less evident in Catholic schools. Psychological insights into child development have also influenced the shape of religious education there too. This may be seen from the second extract, part of an article on 'Contemporary Catechetics' in the introduction to a primary syllabus originating

from the Westminster Archdiocese. Christian formation remains
the goal but the marks of the new catechetics show through here
(as in the syllabus) in the christocentric emphasis, the call for
attention to the interests and capacities of the child and willingness to wait upon their development in introducing him to doctrinal
formulations.[2]

A feature of the changing scene in secondary schools is the introduction of interdisciplinary teaching in the humanities. This is often
referred to as 'integrated studies', though that title may cover differing types of work. The teaching may take the form of the contributory disciplines operating separately but treating a common theme,
or work on an area of inquiry in which the organization is such
that teachers and pupils are working together in ways which
deliberately cross subject boundaries. In either case the activity
raises the question of what (or where) is the integration which is
said to be taking place and – for religious education – what distinctive perspective the subject has to offer in an inquiry. One
answer to the second question is given in the extract from a Schools
Council publication, one of a series on the role of the contributory
disciplines in a humanities programme. Here religious education is
seen as having a special contribution in pointing to the level of
ultimate meaning underlying the empirical level from which an
inquiry may begin. The position is reminiscent of Phenix's view of
religion as concerned with the realm of 'ultimacy' and having a
synoptic function. Close attention to the first question has been
given by the Schools Council Humanities Curriculum Project and
John Elliott, a member of the project team, draws upon their discussions in two papers included in the symposium *Religious Education in Integrated Studies*.[3]

Among the advantages claimed for linking religious education
with other subjects is that it demonstrates religion's concern with
the whole of life. In an excerpt from a monograph originally prepared as evidence to the British Council of Churches' survey published as *Religion and the Secondary School*,[4] Peter Cousins and
Michael Eastman argue that interdisciplinary work and a concern
for relevance should not and need not diminish the use of the
Bible or effective teaching on the Christian faith.

Consideration of the place of religious education in integrated
studies has been given added depth by the case made for the study
of religion in schools as a discipline in its own right by the Schools
Council secondary project at Lancaster. In essence the case is that

summarized in the extract from a paper read at the 1970 Inter-European Commission on Church and School by Sten Rohde, chairman of the Union of Swedish Teachers of Religious Knowledge. Dr Rohde believes that the form of religious studies made possible by the revision of the curriculum in Swedish comprehensive schools in 1969 provides a universal model for teaching about religions in schools. The model has clear affinities with that offered in Working Paper 36 (where Dr Rohde is quoted), not least in the wish to secure both a scholarly treatment of world religions and one which illuminates the existential questions of the pupils.

J. W. D. Smith · *Religious Education in a Secular Setting*

From J. W. D. Smith, *Religious Education in a Secular Setting*, SCM Press 1969, pp.86-93[5]

The real task of the state school is to enrich pupils' inner experience in ways which may awaken religious feeling and provide a pre-cognitive core of meaning which may gradually interpret religious language. This brings us at once to the theme of worship in the primary school.

In early years worship will naturally be informal. It must be adapted to local circumstances and to the outlook and attitude of the teacher. Class-room worship should not involve teachers in conscious insincerity but perceptive teachers may be able to use moments of spontaneous wonder as growing points in the experience of genuine worship. Violet Madge makes many helpful comments on this subject in her book *Children in Search of Meaning* (SCM Press 1965) ...

As children grow older myths and stories from many lands and cultures might be used in association with worship. The great myths of mankind may speak to deeper levels of the developing personality before the mind is able to understand religious concepts. The Epic of Gilgamish contains material which could be used along with the biblical stories of creation and the flood. Such juxtaposition would help to lift the biblical myths out of the category of literal history. It would set them free to speak directly to the levels of feeling and emotion. Musical and dramatic techniques might be used in connection with such myths.

Many stories from the Old and New Testaments might speak in this same way. The stories of Moses at the Bush and of the call of Isaiah create difficulties in religious teaching because irrelevant questions about historicity and literal interpretations destroy their 'numinous' quality. The first of these stories can be used with younger primary classes and the second with older pupils if these irrelevant issues can be avoided. Such stories appeared in 'progressive' syllabuses forty years ago under headings like 'Stories told to Jesus' but few teachers accepted the freedom offered by these words. The limitations of the teachers defeated the intention of the syllabus compilers.

The devil of literalism might be exorcised more successfully if selections from other great religious traditions were included among stories used in the primary school. Even the *Crossing of the Red Sea* might claim a place as a Hebrew 'wonder story' and the 'pillar of cloud and fire' might regain its former power. Such stories should not be taught as part of biblical 'history' and they should not be used for direct religious teaching. They belong to the religious traditions of mankind and they may speak, as stories from non-biblical traditions may also speak, to levels of feeling and emotion which abstract language cannot touch. 'The conquest of literalism without loss of the symbols is the great task for religious education.'[6]

Similar principles should guide the handling of the 'miraculous' elements from the New Testament in the state primary schools. The nativity stories will naturally figure in primary-school teaching. Some Christians would wish to retain the traditional 'supernatural' character of these stories and would regard the miraculous happenings as God's witness to the birth of his Son. Non-Christians, and many Christians, would think of them as the Early Church's witness to its belief about the nature of Jesus. The former view may have its place in Christian teaching. It is not appropriate in the state school setting. Christians differ in the degree of historicity which they find in these stories. All teachers would surely agree that such stories are akin to poetry in their educational value. The clue to their appropriate treatment lies in that fact. When these stories are treated as literal history they raise puzzles for the mind. Primary school pupils know, for instance, that no star could guide men to a house unless it came down out of the sky and hovered directly over the house. When teachers attempt to 'historicize' such a story they are forced to introduce details which are not in the original narrative. In doing so they destroy the simple poetic beauty of the story and they may cause unnecessary perplexity ...

Verbal teaching in the primary school should be factual and preparatory, rather than directly religious in intention. It should be focused on the person of Jesus. Primary pupils in state schools should learn that 'Jesus of Nazareth taught men to trust God's love and to show love to others'. The teaching should show Jesus in his contemporary Jewish setting. It should provide factual teaching which may prepare pupils to understand, in later years, the meaning of the original Christian claim 'Jesus is the Messiah' ...

In older classes it would be appropriate to include stories of men and women in later centuries, and in modern times, who have followed Jesus's way of love in creative social and personal action. Men and women from many lands and from other races should be included. Such story material should not be confined to Christians but should include other great figures from the moral and spiritual history of mankind ...

Story material will always have a place in the primary school and the art of the storyteller will always be a valuable asset in younger classes but modern primary methods recognize the importance of pupil activity in learning. This modern emphasis breaks down the barrier between 'subjects'. The many-sided 'project' is replacing the traditional subjects. The formal element cannot be eliminated from primary education but it should not be allowed to hamper the natural growth and expression of spontaneous interests ...

Goldman's 'life-themes' are an admirable educational device for integrating religious teaching with other elements in the primary school curriculum in ways which utilize pupils' interests and engage their activities. Their weakness lies in their aims and intentions. Goldman seems to think that Christian education is still the ultimate objective of religious teaching in state schools. There are curious inconsistencies in his position. In *Readiness for Religion* he claims that 'Religion is eminently a personal search, a personal experience and a personal challenge'.[7] On later pages he makes other claims. He states that 'The Christian faith is a frame of reference through which everything can be experienced, related and interpreted'.[8] He also writes: 'The unifying principle, spoken by the teacher, or to be assumed by the child, is that all we learn about the world is a knowledge of God's world, of his creation and his power.'[9]

Goldman seems to ignore three important facts. The first is that 'personal search' will not necessarily lead to an acceptance of the Christian faith. The second is that many teachers in state schools would not accept the Christian faith as a 'unifying principle' in all learning. The third fact is that large numbers of boys and girls in state schools today have no experience of Christian belief and practice at home which might provide some inner understanding of concepts which are beyond their intellectual grasp. Many of Goldman's suggestions might be very fruitful within a believing community. The aims and intentions of his life-themes are hardly relevant to the problems of the state school.

Goldman seems strangely unwilling to recognize the implications of his own investigations. The use of the Bible for direct religious teaching in state primary schools has very severe limitations in an age which cannot accept pre-critical literalism. Biblical imagery, the alien idiom of biblical thought, the many layers of moral and religious insight within the pages of the Bible make it an impossible text-book for direct moral and religious teaching in the primary school. But the Old Testament contains essential material for understanding the faith of Israel in which Christian belief and life had their roots. Factual teaching which prepares for such later understanding is the appropriate contribution of the primary school to the Christian element in religious teaching. The living faith of Israel provides a focus for concrete factual teaching. Similar teaching from the New Testament finds a natural focus in the words and deeds of Jesus of Nazareth whom some Jews recognized as their Messiah. The essential methods of the life theme can be adapted to such factual teaching although the aims and intentions would be different.

A programme of religious education for primary classes in state schools should accept two main objectives. It should seek to foster and deepen the awareness of mystery which touches the experience of young children at so many points. Violet Madge refers helpfully to this dimension of mystery in her book. She finds it associated with the wonders of the natural world, awareness of the frontiers of human knowledge, with birth and death and with human relationships. The sensitive and perceptive primary school teacher will find many opportunities for fostering such experiences of 'natural religion'.

What about 'revealed religion'? What place remains for Christian teaching? An objective approach to Christian origins might be acceptable to Christian and non-Christian alike as an element within the secondary-school curriculum. A completely objective approach is hardly feasible in the primary school. Logical consistency is impossible in the present confused situation. Circumstances and attitudes differ greatly from region to region and from school to school. Neither pupils nor teachers can separate themselves from the social and religious influences around them. These influences – as they touch the primary school child – are still strongly coloured by Christian belief and practice. Traditional beliefs will colour the approach of many teachers. It will colour the thinking of many pupils. Complete consistency is impossible.

A clear declaration of objective intent is desirable, however, if Christian and non-Christian teachers are to co-operate in a common policy. Goldman's conclusions suggest that we should not press direct religious teaching on young children. They are not ready for it intellectually. It is not meaningful for them emotionally unless they come from Christian homes. We should be content to limit our verbal teaching to such factual knowledge as may prepare pupils for a later understanding of the source and meaning of Christian love. This would seem to imply factual teaching about Jesus of Nazareth from whom men have learned how to live, in whom men have seen perfect love. Such factual teaching may prepare for the adolescent stage when pupils must find new 'gods' to replace the parental image and the parental law of early childhood.

David Konstant · *Religious Instruction for Catholic Primary Schools*

From David Konstant, *A Syllabus of Religious Instruction for Catholic Primary Schools*, Burns & Oates/Macmillan 1966, pp.19-24

What has been said so far is an attempt to state briefly those aspects of the work of recent theologians which immediately concern the catechist in school and parish. The basis for it all is a return to the sources, to the writings and traditions of the early Church, and first of all to the New Testament 'kerygma', the proclamation of the 'good news' of the saving acts of God and in particular his sending of his Son to share our human life and to dedicate it wholly to the Father. This good news demands from all either a positive response or a refusal. As teachers, we have to proclaim the same Gospel (kerygma) and to explain it (catechesis) in such a way as to encourage a response in faith.

Suppose that we are persuaded of this, of the need for a fresh content, for a shift of emphasis in our religious teaching. What then? Obviously our *approach* will have to change also. First and foremost our whole approach must be *based on Christ*. We are not teaching some abstract philosophical system, or a code of morals, but a person, Jesus Christ, the one Word of the Father, the perfect Mediator between God and man. All we can know about God – and about man – is summed up in Christ, and consequently he must be the centre of all our catechesis ...

There would be little point in going into specific lessons here, but one can at least narrow down the problem by looking at the general methods of working out the syllabus. Modern catechists accept as axiomatic (or at least they did so up till quite recently) the well-known fourfold approach canonized by the Eichstätt Catechetical Conference of 1960. These are: through the Bible, through the Liturgy, through systematic teaching ('doctrine') and through the testimony of Christian living. Here, by the way, is clear proof that recent revivals in different fields of Christian studies are all interconnected. We have a new catechesis because we have a new approach to the Bible, a revival of Liturgy, a new theology, and so on. Each is vital and all are interrelated with one another.

Let us take first the *biblical approach* in catechetics. If it is to have any validity it must relate to Christ, for the Bible itself derives its deepest meaning from Christ, its central point. It is the Word of God we are dealing with in the Bible and its full significance is apparent only in its relation to the perfect Word revealed in Jesus Christ. The Old Testament looks forward to Christ – or rather grows forward, 'for the word of God is living and active' (Heb. 4.12), while the New Testament goes on to present the fruit developed from the Passover of Christ with its seed of future growth for the People of God.

Bible and *Liturgy* go hand in hand. A scriptural approach must refer to the liturgical basis and development of the Bible, while a liturgical presentation will involve the biblical foundations of the Liturgy. And Liturgy without Christ is unthinkable ...

A common objection to the new catechetics is that 'the children don't learn anything', that they 'know nothing about their religion' after perhaps years with an up-to-date catechist. If we take this objection at its face value, then we can only say that such a catechesis as the traditionalists object to is a perversion of the modern view. There is indeed a time for *doctrinal formulations*, especially when based on the creeds and authoritative pronouncements of the Church. Such formulations are an essential part of our attempt to help a young person cope with the questions of the day as an articulate Christian and express his faith to those who enquire about it. But it is of great importance to keep in mind the age, ability and interest of the children in our charge. We would suggest that there is no place at all for doctrinal formulas during the Infant years and little place in the Junior years. In the Secondary years – and this is essential – they must be summaries that follow from the child's understanding of the mystery or salvation event in question, not involved formulas constructed to satisfy the nuances of a theologian's thinking and utterly incomprehensible to the child. The most suitable summaries are often to be found in the New Testament and these will be centred naturally on Christ, who acknowledged that he himself was the Truth (Jn. 14.6).

Let us beware, however, of setting too much store by the learning of formulas, no matter how carefully chosen. It is not knowledge, at least not in the non-biblical sense, that we seek to instil, but a living faith, a full commitment to Christ in response to the good news that we bring of him. It is the fact that such a response is not measurable in the same way as material learned by heart that has led to criticisms of the new methods.

The concentration on learning and assessable acquirements has also led to a certain neglect – even among the catechetical reformers themselves – of the fourth way of presenting the faith mentioned above, namely *Christian witness*. We look for a response in faith – and what better way to inspire the children to it than by bringing them into contact with those who have given shining examples of commitment to Christ, the apostles, the early martyrs, the saints down the ages to our own present day. The children can learn about the following of Christ from their example and inspiration. They can learn too by bearing witness to Christ themselves, so that Christian living and Christian action will themselves be an integral part of our catechetical approach. This is, indeed, the whole purpose of our catechesis. Whether the instruction is at home, at school or in the parish, the aim must always be to create, foster and maintain the spirit of Christian living in the community ...

Right from the outset, also, we must keep our eyes firmly fixed on *the child* before us. As it is, we spend too much time gazing into the crystal ball, treating the child as a prospective adult and forgetting the needs of the moment. Are we ever influenced enough in our catechetical presentation by the ability and aptitudes of the child as they are here and now? If we really want our methods to be adapted to their object, then we must pay careful attention to the work of child psychologists, and not just to those who study religious development. Piaget is just as important as Goldman.

We should learn to start from the interests of the children and not presume that they will be enthralled by something because we ourselves are keen on it. Any teacher of experience knows this, of course, but time and time-table exigencies often prevent his acting on it. It is essential to start from the child's personal experiences. It may even be necessary to put off the religion lesson as such and to concentrate, for example, on a preliminary project on wind, or water, or bread (a pre-catechesis, if you like), so that the child may be fully responsive to the religious teaching when it is presented.

We see, then, that catechetics today involves a reappraisal of both *content* and *approach*. There is in process a re-examination of the content of the faith in relation especially to the teaching about the Trinity, the Incarnation, grace and the sacraments. Secondly we are now more aware of the need to teach through the Bible, through the Liturgy, through systematic instruction and through the testimony of Christian living (and not almost exclusively through systematic instruction). Such a reappraisal of content and approach will not of itself solve all our difficulties, but provided we are always willing to learn it will undoubtedly help.

Schools Council · *Humanities and the Young School Leaver*

Schools Council, *Humanities and the Young School Leaver: an Approach through Religious Education*, Evans/Methuen 1969, pp.10-11

Religion is not an optional extra in the interpretation of human life, nor a last expedient in meeting the demands of life when all else fails. It is, rather, a dimension of all experience. It is the full understanding of the whole of life – life viewed *sub specie aeternita-*

tis. It follows that any problem, if pushed far enough, becomes a religious problem. To single out some problems as more 'religious' than others is to betray a misunderstanding of the meaning of religion.

If what has been said is true, the areas of inquiry for a general humanities programme cannot be distinguished as 'religious' and 'secular', but must be selected for their importance to older pupils. We would, however, advance the view that all programmes should be thought of as requiring three levels of mental activity. It is useful to distinguish these three levels, though they are not completely separable from one another.

(a) *Questions of fact.* The facts of the case; the empirical aspect of the situation. Problems arise because of the conflict between men's desires and the obstinate nature of matter, or between one man's desires and those of another. The first exercise is therefore the patient study of the problem itself – what is known about it, what interpretation is put upon it by the various academic disciplines involved, and how the various intellectual tools can contribute to its solution. At this level the study of the problem is broadly 'scientific' ('science' being taken to include the social sciences).

(b) *Problems of value.* At this level the study is broadly 'humane', in the sense of literary, biographical, artistic, and moral. We are here concerned with the human significance of the facts and the human choices involved in the situation. At the first level the standpoint is that of a spectator, as it were in the audience. At this second level the standpoint is that of an actor in the drama, experiencing it from within.

(c) *Ultimate meaning.* At the third level there has to be an attempt to see the situation *sub specie aeternitatis*. The problem has to be seen against the total story of man's life, the world's history, and the significance (if any) of the whole universe. At this level we are not content to ask: 'What is the matter?' We have to ask: 'Does anything matter? Do people matter as people? And why do they matter? And what difference does our answer make to our view of the particular problem?' Any question likely to be of interest to the pupils we have in mind can be pressed to this point; and, unless it *is* pressed so far, it will not have been properly treated.

It is our experience that the teacher who establishes a deep personal sympathy with his pupils, and who is willing to be honest and without fear of where honesty may lead him, finds that the pupils themselves push the dialogue to the final frontier:

> We ask our parental cause why we had to be.
> Why do we live at all?
>
> GEORGE BARKER *The Weepers in the Sacred Tree*

The religious education specialist has a part to play at each of the three levels distinguished above. At the first level, he is concerned, like the other teachers, with an understanding of the facts; but even here he will contribute a certain critical attitude to the facts (for a 'fact' is an experience interpreted in some framework of thought). Thus he will be moved by the humane and compassionate values that predispose men to attend to some facts rather than others (e.g. the fact of poverty).

At the second level he will be concerned, like all men of goodwill, with compassion and the moral obligations that are generally acknowledged. It is now widely argued that moral values do not necessarily depend on religious sanctions. Whatever view is held on this issue, it must be agreed that it is unwise to tie ethical propositions too closely to religious propositions, lest a later rejection of religion may carry with it a rejection of moral responsibility.

At the third level, the religious education specialist clearly has a part to play. For he poses and invites questions about the meaning of human life, and of the world in general. Is there meaning and purpose in the universe as a whole? And what difference to our attitudes and behaviour in particular circumstances does the answer to the general question make? The teacher will examine this inquiry with the aid of Christian and non-Christian statements. He will also examine the alternative – that there is no ultimate meaning in existence – and its implications. He will examine the nature of belief, and the necessity for making a choice of believing; for to say: 'I do not choose at all' is a denial of human status. The choice itself remains the pupil's own; and the teacher should not measure the success of his teaching by the extent to which his pupils agree with him. What he is called on to do, as a teacher, is to make clear the available choices, and the grounds thereof; and to help his pupils to make their choices and face the consequences of making them.

Cousins & Eastman · *The Bible and the Open Approach in RE*

The Bible and the Open Approach in Religious Education, ed. Peter Cousins and Michael Eastman, Tyndale Press 1968, pp.39-40, 41-44

The catch-phrases currently fashionable are 'Bible-centred' and 'life-centred'. An elliptical approach might appear to do justice to both needs, but the further demand for 'child-centredness' involves geometric complexities to be solved only by mathematicians! We discard the metaphor. But it seems plain that if there is to be any teaching at all of the Christian faith it must include a substantial amount of biblical material. To accept the implication that this will therefore be irrelevant to life involves implicit adverse judgment on the Scriptures. We see no reason why teaching that is based on the Bible should not be child-related and life-related.

Yet we are not altogether happy with the approach that is often adopted of saying, in effect: 'We want to teach the Bible; what are the best ages for teaching which parts?' It seems better to ask: 'Given that these are the aims of RE, what are the best methods of achieving them, and what part has Bible teaching in the process?' We should also ask how far systematic teaching of the Bible is possible and desirable at all stages.

The so-called 'life-centred' approach itself has defects. It encourages using the Bible in snippets (reminiscent of the universally-condemned proof-texts beloved of our fathers in the faith) and may thus lead to a wrong understanding of the way in which the Bible is to be used, a failure to grasp the biblical view of life, and a dilettante approach to the whole question.

To oppose 'life-centred' and 'Bible-centred' in any ultimate way is to divorce the Bible from life, whereas ultimately the two ought to coincide. Basically the question is one of method rather than content, at any rate for Christians who accept the authority of the Bible. A distinction can be drawn between an approach which starts from the Bible as authoritative in a universally-recognized and objective sense, and one which starts from the Bible as a contribution to a continuing debate, in the course of which the

Bible shows itself to be authoritative through its own intrinsic relevance and value.

Secondary school teachers seem to agree that at this stage a good deal has to be broken down. Typical obstacles are a sentimentalized view of the nativity stories, the Cecil B. de Mille approach to part of the Old Testament, a view of Jesus which fails to take Him seriously as a man. Sometimes there seems to be a sort of psychological block; material which was certainly taught at primary level is apparently forgotten, yet when it is raised again pupils 'don't want to know'.

It seems that a 'life-centred' approach is generally desirable for those over thirteen. Local factors will determine whether it is necessary with all pupils, the stage at which it should begin, and the nature of the problems discussed. In general we would expect the approach in the lower forms of the secondary school to be 'Bible-centred' and 'life-related' and that these emphases would be reversed for most pupils by the age of fourteen. As we have already suggested, this does not mean dropping the Bible just when young people reach a stage when it may become particularly relevant, but it does mean making use of the Bible in a different way.

The 'life-centred' method involves several stages. First comes investigation of a situation in which we live and are forced to make decisions. It may be valuable to see how this problem arises in different classes, societies and periods in history. Secondly, arising from this discussion it will appear that in making what may prove to be a difficult decision there are factors other than material which must be taken into account. At this point it is meaningful to proceed to the third stage, the examination of various possible approaches including the Christian one. Discussion of these, and of their implications will lead (one hopes) to a realization that committal is necessary; in the particular case being discussed, committal to a particular course of action based on certain affirmations, but in general, committal to a view of life, and, for the Christian, to a Person.

Before indicating areas of life that are likely to produce this sort of material, it should be pointed out that the Bible is relevant not only at stage 3 above. The issues are often presented very forcefully in biblical narratives, so that stage 1 may involve use of the Bible, which certainly shows the impact of the problems men face today upon a culture which is in many ways completely different.

In suggesting areas for examination we shall be forced to use abstract terms. In practice, issues are almost invariably concrete. Yet behind the most specific and concrete problem there lies an abstract issue; one of the teacher's tasks is to help his pupils begin 'operational thinking' to the limit of their ability while at the same time helping them to arrive at a satisfactory answer to the specific question posed.

One area to consider is human nature. What does it mean to be human? What distinguishes man from other life forms? What ideals should man set himself? What prevents him from attaining these ideals? Standards of personal conduct will be discussed in this connection as will such theological questions as original sin, atonement, eternal life.

Then there are questions about life in society, and social justice, whether seen globally or locally. Why do some men starve while others live in plenty? Are all men born free and equal, and if so, why are so many apparently far from free while society is based on inequality? Is work a necessary evil? What do we mean by good government? What are the ideals which society should strive after?

Another group arises from study of the natural world. Are creation and evolution mutually exclusive? What is the scientific attitude? What are its presuppositions, its strength and limitations? Are these moral issues involved in cybernetics? Or generally in scientific progress – the right use of power, man's dominion over the natural order, *etc.*? Many philosophical questions would in any case arise from the study of such subjects as literature and history. Of the many possible topics we may mention such issues as the significance of experience, physical, emotional, aesthetic, intellectual; the meaning of truth; the nature of reality.

The 'life-centred' approach does not, of course, exclude discussions of specifically religious issues. Religion is, after all, a human activity, and (whether or not Christianity is a religion) the Christian church indisputably is there. The questions that will arise in this connection will include the significance of man's search for God and the distinctively biblical view that the initiative rests in fact with God; the nature and validity of religious experience; the meaning of religious concepts; the possibility of revelation and the place of natural theology; the role of religious beliefs in working out ethical and social problems; and the place of the church in society today.

Pupils in secondary schools are faced with the need to enter into new relationships in various departments of their lives. Discussion of problems of personal relationships and the related moral issues will naturally arise as the class considers individual friendships, family living, peer groups, life at school and in the neighbourhood.

In considering these problems it is important for all to realize that adequate discussion can only be based on facts. Pupils who learn this will have grasped a principle of great importance and universal application. Some of the facts involved will have been dealt with in other lessons; some will be of a type that does not usually appear in school syllabuses; others will be biblical or theological and plainly within the field of the RE department. An approach that takes account of this need for facts will in itself teach a vital lesson about the relation between the Bible and life.

Sten Rohde · *The Teaching of Religions*

From Sten Rohde, 'The Teaching of Religions', *Teaching about Religions*, ed. Geoffrey Parrinder, Harrap 1971, pp.84-93

A Universal Model for the Teaching of Religions

... I believe that Sweden is on its way to a kind of teaching about religions which can function as a universal model in any country. I think we have to look for such a model in a world which in spite of its divisions is more and more becoming one world. We have to find a model for the teaching of religions on which Christians and non-Christians, church and society, can unite. Fundamentally, it should not matter who is responsible for this teaching, though of course in practice differences will be great. But this approach is valid for all kinds of teachings, and there should be no difference in this respect between the teaching of religion, the teaching of science, or the teaching of history. I want to present this model in a number of points, which I hope can serve as a basis for our discussion.

(*a*) School teaching of religion should be a teaching of *religions*, not of one religion.

... The time is far away when Christian leaders believed that within their generation the whole world would be Christian. They foresaw a decay of non-Christian religions. Instead we are witnessing their renewal ... As far ahead as we can see, we shall have co-existence between world religions, which must mean extended dialogue between them. The teaching of religion in schools must bear witness to this fact, giving true information about the religious situation of the world today.

(*b*) The teaching of religion in schools should be a *teaching about* religions, not religious instruction.

This means that the teaching of religion at school has to conform to the secular school milieu. As a matter of fact, the teaching of religion has to accept the secular approach of the pupils even when it tries to be Christian instruction. I have heard teaching of religion which was intended to be Christian, and I have heard teaching of religion which was intended to be secular (objective), without always being able to find any difference. A difference should be that Christian instruction must include exercise in prayer, and in helping and serving our neighbour. But the secular setting of schools today is not a good place for such exercises ... The school of today is mainly intellectual, even though this may be deplored, and the teaching of religion cannot do anything but conform to this pattern, which means no religious exercises, but teaching *about* religion.

(*c*) School teaching of religion has to be *descriptive*, it cannot give religious experience.

This is only another way of expressing point (*b*), that we have to teach *about* religion. The teacher can if he likes refer to experiences of his own, as he can refer to experiences of others, but in any case he will have to describe these experiences. He cannot directly communicate them. Everybody knows how deficient are descriptions of religious experiences. In all religions it is said that you have to do, to act, in order to know ... It is like painted-glass windows in the cathedrals. You see them from the outside, and they are nothing, grey and colourless. You see them from the inside, and they are wonderful, full of life and colour. Without experience dogmas and rituals become grey and sapless. And further, there are so many kinds of Hinduism, Christianity, Buddhism and Islam. You describe a Lutheran doctrine and practice, an Anglican, an

Orthodox, and so on. But which is really Christianity? To these objections against describing religion we have to say that we have no choice. We know that no words can say what we mean by the word God, but nevertheless we have to use words and human symbols. Similarly with religions, we have no choice but to describe the human aspects, knowing that these are only outward expressions of the inner religious realities.

(*d*) The teaching of religion in schools should deal mainly with *living world religions*, not with ancient, dead religions or with the origins of religion.

In this fast-changing world a modernizing of syllabuses is taking place everywhere. Much outdated material must give way to modern knowledge. In Sweden there is a risk that this process may go so fast that contacts with history are broken. Man without history loses his capacity for understanding his own time, which has grown out of history. But this risk in putting old material aside must not prevent us from modernizing all syllabuses. They should not be so modern that they only deal with what is topical, but everything we teach should in some way be connected with the present world, so that our teaching helps pupils to understand what is happening today. In order to understand the conflicts in Palestine they have to know something of Jewish and Muslim faiths and traditions. In order to understand something of events and conflicts in India, they must know something of Hinduism. They have to know that Hinduism can mean many things, from social, liberal Rama-krishna Mission to orthodox, violent Mahasabha Hinduism. Zen Buddhism and yoga-techniques are popular also among Europeans and Americans, and our students are eager to learn about these. Formerly much of the short time devoted to non-Christian religions was given to so-called primitive religion and the general phenomenology of religion, explaining such terms as magic, totem, mana, taboo. I do not think we shall give much attention to these things, or to speculations about the origins of religion, something we do not know anything about. But so far as the primitive religions are finding renewal and influence in Africa today, we shall have to deal with them.

(*e*) Teaching of religion in schools should deal with *existential questions*, not with curiosities.

It is often pointed out nowadays that theology and preaching too often try to answer questions in which nobody is interested except theologians and ministers. The lack of interest in the teaching of religion in schools is due to the fact that it is echoing theology. Some years ago Harold Loukes pointed out that English teaching of religion needed to start with the real-life questions of the pupils. In Sweden the results of some research into the real interest of ninth-graders were published in 1969. The Swedish research was carried out in order to discover how the revised syllabuses of religious teaching in the upper levels of the compulsory school could be made relevant to the real-life problems of the pupils. The conclusion was that questions which might be termed 'existential' were regarded as important, while questions expressed in traditional Christian terminology were regarded as unimportant. Important were questions about life and death (how life is created, the moral right to take life, life after death), about race and social equality, about war and peace, about suffering and evil, about solitude and companionship, about sex and family, about faith and reason. Unimportant were questions about Jesus and salvation, about Church and confession, about prayer and sacrament.

This research was made in one age-group in one country. Would the same results have been reached in other age-groups and in other countries? How far are the existential questions independent, how far are they dependent on age and cultural environment? Paul Tillich has pointed out that existential questions are verbalized in various ways in various periods of history. Teachers of religion must learn from him, and find out how existential questions can be expressed in various situations, and then apply fitting formulations of the religious answers. It belongs to the essence of religion to give answers to existential questions. Different religions sometimes give similar answers, sometimes differing ones. Teaching in schools about religions has to present both what is similar and what is different. But it should not deal with differences which merely satisfy curiosity, telling strange stories about cannibals and cows.

(*f*) The goal of the teaching of religion should be to bring the pupils into *living dialogue* with religions, not to inform about separate facts.

This is another way of expressing point (*e*), about taking up existential questions. There has been much debate about content-centred and pupil-centred teaching. I do not think that the circle with its one centre is a good graphic model for teaching. A better model is the ellipse with two foci: the content and the pupil. There must be a dialogue between content and pupil, and the job of the teacher is so to present the content that a dialogue is created. Teacher and pupils together should form a team working with the existential questions, and their religious answers.

(*g*) Teaching of religion in schools should build on *primary sources*, not on second-hand knowledge or subjective evaluations. If the needed dialogue between pupils and religions is to take place the religions must be represented in forms that are felt as real answers, not in forms which lack real meaning. Sometimes it is possible to have representatives of different religions present, but this is not always possible. The presentation made by the teacher must, however, always be such as could be made with living representatives present. If they are not there corporally they must be there spiritually. Textbooks should not give easy evaluations but real texts, both ancient and modern, though the selection must be related to the age group. The aim must be to use the finest and most important texts. Extracts from the Bible should be studied together with extracts from the Qur'ān, the Upanishads, the Bhagavad Gitā, the Dhammapada, etc. Holy texts are easily misunderstood when they are divorced from their milieux, and the study of religious texts demands many commentaries. Text studies should be supplemented by audio-visual material: pictures and music from churches, temples, pagodas, mosques, synagogues. When choosing this material one must have in mind the great differences within the religions, so that the presentation will not be too one-sided.

(*h*) In all schools the teaching of religion should be a separate subject, co-operating with other subjects but not integrated into them.
Because of the controversies about the teaching of religion it often happens that the religious material is assigned to other subjects: history of religion to history, religious texts to literature, and so on. Sometimes a separate subject called ethics is created which includes non-controversial religious material ...

It is not right that controversial religious material should be kept outside school. Teaching must be meaningful and existential, not dull and harmless, and this means bringing in even what is controversial. But religious material is difficult to handle, and needs special training of the teachers. A teacher of history, dealing mainly with political and economic history, is not the right man to deal with the history of religions. A teacher of literature, skilled in novels and lyrics, may not be the right man to teach about the basic religious texts. Moral abstracts from religions do not give a true description of religion. Teaching of religion has to be a separate subject, because the teachers need special training. The extent of this training must vary according to the level at which the subject is being taught, and the extent of the whole teacher-training. At levels where the teacher is expected to teach many subjects, special training has to be shorter than at levels where teachers have to teach only one or two subjects. Religions must share the same fate as other subjects, demanding neither more nor less. I suppose every subject claims what is certainly true of religion: it is so vast that adequate training of teachers takes much longer than is at present possible. In the limited time for teacher-training the students should learn something about the backgrounds and contents of Indian religions, of East Asian religions, of Middle Eastern religions, of African religions, of religious philosophy, psychology, and sociology.

If the teaching of religions is to be kept separate from other subjects there should be close co-operation with them. Pupils should learn that reality is one, and has many aspects, the biological, the physical, the historical, the literary, the religious, and so on. This co-operation can sometimes take place in planned projects in which teachers co-operate. In the Swedish revised school plan of 1969 important attempts at such co-ordinated teaching, including the teaching of religions, are made. Projects are sometimes geographical, such as on Africa, Latin America; sometimes existential – such as, The Use of Violence, or What is Man?

(*i*) Teaching of religion in schools should be given to *all pupils at all levels*, not to separate groups, or at some levels only.

This principle should not exclude the teaching of religion also being restricted in practice to certain levels and to specially interested pupils. Such arrangements depend on the whole school curriculum, and religion has to share the same conditions as other subjects. But in principle the teaching of religion has its place at all levels and for all pupils. There is so much content that it will always be possible to find new material for different levels. It is for the psychologist to discover what kind of material is most suitable at various levels. Probably young children will be told mainly stories and myths from the religions; when they grow older they will be more interested in the visible expressions of religion (churches, organizations, rituals, festivals), and in adolescence they will want to discuss questions about faith and reason, religion and society.

There should be no separation into denominational groups, such as is now the case, for instance, in Germany. The presence of pupils with varying religious backgrounds guarantees a living dialogue, in which justice is given to various positions. Confessional teaching about religions will too easily present the absent religions in a polemical way. Just as pupils are taught together in science, history, literature, mathematics, so they should be taught together in religion.

(*j*) Teaching of religion in schools should be complementary to and *supplemented by the teaching of religion outside school* (*e.g.* in churches), not be in opposition or rivalry to it.

Sometimes there has been or is rivalry and opposition between general teaching about religions in school and Christian teaching of religion in the church. There is no reason why it should be like that.

Why should not the Churches be positively interested in the general teaching about religions which the school can give? Christianity tells us to love our neighbours, and that means that we have to be interested in them and in their thinking and habits, which are often religiously motivated. Our neighbour is not only Christian, he is also Muslim, Hindu, Buddhist, Jew, whether he lives nearby, or in Asia, or Africa. But teaching about religions is not the same thing as teaching the observation of all that Christ commanded – the words in Matt. XXVIII which are the basis of Christian education. This Christian teaching must take place outside school for those wanting it. The secular school should have no objection to it. Religious freedom implies that the Churches should have the freedom to teach according to the commands of their Master.

Contacts should be kept between Christian educators in the Church and school-teachers. Many pupils take part in both kinds of instruction, and what is taught in church has much in common with what is taught in school, though the syllabuses cannot be identical, as I have stated earlier, in point (*b*).

(*k*) The teaching of religion in school has to do a pioneering job, it cannot merely follow the lead of university or Church theology to tackle the problems of the meeting of religions in the world today.

5 · Some Theological Perspectives

Roman Catholic thought and practice in catechetics has been closely linked with theology. Changing practice in the one field can often be seen to be related to developments in the other. For the county school the lines of connection are less direct. In discussions of religious education *there* overt theological considerations do not appear at first sight to have loomed large.[1] Certainly in the post-war period appeal has been more often made to educational and social than to theological factors in arguing for change in religious education. Theology has usually played only a supporting role. Thus the work of Paul Tillich was frequently cited during the 'sixties in justification of the life-centred style in religious education.[2] However, it was rather that Tillich's theology provided a timely and useful support for what was on educational grounds deemed to be a necessary change in approach and which was already taking place than that the approach had been instituted in the light of his theological system and its principle of correlation.

The fact that catechetics is seen as directly the work of the church in the exercise of her teaching office may be taken as sufficient explanation for the apparent close alliance of theology and catechetics in catholicism. That the actual Roman Catholic situation is not quite so simple is indicated by the first excerpt of this section in which Gabriel Moran, whose *Theology of Revelation* made a powerful contribution to the catechetical movement, stresses the need for a renewed theological seriousness in catechetics.

It is probably equally over-simple to attribute the seeming absence of the theologian (as distinct from the biblical scholar) from the religious education conference table to the fact that the subject in county schools is carried on at one remove from the churches. Until very recently religious education too was seen as the communication of the Christian faith and close to the concern of the churches in Britain. The apparent neglect of, or at best selective attention towards, theology in religious education circles may arise not so much from a conviction that theology is an unnecessary complication in a primarily educational task but from the dominance in religious education of a particular theological position, broadly that of liberal protestantism, which has seemed so obviously right (despite restiveness on the part of some evangelical Christians in education) as not to require defence, and so deeply embedded as to resist any attempts at displacement which might have been made.

To identify this theological sitting-tenant simply as liberal protestantism is inadequate, for the position owes as much to that strain in English religion represented by Richard Hooker, which sees no conflict between reason and revelation, as it does to Schleiermacher or Ritschl. However, two of the central themes of liberal protestantism proper appear in much writing on religious education and have influenced practice in the schools. The first of these themes is the view that man is by nature religious so that there exists in all human beings an awareness of God or a sense of the sacred and a capacity for response to religious truth which it is the task of religious education to nurture and refine. This view is expressed with characteristic warmth and lucidity in the excerpt from Victor Murray's *Education into Religion*. Essentially the same view of religious education as the cultivation of natural religion is evident also in phrases about the intuitive understanding of God in young children or the religious quest in adolescents which have characterized advocacy of more recent approaches in the subject.

No less important than this immanentist emphasis has been the basically optimistic view of human nature and secular culture characteristic of liberalism. This leads to a view of religious education as, on the one hand, a translation into religious terms of the personal and social aspirations of the young and on the other a commendation of the Christian faith by restating it in terms which take up, rather than conflict with, the insights reached by the intellectual enquiry carried on in other aspects of the curriculum.[3]

Both of these foundation assumptions are criticized, as they appear in the context of nineteenth-century Protestant theology, in the excerpt from Karl Barth.[4] It is, however, an indication of the strength of the liberal tradition in religious education that Barth's theology, which might have been felt to call into question the whole enterprise, while it had some influence upon academic theology in England, made no discernible impression upon religious education. Equally it is perhaps an indication of the resilience and self-assurance of this liberal tradition that religious education has been able to interpret Bonhoeffer's admittedly fragmentary thoughts on religion and 'man's coming of age' as a confirmation of the essential rightness of its position rather than an attack upon its aims and presuppositions.

Where religious education passes into religious studies on the pattern advocated by the Lancaster Schools Council project, then the search for a theological basis may be thought less appropriate than an analysis of the nature of religion which will guide the study of that phenomenon. Such an examination of the 'logic of religion' is undertaken in the excerpts from Ninian Smart. Nonetheless, for the Christian teacher operating professionally in the field of religion, whether in Lancaster terms; adopting the necessary procedural neutrality in using the material of the Humanities Curriculum Project; or in more traditional modes, some theological orientation is needed if he is to understand the relation of his professional task to the faith he holds and to live with the tensions that may produce.[5] In this connection H. R. Niebuhr's *Christ and Culture* remains a classic exposition of the problems expressed in its title. His short summary of some typical attempts at its resolution forms the final reading of the chapter.

Gabriel Moran · *God Still Speaks*

Gabriel Moran, *God Still Speaks*, Burns & Oates 1967, pp.38-43

The catechetical movement has from its inception hovered on the brink of trivialization; it continues to hang there. It will never be accepted as more than a realignment of tactics, a redefining of technical words, a reassessment of methodological gimmicks, unless it incorporates into itself the best that is available in fields such as philosophy, anthropology, and psychology. It must wrestle with the exegesis of Scripture and deal with the history of the Church. At the very least, catechetics ought to recognize that theology is its chief ally and not an enemy or an estranged relative. It is time to put to definitive rest the implication that theological reflection upon Christian faith is mostly irrelevant and perhaps a bit dangerous to the Christian life. Some catechetical writing seems to be oblivious of what has been going on for the past thirty years in theology. Such a position is difficult to understand considering the role of theology in the Second Vatican Council. Theology is not an irrelevant game being played by professors; it is the driving force in the Church today that will make or break any catechetical movement.

Advances in religion teaching have, in fact, come about through the influence of improved theology. However, the effect has not been greater because of a simplistic opposition between theology and catechetics that still pervades catechetical writing. For example, the statement is often made in catechetical literature that theology deals mainly with 'doctrine' but that catechetics is concerned with the 'message'. There is a difference between theology and catechetics that is vaguely hinted at by this terminology, but the opposition of doctrine and message does not come to grips with the issue and may do nothing but cause confusion. Theology is just as concerned with the 'message' as is catechetics. Conversely catechetics is at all times doctrinal, not only because human reflection leads to doctrinal understanding, but because even the most primitive 'message' of Christianity is already a doctrinal formulation. The chief interest of both theology and catechetics is the revelation of God in Jesus Christ. This revelation is neither doctrine nor message, but is a real, personal intercommunion. When trying to convey some insight into this inexhaustible reality, both theology and catechetics use a doctrinally formulated message.

A sharp opposition of doctrine and message seems to be based on the assumption that the more primitive the formulation, the closer one is to the 'pure' revelation. But the fact that one teaches the earliest apostolic discourses is no guarantee that one is conveying God's revelation in unadulterated simplicity, nor even that one is approaching more closely to it. Indeed, the attempt to avoid theological reflection upon the most primitive records of revelation does not succeed in getting rid of theology, but only in ingesting bad theology. Thus today there is building up in catechetical writing a new theological vocabulary not always supported by careful theological reflection. These new words are at first sight more personal and concrete, more 'existential' and relevant, than the tired, old scholastic words. But the very reason why they are more immediately appealing is the same reason that they more quickly degenerate into jargon. What is needed to resolve this problem of terminology is not to create a new and still simpler vocabulary, but to stop hoping that the problem can be solved at this level and with these tools. What is needed today is not a further stripping away of theology, but more and better theology both in the preparation of religion teachers and in discussions concerning catechetical theory. Otherwise, with theology and catechetics removed from one another or sharply contrasted, catechetical writing turns in upon itself and ends by creating a new system of technical words – the very thing the catechetical movement set out to get rid of.

One catechetical writer, maintaining that the catechism should not be a summary of theology, goes on to say that 'it is necessary to distinguish between knowledge concerning God and knowing God, intellectual assimilation and vital assimilation, doctrine and message, notional assent and real assent, a faith of principles and a faith of concrete realities, a faith that is simply knowledge of things of faith and faith as a way of salvation.'[6] The question that must be raised with reference to such statements is not whether catechists are or should be in favour of the second set of aims as opposed to the first. The questions that must be asked are whether anyone prefers the first set over the second, whether this whole schema clarifies the relationship between theology and catechetics, and whether these contrasts are any help at all to teachers trying to understand their role in religious education. Obviously, catechists are more interested in the students knowing God than in knowing about God, but the serious questions are how catechists can make any contribution to the student coming to know God, and what the possibilities and limitations of any human being are in helping another to know God. A deep probing of these issues behind the new phrases is not always evident in catechetical writing. This, I would claim, is the great crisis of catechetics today: not the dying catechism and manual, but the still rising hope that the education of hundreds of millions of people in an incredibly complex world can be carried out with a bit of Scripture and liturgy and much sincerity and good will. This simply is not enough. There is need for patient inquiry, deep understanding, and detailed knowledge.

It is often said in catechetical writing today: In the past we merely instructed the intellect in revealed truths; now we must concern ourselves with 'forming the whole man.' Some people may understand clearly what they mean to say with this formula, but some very dangerous ideas could easily lurk beneath the surface.

Certainly, it is true that teaching 'revealed truths' to the intellect of a child is insufficient (I would go further and say it is impossible). One must ask, however, whether the situation that practically everyone today revolts against has been understood, and more important still, whether the supposed remedies might not worsen the situation. It is very strange that catechetical writers keep saying that Catholic religion teaching has been too centred on knowledge and has neglected everything else. In actual fact, it would seem that religion books and religion teachers have never been wanting in exhortations to avoid sin, in imposing devotional and ascetical practices, in insisting upon frequent reception of sacraments, in maintaining strong external discipline, and so forth. The juxtaposition of these and numerous other things with the 'holding of true doctrines' has never been lacking; and this is what constitutes a large part of our difficulty. The assumption that we have dealt too much with intellectual understanding and not enough with emotion is wrong on both counts.

On the one hand, we have never had in the teaching of religion too much concentration upon knowledge and understanding; we have had only too little of it. What has been most painfully lacking and what is most desperately needed is some intellectual seriousness and competence in the teaching of religion. It is preposterous to say that the ordinary catechism or theology manual is overly intellectual, too philosophical, excessively theological. 'The fact that our textbooks are so little alive, serve proclamation and witness so little, is not due to their superabundance of scholastic and scientific theology but because they offer too little of it.'[7] In the teaching of religion our problem has not been in stopping at knowledge and understanding; would that we could get so far. We have not dealt exclusively with the intelligence of students precisely because the only way that their religious understanding could be reached would be through historical, bodily, and social experience.

On the other hand, if religion teaching has not succeeded in reaching the child's understanding, one must then ask where the real, operative, religious motivation has been coming from. The answer, it would seem, is that it has sprung from emotion, a distorted and dehumanized emotion because separated from understanding and freedom. In other words, while paying lip service to 'intellect', religion teaching has usually been concerned with emotional reactions, particularly sentimentality and fear. We do not need more manipulation of children's emotions; we ought to have far less of it. While letting children experience their world, teaching ought to be directed to the intelligence of the children so that they may be freed from their fears. The constant refrain today about the need of less concern for intellectual learning in religion and more 'training of the heart' not only misses what has been wrong in the past, but threatens to point us a hundred-eighty degrees in the wrong direction.

At the very moment when the Church stands in greatest need of an intellectual apostolate there is implicit in much catechetical writing a devaluation of intellectual understanding. Of course, it is always admitted and even strenuously asserted that the transmission of knowledge (the 'revealed truths') is a necessary step along the way to forming Christians, but this shows an inadequate conception of the nature of Christian revelation. One must come to realize what it means to stand in the truth which sets men free. What is necessary is not something in addition to the 'revealed truths' but a much deeper comprehension of Christian revelation. When this task is accomplished it will become apparent that the understanding of what it means to be a Christian is not a preliminary to be gotten through as an embarrassing preamble, but is itself the radical grasping hold of (or being grasped by) the Father of Truth.[8]

A. Victor Murray · *Education into Religion*

A. Victor Murray, *Education into Religion*, James Nisbet 1953, pp.92-95

The sense of God comes to us as that of a power not ourselves making itself known in creation, in beauty, in conscience and in fear. Sometimes it comes in darkness and terror, in the piercing shriek of the hurricane, in the upheaval of a mountain, in the horrors of plague, or in tragic changes of fortune. 'Fear created the gods', said Statius, and this fact was well accepted in the Middle Ages. But there are other manifestations of the unseen that are more kindly and gentle. They steal upon us almost unawares in the experience of human love, in the painful beauty of the setting sun, in moonlight over the sea, in the sweetness of Mozart's music, or in haunting appeal of a single line of poetry:

A rose-red city half as old as Time –

but in whatever way they come they authenticate the existence of an unseen world of spirit with which at one and the same time we have a sense of affinity and a sense of strangeness. It is in this contact with nature in all its forms and the conviction of something over and above the evidence of the senses that we have to look, in Dr. R. R. Marett's notable phrase, for 'the birth of humility'.

> When I consider thy heavens, the work of thy fingers,
> The moon and the stars, which thou hast ordained;
> What is man, that thou art mindful of him?

This psalm puts into a personal form an experience of which everyone from the most primitive even to the most sophisticated has some knowledge. It comes not only through nature but also through beauty of every kind – of sight, colour, sound and personal relationship. It takes different forms in different religions; sometimes it is expressed as abjectness and sometimes as exhilaration, but in every form it is a recognition of the existence of something outside ourselves that is 'from everlasting to everlasting', against which the life of man is but a shadow.

This intuitive sense of God is, as we have seen, the beginning of religion, and like the growth of a tree this earlier growth remains at the heart of every later development. Deep within all our different forms and revelations there is natural religion – the sense of God in nature and in the unsophisticated mind of man. The historical religions explain it, give it a name, criticize and discipline it, but they do not, and cannot, explain it away. The intellect is driven by this sense of the unknown to seek to make it known, and scientific curiosity is itself a witness to the mysteriousness of the universe. Pride takes hold of the intellect when it is cut off from this source, and men imagine that in their own thinking is the beginning of all science and all religion. This is a common theme of Greek tragedy, the pride of men in their own cleverness forgetting God, and also of primitive mythology, the giants that scale the heights of heaven and are hurled headlong 'with hideous ruine and combustion'.

This natural religion shows itself very strongly in the time of adolescence, for it is the biological changes of puberty and the pains of adaptation to modern society that bring the civilized man back to the experiences of primitive life. The interest of this period lies in the coincidence of primitive impulses and an informed modern curiosity. The adolescent is thus a good deal more primitive than the child. There is in his experience a sense almost of disintegration, sometimes pleasant, sometimes very painful, and objects of concern group themselves round three main feelings: the sense of the littleness of human life compared with the vast span of the ages and the incredible size of the universe; the sense of incompleteness and frustration in all experiences that are enjoyable; and the sense of the sacred as something which is at once overwhelming and attractive. These experiences are the raw material that is misused by Romanticism but they represent, so to speak, an outcrop of natural religion with which education is very vitally concerned.

Nevertheless, for the natural man this experience is one of contact with a world that is anonymous. He does not know with what or with whom he has to do. This anonymous Presence therefore needs to be given a name and the unseen world itself needs to be 'informed', to be given form. This happened in the beginnings of history in folklore and mythology. The powers of nature were personified and familiarity drew the sting of their awfulness. But it has better come about through men's reflection on their own experiences, through the insight of persons particularly sensitive to spiritual qualities, such as the Hebrew prophets and the prophets and poets of every age and country, through the pattern that gradually shows itself in the history of the race, and through the accumulated records of the experiences of men in this sphere. Looked at from one side these have all been men's discoveries about the unseen world. From the other side they are God's revelation of Himself. In this sense, therefore, there is not and there never has been 'religion without revelation'. It is the same God who was there in the first nuclear fission whom we now believe to be 'the father of our Lord Jesus Christ'.

When, however, our own interpretation of the unseen world becomes so familiar that we cease to question it, a new problem arises.

A moral difficulty in the case of historical religions is that they express themselves in words so fully that God is apt to become narrowed down to the compass of our own thought. Hence arises that familiarity in the things of God which is the sin of idolatry; it is to worship that which our minds have made. From this spring all manner of censoriousness and superciliousness whether in doctrine or in morals. In this context clarity of thought is often the foe to humility. On the other hand, face to face with the natural universe, with the God of the bright sky or the storm cloud, of the mountain and the plain, a man feels his own littleness, and this natural religion is an integral part of the Christian religion and of Judaism. To the prophet Amos, the God who insisted that judgement should roll down as waters and righteousness as a mighty stream was the same God who made the Pleiades and Orion. The unknown prophet of the Exile reminds contemporaries that the God whom they appear to know so well is 'he that sitteth on the circle of the earth and the inhabitants thereof are as grasshoppers'. And Jesus Himself gave the same warning to those who light-heartedly take oaths: 'the heaven is the throne of God and the earth is the footstool of his feet'.

Now concentration in religious education on the historical and literary side of the Bible may expose people to precisely this temptation of familiarity. They may easily mistake religious knowledge for religion. An earlier generation valued knowledge mainly for its *form*: the present generation is apt to value it mainly for its *content*. Yet the alternative is not an authoritarian creed, for the authoritarian may be just as much the victim of his own intellect as the modernist: he is apt to be concerned with propositions intellectually conceived, and he is looking for certainty. The real alternative is to recognize that the goal of all our endeavour in religious education is to help a child to be at home in the universe, which is his Father's house, and to behave accordingly. This means natural religion interpreted and not superseded by Christianity, and a spirit to which all pettiness is alien and all self-seeking impossible.

Karl Barth · *Evangelical Theology in the Nineteenth Century*

Karl Barth, 'Evangelical Theology in the Nineteenth Century', *The Humanity of God*, Collins Fontana 1967, pp.20-22

The theologians of the 19th century proceeded fundamentally along the lines of the 18th-century Christian Enlightenment. Their particular venture became questionable, however, as they set out to prove the possibility of faith in its relatedness to, and its conditioning by, the world views which were normative for their contemporaries and even for themselves. More precisely, they tried to find that point of reference in the world views where voluntary acceptance of the Christian message and the Christian faith suggested themselves more or less convincingly and were viewed at least as possibilities. It is evident that for this purpose the theologians had to make a particular world view their own and had to affirm its validity. This was all the easier for them as acceptance of a prevailing philosophy was precisely the presupposition for their work. The world views changed in the course of the century; but there were always theologians who went along, more or less convinced, if not enthusiastic, and who started the theological task afresh within the new framework.

In contrast to Enlightenment theology, the 19th-century theologians focused their attention on one particular point in relation to all the various world views of their time: man's supposedly innate and essential capacity to 'sense and taste the infinite' as Schleiermacher said, or the 'religious *a priori*' as later affirmed by Troeltsch. There was scarcely a theologian who did not also consider himself a professional philosopher. These philosophers of religion, more or less faithful or sophisticated advocates of one of the current world views, were busily working out a general epistomology, a system of metaphysics and ethics focusing on this very capacity. In these terms they sought to validate the potential for religion, including the Christian faith. The great efforts undertaken in the steps of Schleiermacher by men like De Wette, Biedermann, Lipsius, Kaftan, and Lüdemann were highly commendable.

And yet these efforts were surrounded by two questions which we may find difficult to answer in the affirmative.

First: Were men prepared to take such lessons from the theologians? Did they permit having their world views supplemented? Were they sensitive to man's openness towards religion and the Christian faith, and desirous to make any use of it? The revelation theology of Schelling during his later years should not be forgotten at this point. And we must not overlook that later philosophers like Lotze, Siebeck, Dilthey, and Eucken actively shared in their own way in the work of the theologians. But it was a bad omen that Goethe either ignored or viewed with displeasure what was happening. He disliked Schleiermacher's *Speeches*, quite apart from their romantic garb. The same can be said of Hegel, the other great master of the century. The efforts of Schleiermacher and of his successors did not acquire any significance for the broad mass of the 'cultured' to whom Schleiermacher had addressed himself so impressively with his proof of the roots of religion in the structure of man's spiritual life. The thinking of the awakening labour class of the 19th century was even less influenced. The response to the efforts of the theologians was really not encouraging. If this does not necessarily speak against the excellence of what these philosopher-theologians did, it is yet a quite serious matter when compared with the explicit intention of their work.

The second question is more serious. Could the Christian message and the Christian faith be a subject for debate while the validity of a general world view was presupposed? Is there any proof that acceptance of a particular world view will make Christianity generally accessible or even possible? Even granted the existence of man's religious disposition, can the Christian faith be called one of its expressions, in other words a 'religion'? Nineteenth-century evangelical theology assumed that it was so. But it could not do so without subjugating the Christian message and the Christian faith to that interpretation and form by which Christianity could achieve validity and general accessibility for the proponents of the prevailing world view. The Christian faith had to be understood as a 'religion' if it was to be generally accepted as valid. What if it resisted this classification? What if acceptance was so eagerly sought that Christian faith ceased to be Christian faith as soon as it was interpreted as 'religion'? What if the attempt to give it the 'firm' basis actually removed the real ground from under it? Nineteenth-century theology did not raise these questions. One wonders, therefore, whether its most typical spokesmen were not primarily philosophers and only secondarily theologians. This might explain the failure of their missionary task at a deeper level. Was it possible to win the 'Gentile' point of view, in order to commend to them the Christian cause? Could this procedure impress the 'Gentiles'? Would it not have been necessary first to be innocent as doves in order to be wise as serpents?

Ninian Smart · *Secular Education and the Logic of Religion*

Ninian Smart, *Secular Education and the Logic of Religion*, Faber 1968, pp.12-14, 15-18

We must note then that the term [theology] usually makes two big assumptions: first, that there is a God, and second that it is the Christian tradition with which it is essentially concerned.

Now it might be replied to this that there is a sense of the term which at least does not make the first assumption. Can we not simply study Christian texts, Christian history and so forth from an object-ive, scientific point of view? Such a study yields results independ-ently of any faith in the truth of the Bible as a record of God's self-revelation. Is this not the proper sense in which we speak of theology in the secular university?

The objection is well taken, for it points to the fundamental ambiguity in the knave of arts. The fundamental ambiguity is that one can approach religious studies in two quite different ways. We can consider religious phenomena and beliefs from a purely histori-cal and descriptive point of view on the one hand; and we can approach them as relevant to, or as enshrining, claims about the nature of reality. We can, that is, treat religion historically or doctrinally. This is so, whether our standpoint be religious or atheistic. The atheist who argues for the falsity of belief in God is going beyond a simply descriptive account of religion. Likewise the Christian who preaches, or who engages in apologetics, is doing more than making historical and descriptive remarks about Christianity.

I have used the terms 'historical' and 'doctrinal' to point to the contrast between the two approaches. But the latter expression is not altogether a good one for the purpose. Although a religion such as Christianity teaches certain doctrines, doctrines are by no means everything. The Christian faith has prescriptions about conduct, a right mode of worship (or modes thereof), an institutional vehicle, the Church, and so on. As we shall see, a religion is a multi-dimen-sional thing, and the doctrinal side represents only one dimension.

One needs then a wider word. It is required to cover cases of commending the faith, of arguing for its truth, of endorsing religious values, etc., and cases of doing the reverse (as when one may criticize a faith as untrue, or dangerous, or decadent, or pernicious, or nonsensical, etc). In all these cases one is not disputing that John XXIII was a Pope or that Christianity is nearly two thousand years old or that there are many Christians in Italy. One is rather taking some stand about or arguing about the validity or value of a faith or of some aspect thereof. The distinction between making a religious claim and asserting something descriptive about religion is used in the joke about the man who asked another 'Do you believe in baptism?' 'Believe in it?' the other man answered: 'I've seen it done.'

If in a broad sense we can say that descriptive studies are historical (even if they are sometimes about contemporary events or transcultural analogies and so on), then it may be useful to employ the term *parahistorical* to refer to those studies and arguments which concern the truth, value, etc., of religion.

The question of whether Jesus lived in Galilee is, on this usage, an historical question; but the question of whether he died for men's sins is parahistorical (but note that the question of whether he thought he died for men's sins reverts to the historical side). The question of whether mystical experience contains an unvarying central core is an historical question; but the question of whether one knows God through mystical experience is a parahistorical one. The problem of the degree to which a particular religion is sociologically determined is an historical problem (on this usage); the question of whether its moral teachings are right is a parahistorical question.

It is of fundamental importance to bear this distinction in mind. The very notion of religious studies takes on a very different meaning according as we include in them, or fail to include in them, parahistorical questions. I shall argue later that they need to be included, because of the logic of the subject: but I shall also argue that this can only rightly be done by liberating theology from the narrow confines of its past.

Now whether or not we think that parahistorical approaches to religion are a proper component of formal education – they are, of course, entrenched in school education by virtue of the 1944 Education Act – they obviously are important. They belong to the general problem of deciding about the truth of ideologies. Whether, for instance, we are committed to a political liberalism which makes Humanist assumptions, or to Marxism, or to Christian Democracy in the European sense, our commitment will make some difference to the tangled ongoings of history. It will make some difference to our personal and professional conduct. It will in some degree influence our emotional reactions to the world into which we have been pitched. One cannot for these reasons divorce ideological from religious issues. Consequently, the parahistorical questions about religion are part of the general problem of ideology – or if you like, metaphysics.

In claiming that a theology or doctrinal inquiry is not just a free-floating affair, I am attempting to put proper weight on the fact that religious ideas are not just ideas but *religious* ideas. One can see this point more clearly by observing the nature of religion, which is a complex object – a six-dimensional one, as I shall argue.

One dimension of religion can be epitomized in what we have already started to discuss: namely the fact that religions typically teach *doctrines*. In Christianity, there is, for instance, the Trinity Doctrine, the doctrine of Creation and so on. In Buddhism, there is the *dharma*, summed up in such formulae as the Four Noble Truths. It is true that many ethnic religions in technologically primitive and pre-literate cultures do not formally enunciate teachings about the nature of God, the world man, etc. They tend to spell out religion in myths. But it is typical of the major religions of the world – in the Indian, Semitic and Chinese cultures – to teach doctrines. It is therefore useful to speak of the *doctrinal dimension* of religion.

Secondly, a religion typically contains beliefs which are cast in story form, whether the stories concern actual historical events interpreted religiously or non-historical 'transcendental' or sacred events. Such stories of the gods, of God, of God's activities in history, of the career of the sacred teacher – these can, by a generous extension of the term, be called myths. I am in using this last word not intending any judgment about truth or falsity: I am not using the word in that everyday sense where 'myth' just means a false belief or what have you. On my usage, the Exodus, the stories of deliberations on Olympus, the Buddha's career, the accounts of the gods in the Pali canon – these belong to the *mythological dimension* of religion. Sometimes, we may note, it is not easy to draw a line between doctrine and myth. Sometimes the doctrine, indeed, results from reflection on and refinement of what is initially cast in mythological form: thus between *Genesis* and Aquinas' theology of Creation there is a transition of this sort.

Thirdly, a religion prescribes an ethical path. Its ethics are often woven in part out of doctrinal and mythological threads. Jesus' death on the Cross illuminates the meaning of Christian love, for example. We may call this the *ethical dimension* of religion.

These three dimensions can be said to represent the teachings of a religion: they sum up its *Weltanschauung*: they express the perspective in which the adherent views the world and himself. But even if we have gone beyond the notion that the world-view of a religion is simply expressed in doctrinal propositions, for it is clothed too in myth, symbolism, ethical prescriptions, we must go further and see the relation between these three dimensions and the living practice of a faith. The doctrines, myths and so on cannot be properly understood save by reference to the characteristic patterns of religious activity in the faith in question.

Thus Christianity involves the worship of God, the sacraments, etc. If God indeed were not to be worshipped would he be properly called 'God'? In some forms of religion, worship is rather unimportant, but other activities are more central. For example, in Theravada Buddhism there is no worship of the Buddha (though reverence is paid to the departed Teacher): what is central is the treading of the Path which culminates in the practice of contemplation. This contemplative life – yoga in the broad sense of the term – has its analogies to the contemplative life of Christian mystics, such as Suso or Ruysbroeck, even if its goal is interpreted very differently in Buddhism. But just as it is impossible to understand properly the concept of *God* or *sacrament* in Christian theology without entering at least imaginatively into the milieu of worship, so one cannot understand the idea of nirvana in Buddhism without entering at least imaginatively into the meditative life which takes one towards the goal. Since in the West we are more used to the religion of worship of God, and since worship is a form of ritual, I shall call this practical aspect of religion the *ritual dimension*.

To avoid misunderstanding, let me emphasize two points. First, I would not wish ritual to be confused with ritualism. The latter is an opprobrious term we sometimes use to designate ritual activities which have become merely mechanical or over-elaborate. It is a disease afflicting religion when ritual is divorced from inner experience, from genuine concern, from religious sensitivity. Moreover, it is worth noting that ritual need not be elaborate: it can be very simple and informal. When I close my eyes in prayer, when a few are gathered together to sing a hymn – these are as much cases of ritual as a High Mass. Second, I want to include in the ritual dimension the contemplative practices to which I have referred in the case of Theravada Buddhism and Christian mysticism. This is perhaps artificial and a little strained. But mysticism is in the West treated as a form of prayer; and the function of contemplation in Buddhism, say, is analogous to the function of worship, etc. It is a response to and a quest for the transcendental world.

But we cannot fully appreciate religion or its meaning without paying attention to the inner life of those who are involved in the life of the dimensions we have so far considered. Indeed, many of the seminal moments of religious history have involved religious experiences of a dramatic kind: the Enlightenment of the Buddha, the visions of Isaiah in the Temple, the conversion of St. Paul, the prophecy of Muhammad – we could scarcely explain the directions religious history has taken without referring to such moments. At a humbler level there is the testimony of countless religious folk who believe themselves to have had moments of illumination, conversion, vision, a sense of presence and so on. We may refer to this aspect of religion as the *experiential dimension.*

Finally, though the continuance and development of religion may be nurtured internally (so to speak) by experience, they also depend on social institutions, such as the Church in Christianity and the Sangha in Buddhism. More widely, religion has its social roots and effects. All this can be referred to as the *social dimension* of religion.

H. Richard Niebuhr · *Christ and Culture*

H. Richard Neibuhr, 'The Typical Answers', *Christ and Culture*, pp.39-41. Copyright © 1951 by Harper & Row, Publishers, Inc. Used by permission of the publishers

Given these two complex realities – Christ and culture – an infinite dialogue must develop in the Christian conscience and the Christian community. In his single-minded direction toward God, Christ leads men away from the temporality and pluralism of culture. In its concern for the conservation of the many values of the past, culture rejects the Christ who bids men rely on grace. Yet the Son of God is himself child of a religious culture, and sends his disciples to tend his lambs and sheep, who cannot be guarded without cultural work. The dialogue proceeds with denials and affirmations, reconstructions, compromises, and new denials. Neither individual nor church can come to a stopping-place in the endless search for an answer which will not provoke a new rejoinder.

Yet it is possible to discern some order in this multiplicity, to stop the dialogue, as it were, at certain points; and to define typical partial answers that recur so often in different eras and societies that they seem to be less the product of historical conditioning than of the nature of the problem itself and the meanings of its terms. In this way the course of the great conversation about Christ and culture may be more intelligently followed, and some of the fruits of the discussion may be garnered. In the following chapters such typical answers are to be set forth and illustrated by reference to such Christians as John and Paul, Tertullian and Augustine, Thomas Aquinas and Luther, Ritschl and Tolstoy. At this point brief and summary descriptions of these typical answers is offered as a guide to what follows. Five sorts of answers are distinguished, of which three are closely related to each other as belonging to that median type in which both Christ and culture are distinguished and affirmed; yet strange family resemblances may be found along the whole scale.

Answers of the first type emphasize the *opposition* between Christ and culture. Whatever may be the customs of the society in which the Christian lives, and whatever the human achievements it conserves, Christ is seen as opposed to them, so that he confronts men with the challenge of an 'either-or' decision. In the early period of church history Jewish rejection of Jesus found its counterpart in Christian antagonism to Jewish culture, while Roman outlawry of the new faith was accompanied by Christian flight from or attack upon Graeco-Roman civilization. In medieval times monastic orders and sectarian movements called on believers living in what purported to be a Christian culture to abandon the 'world' and to 'come out from among them and be separate'. In the modern period answers of this kind are being given by missionaries who require their converts to abandon wholly the customs and institutions of so-called 'heathen' societies, by little groups of withdrawing Christians in Western or 'Christianized' civilization, and in partial manner, by those who emphasize the antagonism of Christian faith to capitalism and communism, to industrialism and nationalism, to Catholicism and Protestantism.

Recognition of a fundamental *agreement* between Christ and culture is typical of the answers offered by a second group. In them

Jesus often appears as a great hero of human culture history; his life and teachings are regarded as the greatest human achievement; in him, it is believed, the aspirations of men toward their values are brought to a point of culmination; he confirms what is best in the past, and guides the process of civilization to its proper goal. Moreover, he is a part of culture in the sense that he himself is part of the social heritage that must be transmitted and conserved. In our time answers of this kind are given by Christians who note the close relation between Christianity and Western civilization, between Jesus' teachings or the teachings about him and democratic institutions; yet there are occasional interpretations that emphasize the agreement between Christ and Eastern culture as well as some that tend to identify him with the spirit of Marxian society. In earlier times solutions of the problem along these lines were being offered simultaneously with the solutions of the first or 'Christ-against-culture' type.

Three other typical answers agree with each other in seeking to maintain the great differences between the two principles and in undertaking to hold them together in some unity. They are distinguished from each other by the manner in which each attempts to combine the two authorities. One of them, our third type, understands Christ's relation to culture somewhat as the men of the second group do: he is the fulfilment of cultural aspirations and the restorer of the institutions of true society. Yet there is in him something that neither arises out of culture nor contributes directly to it. He is discontinuous as well as continuous with social life and its culture. The latter, indeed, leads men to Christ, yet only in so preliminary a fashion that a great leap is necessary if men are to reach him or, better, true culture is not possible unless beyond all human achievement, all human search for values, all human society, Christ enters into life from above with gifts which human aspiration has not envisioned and which human effort cannot attain unless he relates men to a supernatural society and a new value-centre. Christ is, indeed, a Christ of culture, but he is also a *Christ above culture*. This *synthetic* type is best represented by Thomas Aquinas and his followers, but it has many other representatives in both early and modern times.

Another group of median answers constitutes our fourth type. In these the duality and inescapable authority of both Christ and culture are recognized, but the opposition between them is also accepted. To those who answer the question in this way it appears that Christians throughout life are subject to the tension that accompanies obedience to two authorities who do not agree yet must both be obeyed. They refuse to accommodate the claims of Christ to those of secular society, as, in their estimation, men in the second and third groups do. So they are like the 'Christ-against-culture' believers, yet differ from them in the conviction that obedience to God requires obedience to the institutions of society and loyalty to its members as well as obedience to a Christ who sits in judgment on that society. Hence man is seen as subject to two moralities, and as a citizen of two worlds that are not only discontinuous with each other but largely opposed. In the *polarity* and *tension* of Christ and culture life must be lived precariously and sinfully in the hope of a justification which lies beyond history. Luther may be regarded as the greatest representative of this type, yet many a Christian who is not otherwise a Lutheran finds himself compelled to solve the problem in this way.

Finally, as the fifth type in the general series and as the third of the mediating answers, there is the *conversionist* solution. Those who offer it understand with the members of the first and fourth groups that human nature is fallen or perverted, and that this perversion not only appears in culture but is transmitted by it. Hence the opposition between Christ and all human institutions and customs is to be recognized. Yet the antithesis does not lead either to Christian separation from the world as with the first group, or to mere endurance in the expectation of a transhistorical salvation, as with the fourth. Christ is seen as the converter of man in his culture and society, not apart from these, for there is no nature without culture and no turning of men from self and idols to God save in society. It is in Augustine that the great outlines of this answer seem to be offered; John Calvin makes it explicit; many others are associated with these two.

When the answers to the enduring problem are stated in this manner it is apparent that a construction has been set up that is partly artificial. A type is always something of a construct, even when it has not been constructed prior to long study of many historic individuals and movements. When one returns from the hypothetical scheme to the rich complexity of individual events, it is evident at once that no person or group ever conforms completely to a type. Each historical figure will show characteristics that are more reminiscent of some other family than the one by whose name he has been called, or traits will appear that seem wholly unique and individual. The method of typology, however, though historically inadequate, has the advantage of calling to attention the continuity and significance of the great *motifs* that appear and reappear in the long wrestling of Christians with their enduring problem. Hence also it may help us to gain orientation as we in our own time seek to answer the question of Christ and culture.

Religious Education and Moral Education

Faith and Reason and Moral Situation

6 · The Relationship Considered

This section forms a bridge or watershed between the other parts of the Reader. In the Preface we stated our belief that religious education and moral education are separable and we have treated them as such. But we are aware of the relationship between these two activities in schools and the underlying questions about the relation of morality to religion which that raises. The extracts in this section show the educational relationship considered, first by those engaged in religious education and then by those whose chief concern is with moral education or moral philosophy.

If the relation between religion and morality has been almost a standing item on the agenda of theology and philosophy, that between religious education and moral education has only recently come up for discussion in this country. The strong moralistic strain in British protestantism provided the grounds for a general assumption that religious and moral education were virtually synonomous, or if differentiated then only to the extent of making it clear that it was hoped the first-named would produce some progress in the second as its result.[1]

A realization that a fresh look at the traditional assumption was needed arose first from practical rather than theoretical considerations. From the religious education side some unease grew, even among those Christians who held that there was an essential connection between religion and morality, about the tendency to defend the subject's place in schools on grounds of its desirable moral outcomes. Such efforts at providing additional support to religious education's cause seemed to some Christians to be mistaken and damaging. Religion must be taught because it was true and important, they felt, not because it was socially useful.[2] Secondly, some secular humanists reasoned that since religious education had proved a contentious subject with a disappointing track record in

maintaining moral standards among the young there was everything to be said for replacing or supplementing it by direct moral
education.[3]

From this initial discomfort on each side at being encumbered
with the other, there has since been a move to more intensive
examination of the relation between the two as activities in the
county school and of the common ground between them.[4] The
discussion has not gone unnoticed in Roman Catholic circles, and
has some relevance to the Vatican II 'Declaration on Religious
Freedom', but it has not substantially affected practice in Roman
Catholic schools. The Roman Catholic church through its Thomist
tradition is well able to conceive of a basic morality available to
all men apart from revelation. However, in the education of
Roman Catholic children moral education is not separated from
the religious task of nourishing 'a life lived according to the spirit
of Christ'.[5]

We turn now to examples of views from writers on religious education. The article written in 1966 by Philip May of the Department
of Education at Durham represents a conservative view of the in-
dispensability of the Bible and Christian faith as a basis for moral
education. It is one which would find echo among many of his
fellow Christians. But not all. Harold Loukes, in the second extract,
takes the view that while there is a clear role for the teacher of
religious education in moral education, not only in promoting concern for it but in seeing that the ultimate questions to which it may
lead are raised, nevertheless moral education is not dependent for
its justification or procedures upon religious education as a carrier.
The third extract, from the Schools Council Working Paper 36, is
in broad agreement with Loukes and with the much more detailed
exploration of the question made in chapter three of the Durham
Report. It provides a convenient summary of the mediating position
which recognizes both the autonomy of moral education and the
distinctive contribution which religious education can make in that
area of study.

Modern writers on moral education have tended to write more
about developmental stages, the psychology of moral behaviour
and about the pervasiveness of moral education throughout the
school curriculum, than about its connections with religious education. The attitude that moral education can be treated as distinct
from, but not entirely unconnected with, religious education is thus
strongly implied by their work and this will be seen in later chap-

ters. In this they appear to have been influenced very much by one side of a long-standing philosophical debate about the possible dependence of morality upon religion.[6] The view that moral education is separable from religious education is strongly argued by two philosophers of education, Paul Hirst and R. F. Dearden. Professor Hirst's paper, 'Morals, Religion and the Maintained Schools' is important and influential but not given here since it is already available in more than one place.[7] Similar arguments are forcibly put by Dearden in the extract given here which is taken from his book, *The Philosophy of Primary Education.*

Our extract by John Hospers deals with a point that has worried many educators, namely, is not religion necessary to the moral life because of its motivational force? Would not people drop morality altogether if dissociated from religion?[8] J. S. Mill had taken up this point in 1874[9] and our extract shows a modern philosopher engaged in examining Mill's views. It is interesting to see philosophers taking seriously a view often put forward by teachers and parents.

The final extract shows how all this looks to someone with a practical responsibility for conducting research in moral education. John Wilson, writing as Director of the Farmington Trust Research Unit in Moral Education at Oxford, offers here his reasons for the kind of neutral approach adopted by his research team.

It must be said, of course, that none of these writers has suggested that teachers of religious education should have nothing to do with moral education; they only say that other teachers can and should engage in this field as well, and that parents who would declare themselves non-religious would still wish schools to provide moral education for their sons and daughters. This is also the view of the editors and accounts for our section divisions.

P. R. May · *Moral Education and the Bible*

P. R. May, 'Moral Education and the Bible', *Learning for Living*, November 1966, pp.10-12

No one has ever seriously doubted that education is a major form of social control. The school is a community the bonds and pressures of which are primarily moral, and the office of teacher, in a democratic society particularly, is one of great power and authority. While rejecting the assertion quite frequently made today that the principal responsibility for the moral training of children is the school's, teachers agree that they must undertake, with the parents, the moral education of the nation's young. What the content of this education is to be, and how it is to be taught, are problems of increasing perplexity for many, as conflicting solutions are proposed from a variety of sources. It is said that the old codes have no relevance in modern society, that the Ten Commandments are sub-Christian, legalistic; Canon Rhymes has asserted that the Church has nothing to offer in the present situation but the law (has he not heard of Christ?), and the answer to our twentieth century needs is therefore not law but something called love. C. S. Lewis pointed out that love in the Christian sense 'is a state not of the feelings but of the will; that state of the will which we have naturally about ourselves and must learn to have about others' (*Mere Christianity*, p.113). The Bible goes further. It rejects the view that love is its own law by stressing that Christian love and law are inextricably connected. 'Thou SHALT love the Lord thy God. . . .' John Murray comments on Christian ethics in his *Principles of Conduct* that 'law prescribes the action, but love it is that constrains or impels to the action involved'. Christian love involves obedience, indeed reveals itself most truly and effectively in obedience – 'If ye love me, keep my commandments.'

C. S. Lewis argued that morality was concerned with three things. 'Firstly with fair play and harmony between individuals' (and he adds that we concentrate too exclusively on this). 'Secondly with what might be called tidying up or harmonizing the things inside each individual. Thirdly with the general purpose of human life as a whole: what man was made for.' (*Mere Christianity*, p.66). But what is the basis of morality? Some say it is the group, one's immediate circle, one's social group, and most obviously of all the society, nation, in which one lives. This may be a pragmatic solution for one's immediate future at least. But it poses the question of each member: Does he fit in? And each member's legitimate question of the group: How right is the group anyway? Others say that the basis of morality today is personal preference, which is not really a preference but a sort of glandular determinism which ignores the area of free moral choice open to man and which destroys all authority since always to uphold the right of every individual as against the right of society is to produce anarchy.

Orthodox Christians argue that ethics must be God-centred because true morality expresses something of the *nature* of God. According to the Bible, man's confusion and lack of harmony with himself and his fellow creatures is a direct result of his rebellion against and disharmony with God. Thus he needs a frame of reference outside, above himself. To take one aspect of his own nature or experience, as he often does, and to absolutize it as the goal of life – for example, love of mankind, or the welfare of society, whatever these phrases mean – is inevitably to distort, twist, confuse. The law of God for man, however, as declared in Holy Scripture, expressly provides directing principles, which are centred upon and stress the will of God for men, not human achievements and attitudes.

Thus the Bible's teaching on morality is crucial in the moral education of children. Christianity has always taught that the basic notion of right and wrong is built into every human heart and that the law of God has universal application laying claim upon the consciences of all men. Biblical ethics are concerned first with the 'heart', man's basic disposition, from which all his actions spring, and the purpose of the law of God is at least fivefold. Firstly it provides accurate information about the character of God and His requirements of us as creatures. Secondly it exposes sin for what it is. Thirdly it aims to awaken and deepen the conviction of sin in both individuals and nations. Fourthly it brings the awakened sinner to Christ, and fifthly it is a rule for Christian behaviour. God's law is not merely ethical, it is soteriological, nor should its didactic function be overlooked. Obedience is the basic principle – the only true response of the creature, the condition of the old covenant, and the evidence of the new.

Dependence on God is at the centre of Christian morality. Conscience is no final standard, but the judgement of God. Thus the central issue for the Christian teacher of Christian morality is not goodness but holiness, 'the state of mind', as Charles Hodge magnificently puts it, 'when the soul is full of God'. 'Be ye holy, for I am holy.'

Is all this applicable to the moral education of children and young people in our state maintained schools? In an officially Christian country, whose ethical, moral and legal codes owe so much to Scripture, and the vast majority of whose members wish their children to know about and understand Christianity (with definite reasons for that wish, as my present research is showing),[10] the answer must be in the affirmative. It is misleading to argue as a few do that moral education should be separated from religious education on school timetables on the ground that if some children reject Christian theology they may well also reject Christian morality and be left without any moral foundation. This argument implies that the end of religious education in schools is to indoctrinate and induce acceptance of Christian teaching. It is *not* the aim of religious education in state schools to teach for commitment, even though Christian teachers of Religious Instruction dearly hope that their pupils will one day come to have true faith in Christ. Their teaching is principally designed to give their children an understanding of religious belief, especially the Christian faith, linked to the developing nature and needs of each child, leading to an appreciation of the Christian view of the world and society and the significance of Christian commitment. Biblical morality with its absolute standards and relevance not to one but to all societies cannot be divorced from this teaching. Any study of the Christian religion is bound to involve the study of ethics. Also, Christianity is concerned with ultimate purpose, and without this purpose morality becomes merely a legal code. The Bible stresses every social relationship – between husband and wife, parents and children, employer and employee, friend and friend, citizens and the state, nation and nation, God and man, Christian and unbeliever – and sets up standards and claims for itself which no other religion or man-made moral code can equal. Also, Biblical morality respects the sanctity of every individual and his freedom to work out its precepts for himself. Thus New Testament ethics can be commended as the ideal core of content for a syllabus of moral education in which a section on 'comparative ethics' might well be advantageous for the pupils' wider understanding. And the aim of all these special moral education lessons is to encourage sympathetic understanding and awaken insight. There must be no indoctrination or teaching for commitment here either.

It is significant that when adolescent attitudes to religion and morality are investigated, in all their confusion of thought there is still clearly present, as the research of Loukes and others shows, an innate respect for moral law. This is not really surprising to Christians since, for them, moral laws are universal. We discover the law of our being when we discover a moral law – that something is right or wrong. If adequate time were given for religious and moral education – the really urgent need to ensure effective teaching – then realistically helpful, balanced yearly courses could be devised. This is not to forget that the development of character and training in responsibility is a task for the school, not merely one or two teachers. A balanced curriculum, community living, individual subjects, extracurricular activities, positive discipline, all contribute here. But the Bible emphasizes the need for direct training in moral awareness. This instruction must be balanced, including both positive and negative aspects, and should include opportunities for the practice of precepts taught, for real experience, with freedom for individuals to opt out of those activities in which they are particularly reluctant to take part.

No aspect of our life in society is morally neutral, nor, Christians would add, outside the sphere of God's command. Moral education apart from the religious imperative is purely relativistic. The Christian ideal situation is one in which all relations are governed by that 'state of the will' called love, and all acts by Scriptural principles. We can confidently look to the schools to give instruction in the moral law and training in habits of obedience. 'Moral education,' said A. N. Whitehead, 'is impossible without the habitual vision of greatness.' Christianity supremely offers this in the teaching and example of Christ who, of all teachers of righteousness, alone also offers the power to obey His commands. One endorses the fifteen year old's recent comment to me when, realizing the truth of this, he said, 'That's *really* living, man'.

Harold Loukes · *An Approach to Moral Education*

Harold Loukes, 'An Approach to Moral Education', *Learning for Living*, January 1970, pp.20-23

One of the curious assumptions in the current argument about moral education is that here we have something we are all broadly agreed about, in which it will be comparatively easy to make progress. Religious education, we are all agreed, has somehow become very difficult. Some people are against it, some are for it, with no apparent ground for concern from which to reach an agreement. Those who are for it are not agreed about what it is, and here again, though there is some common ground between the parties, the fundamental differences are too wide to be bridged in the immediate future. So now, the assumption goes, we must settle for moral education. We are all agreed, at any rate, that it is good for people to be good: let us devise a broadly based plan of action about making them good.

Unhappily, as those of us involved in research into moral education are painfully discovering, we are not in the least agreed about what moral education is, about what we want; and there is a frightening lack of firm evidence about what would help us to get it if we did. There are still a few people who think morals is something to do with sex, and don't want us to go round probing into our children's sex life. There are many more who think that morals are about persuading the young to accept a clear moral code, called Christian ethics; and think all we have to do is to find an improved pedagogy to 'put it across'. There are others, at the other end of the spectrum, who see it as a matter of finding some kind of impregnable justification for lines of conduct, with a rational justification so convincing that it cannot be denied – and since this kind of justification is in the present climate hard to come by, there is not much to be done by way of moral education at all. These last talk earnestly about indoctrination, as a very wicked thing; and they have had such success that many of my students say in their essays things like, 'But we must be careful here, or we shall be merely making a value-judgement . . .' as if that is a rather naughty thing to do.

In the meantime, our young people are growing up puzzled. I do not myself believe they are growing up wicked. The crime-rate admittedly is going up, but certainly no faster than the adult crime rate, so what is happening here is simply that our moral education, in the sense of teaching the young to accommodate to the mores of their elders, is going according to plan. Admittedly they are having more fun with sex than their grandparents did, but there is a genuine puzzle, which their elders feel as much as they do, about what moral means in this context; and here again it is not at all clear that adolescent behaviour is startlingly different from adult behaviour. And in any case, it does not seem to me that young people go around notably immorally, nor that in their conversations with us they have immoral assumptions. They ask 'What is moral?' more than their parents did, but that seems to me a very moral question to ask.

But though I see no signs of the moral breakdown we hear mentioned in the weekend conferences, it is clear that the young are puzzled. They do not know how we are to think out moral issues, how far authority is to be taken seriously, just how anyone decides whether anything is good or bad. And this is presumably what moral education is about: not a kind of skill training, or persuasion to adjustment, but learning how to think and judge, learning to appraise the authorities, establishing the criteria of evaluation. And if this is so, it is also clear that we have to revise our old assumption that religious education was the best vehicle of moral education.

This we must do most urgently because of the brute fact that our religious education is, broadly speaking, not taking. Just what is wrong with it is still a matter of controversy; but that it is largely ineffective in making, say, the majority of our young people religious, in any normal sense of the word, is undeniable. We cannot now appeal to any kind of religious authority in support of a moral proposition and expect it to work. If a youngster were to ask us, 'Why ought I to do the right?' and we were to say, 'Because it is God's will', we should not only be no further on, we should be some way further back. To this crude, pragmatic argument I should add others, perhaps not so uncontroversial. I am not sure, for one thing, that even for most Christians, as they actually go about the world, the concept of the will of God is continually in their consciousness. I do not drive my car thinking about God, but about the Highway Code and the other drivers and my own image of myself and my own desire to survive; and these are the elements of my moral choices. If you pressed me on how I justify the Highway Code and the claims of other drivers and my desire for survival, I might well, in the end, begin to use theological language; but if I entangled myself in theological language while I was actually driving, I should be a worse, and therefore more immoral, driver. And if it is argued, as it sometimes is, that religion is the ideal vehicle for moral *education*, for acquiring a moral standard and scale of values, I should reply that on the contrary, the best way to learn the Highway Code is to learn the Highway Code.

The connexion between religion and ethics is, indeed, acutely difficult to describe. That there is some connexion I do not doubt, but it is difficult to state without landing ourselves in all sorts of absurd corollaries – that religious men are good and irreligious men are bad, or that the seventeenth century must have been more moral than the twentieth, or that Northern Ireland is more moral than Kent. I should like to be clearer than I am about all this, but I am already clear that I hope it will never be demonstrated that man needs religion in order to bolster up his ethics. Unhappy is the man, said Voltaire, who needs the support of religion in order to be honest. And it would seem to me a pity, a sad comment on human nature, if man could not be expected to see that it is right to do right, just as it is right to get one's sums right.

Then what is to be done to help young people to get their sums right? The overriding problem, first and last, is motivation. Unless they want to do right, no amount of skill in moral thinking will be of any use. The question 'Why should I?' is really unanswerable if it is asked by someone who does not already half see why he should. Here moral education is in no different case from any other sort of education: a child does not get his mathematics right or his geography or his physics unless he wants to. He has to believe that it matters in some way: he has to be interested, in the deepest sense of the word. When he *is* interested, he is prepared to attend to the complex operations of moral thinking: to learn how to balance one interest against another, to consider cause and consequence and the facts of the situation, and to find a principle in the situation which chimes with a principle applicable in other situations, a generalization that will hold up under various pressures. This is the area we would describe as ethics; and though it is complex, we are not entirely lost in it – we do know our way about it to a certain extent. And from our experience of the contemporary teenager, most of us would say that it is an area he is prepared to pay attention to: when he is once interested, in the radical sense of involved and motivated, he finds it interesting, in the more superficial sense of stimulating and provoking, fun to do. And when this has all been done, there remains the question, Will the young moralist, who broadly wants to do the right thing, and is skilled in discovering what the right thing is, actually do it? 'For the good that I would I do not: but the evil which I would not, that I do.' We are here obviously back at motivation, which I have called first and last, but we are somewhere else, in some kind of hierarchy of impulses, habit of self-control, unified and effective self-image.

I thus distinguish three areas, or perspectives, or aspects, of moral education: motivation, insight, commitment. It will be observed that there is here a parallel with the old-style psychological trinity of feeling, knowing and acting. There is also a parallel with the six moral components, the elements of the morally educated man, as outlined by John Wilson: the first two being the capacity to take other people's interests seriously and to understand and enter into their feeling; the second two being the capacity to understand the facts of the situation and the consequences of particular actions and the capacity to work out a principle of action; and the last two being a readiness to accept the principle of action as binding on oneself and actually to obey it. These various elements can be described, if you like, as moral or social skills: some of them can be measured; they can all be recognized as they are actually practised; they can all be to some extent attended to: they are susceptible to education. But what are the agencies of this education, and how can it be done? It is already plain, and it will become plainer when more research has been done, that most of it goes on outside the school altogether. Fundamental motivation is a matter of early childhood (if a child is not loved into the world, he will find it hard to love himself back into the world) and of the society into which he grows up (if the world does not love him into adulthood he will not be likely to love it with his adult being). The fundamentals of moral education are thus a matter of the psychology of child-rearing and the sociology of human relations, and behind these of the active values we express when we bring up our small children and deal with each other in society. And while we can already say a good deal about these two areas of experience, not much of it bears on the task which the school performs between 9 and 4 on two hundred days a year. At its best, the school remains a sort of transit camp where youngsters pause on their way from one home to another, where they indent for their equipment and perhaps acquire a rough sketch-map of their route, which they will certainly revise for themselves in the light of experience.

Yet the transit camp does touch them a little. It is only a camp, true, but the human situation is as real in a camp as in a home. It is a place that can love them into itself: and the reason that moral education does actually go on is that our schools do just this; and the better the schools, the more so. A good teacher, even in the narrowest sense of a good O-level-getter, has to love his children: to take them seriously into account, to listen to their difficulties, to feel their condition. He has to do something very similar to moral thinking: to balance interests, to consider cause and consequence, to look for principles. And he has to secure commitment: to involve his pupils in acceptance of the need for standing by principle, for doing 'the good that he would'. Good teaching is inescapably moral: and there is much good teaching about, working in a moral way. A school organized for good teaching is a school organized morally: making pupils feel they matter, sensitive to their needs and wants, organized consistently, so that actions do have consequences, and are dealt with on principle and not on whim; and organized for responsibility, so that pupils see themselves as playing a part, and actually play it. This is the meaning of the old talk about the need for a school to be a Christian community: today we should prefer to talk of its being a moral community, in which moral experience is real.

Further, there is a place for explicit moral discourse: not, I hope it will be apparent, for moralizing and exhortation, but for the use of literature and history and geography, yes, and physics and biology, as a means towards insight into the reality of other people, the results of human action, and the principles that can be derived from such insight. The curriculum, I hope we are all now agreed, is not an object called knowledge: it is experience of what men know, and its ground word is men knowing. Somewhere within the curriculum there will be specific attention to ethics, but I suspect this will in the end prove less important than the ethical dimension of all knowledge. There is as yet no case for a new subject, ME to oust RE. But there is a strong case for all teachers who care about their pupils as persons to explore, and to import into their teaching, the moral meaning of their studies. In particular, the general humanities programme now being adumbrated by the Schools Council will run away into quiz games if it is not sustained throughout by a moral purpose.

I say this is a task for 'all teachers who care about their pupils as persons'. It *must* be this; if morals continues to be thought of as the special affair of the RE specialist, it will be judged not particularly important. It must be seen as the underlying concern of all responsible adults; and the agnostic and the atheist must be brought in. Is there any special role here for the RE specialist as he at present exists? I suspect there is a very clear role as a promoter and initiator of moral education. He has already opened up lines of communication, and he may well be the person who can broaden them. When the Oxford curriculum project in moral education invited teachers to an open conference on moral education, the majority of those attending were RE specialists; and I suspect that without them the new approaches will be slow to come. There is also a special role for them to play in the ethical dialogue. I have argued that we most of us go about most of the time without raising ultimate theological questions; but somewhere along the line ultimate questions have to be raised – and our present generation of young people will not let us rest without raising them. To refuse to raise them, is to indoctrinate with the belief that they do not matter; but this, we should agree, is not yet agreed. The RE specialist may have a task here, in showing how they *do* matter. He can no longer expect to settle them in any way, by appeal to authority or the use of special emotive devices; but he can see that they are raised. And no man is the worse for having faced them.

Schools Council · *Religious Education in Secondary Schools*

From Schools Council Working Paper 36, *Religious Education in Secondary Schools*, Evans/Methuen 1971, pp.67-70

Moral philosophers argue that the study of ethics and the study of religions are separate and distinct academic disciplines or areas of study. So, Atkinson:

> Morality, if autonomous, is equally distinct from and independent of science and religion – a position disappointing to those believers who want to subordinate morality to religion, to argue that it does not make sense to think of morality apart from religion, but encouraging to others who want rather to proceed to religion by way of morality.[11]

None the less, in schools in this country today, religious and moral education are widely regarded by pupil, parent, and teacher as interconnected. There is a general feeling that religious education (by which is usually meant the exposition of selected biblical passages, particularly those that contain the core of the Christian ethic) has as its principal educational aim the development of right moral attitudes in the pupil. An example of this thinking can be found in the Plowden Report where, until the general title, 'religious education', the following paragraph (568) is introduced without the authors having first made any reference to the relationship between religion and morality:

The school should be a community within which children should learn to live *the good life.* ... By example at first hand children can learn to love and care for others, to be generous, kind and courageous. Good experiences in personal relationships in early life will make a most important contribution to an understanding of *spiritual and moral* values when children are older. [Italics ours.]

There are a number of reasons why religious and moral education should be so linked in the minds of many educationists today. Some of these reasons have to do with the nature of the subjects themselves, and some, following from this, have to do with the history of education in this country.

Firstly, all of the great religions naturally prescribe for their adherents principles or codes for the ways of life they teach. Some of these prescriptions are more directly connected with the ritual or liturgical aspect of the religion than with the more specifically moral behaviour of the faithful – the offering of sacrifices, the observance of feast days, acts of communal and private prayer and worship. In the Christian religion this is sometimes described as the believer's 'duty towards God' and is an expression of what is always regarded as the first and great commandment – love towards God. But, in addition to these 'liturgical' prescriptions, all great religions require the believer to direct his present life in accordance with certain moral codes or principles. In this way the faith of the believer directly affects his moral behaviour towards other people in the community, within his family and in his own personal life. Hence no study of religion is complete if it does not examine the moral code or moral principles which form an important and essential part of each religion.

Secondly, religion and morality have many features in common. Each is concerned with attitudes and beliefs; each pronounces on right and wrong forms of behaviour ...

Thirdly, the religious belief of the majority of people in this country in the past has, as a matter of fact, had a direct and important effect upon the moral code which is enshrined in the law and is still widely accepted even by those with no specifically Christian belief. This is not to argue that morality should be thought of as subordinate to religion, nor that 'it does not make sense to think of morality apart from religion'. It is simply to state the fact that Christian ethical teaching lies at the core of Western morality and that this, in part, accounts for the link between moral and religious education in British schools.

Fourthly, it happens that the Christian Church has played a central role in the history and development of education in this country. This was discussed in the opening section of this working paper ... It is then not surprising that moral education in schools should for centuries have been taught in the context of the religious beliefs of the educators and that this legacy should remain with us today.

However, this close link between moral and religious education has led to reactions. There have been, and are today, sincere men and women who campaign for the rigid separation of moral and religious education, in some cases to the point of advocating the replacement of RE by 'ME'. As early as 1897 the Moral Instruction League was formed in an attempt to oust religious instruction given statutory recognition by the 1870 Elementary Education Act, and to replace it with a syllabus of ethical and moral teaching. The members of this league were avowedly anti-religious and believed that a moral code could be developed from natural reason and human experience. The league was shortlived. Its chief mistake was, perhaps, to present moral education as an alternative to religious education instead of as a complement to it. It was really proposing another set of vested interests and prejudices in place of those it was attacking.

Educators whose primary interest is moral education and those whose primary interest is religious education still continue the debate, but, happily, the tendency to polarize these interests and to regard them as exclusive alternatives is less common. Many of those concerned with RE are fully aware that morality is an autonomous area of study, that religious perception and moral perception are as distinct as historical perception and aesthetic perception. Likewise, many whose interest is moral education recognize that the insights and accumulated wisdom of the great world religions cannot be ignored in any comprehensive scheme of moral education.

This attitude of mutual understanding and respect already promises to be more constructive and beneficial to the child than the former rivalry and antagonism. One example of such constructive cooperation was the publication of a joint statement by a group of Christians and Humanists based at the University of London Institute of Education. The following is an extract:

We go on to ask whether there are any elements in the traditional approach to religious and moral education that are making the school's task even more difficult than it need be. Their attempts at moral education are sometimes vitiated by being so closely tied to religious education that at a later stage rejection of religion may well leave the adolescent without any moral foundation. But ... we are not recommending that there should be in county schools two alternative courses, religious education and secular moral education, of which one or the other could be chosen by parents ... The proposals outlined in this paper ... involve a new approach at many points to the task of religious education in county schools, and also more definite planning for moral education, but each considered as closely related to the other.[12]

There are currently several projects – such as the Schools Council Moral Education Project and the Farmington Trust Research Unit – engaged on research into moral education. We would like to contribute one further point to the discussion.

Attempts to take the moral teaching of a religion and to ignore the rest are bound to be unsatisfactory. Such moral teaching is part of an integral whole and is not the same if it is torn from its roots. For example, some have attempted to develop 'situation ethics' based on what 'love' dictates. This term 'love', however, can mean any one of a number of things. Those who appeal to it usually have in mind the Christian use, agape, described in St Paul's first letter to the Corinthians. In context it is part of a discussion of spiritual gifts granted to Christian believers. Out of context it loses its dynamic and its warrant. Many of the moral values which secular Humanists claim are drawn from 'the common pool of natural moral principles that all share' have really got into the pool from Christian springs. They would not be so taken for granted in a society untouched by Christianity.

Perhaps a comparative study of morals is required!

To sum up:

1 Moral knowledge is autonomous: it is perfectly possible to have moral education without reference to religious sanctions or presuppositions.
2 Schools should beware of linking morals too closely with one religious viewpoint, since some pupils who abandon that viewpoint may be left with no considered basis for morality. This

applies particularly to voluntary aided schools and to independent schools having a religious foundation.

3 You cannot successfully take the moral code from a religion and leave the rest: the moral code of a religion is part of an organic whole; it is not the same thing when lifted out of its religious context.

4 There would still be a case for the study of religion in schools, even if it were not regarded as a fount of virtue.

5 If morals are not founded upon a religious view of life, they must have some adequate foundation; you cannot get far by an appeal to self-interest, or by appealing to a child as a rational moral being.

6 Although moral knowledge is mainly gained from experience, without explicit reference to religion, *ethical* religion adds a new dimension: wrongdoing is seen as having more than temporal significance; and, conversely, man's moral life is given an added dignity and significance if it matters to God.

7 There is no reason why moral education in school should be regarded as the responsibility of the RE department; much might be gained by a widespread recognition that this is a task for the whole school. When all departments contribute to this, it will be easier for the RE department to concentrate on its main task.

8 At the same time, whether in autonomous religious studies or in a course of integrated studies, the RE teacher has a special contribution to make to moral education, showing the links between moral problems, and moral concepts, and religious belief.

R. F. Dearden · *The Philosophy of Primary Education*

R. F. Dearden, *The Philosophy of Primary Education*, Routledge & Kegan Paul 1968, pp.153-161

Morality and Religion

There is, of course, no *one* way in which morality and religion are connected. There are many such ways, not all of them relevant to our present purpose. For example, there are historical questions to be asked about the origins of our present social morality, but such origins are no more relevant to the validity of this morality than the origin of geometry in Pythagorean mystery religion is relevant to the proof of Pythagoras' theorem. The fact that a moral rule originated at some particular time and place is logically neither here nor there if our concern is with what ought to be done now. Similarly, administrative questions to do with the *utility* of religion in curbing the inclination of 'the masses', or of 'the populace', do not concern us. When religion is viewed by a governing class in such a purely utilitarian fashion as that, questions to do with truth or validity cease to be of any importance at all: any religion will do, so long as it 'works'.

A third connection, which is again irrelevant to our purpose but nevertheless of great topical interest, deserves mention. This concerns the reduction of religion to morality, as exemplified in R. B. Braithwaite's lecture 'An Empiricist's View of the Nature of Religious Belief'.[13] On this view, religion is just a picturesque and perhaps psychologically useful way of talking about being kind and loving to people, helping the other chap, etc. Thus for Braithwaite, a religious assertion is to be interpreted as 'the assertion of an intention to carry out a certain behaviour policy, subsumable under a sufficiently general principle to be a moral one, together with the implicit or explicit statement, but not the assertion, of certain stories. Neither the assertion of the intention nor the reference to the stories includes belief in its ordinary sense' (op. cit., 71). As can easily be seen, even atheists could be regarded as being 'really religious' if such a reduction were allowed. But by 'religion' in this chapter will be meant at least a belief in a transcendent being who is to be worshipped and who exists whether we believe him to exist or not. In that sense, then, can there be any morality apart from religion?

The autonomy of ethics. An immediate answer to this which has gained some acceptance amongst philosophers in recent years is that ethics is autonomous, and hence *must* be possible apart from religion. Some sort of mistake would be involved in thinking that the matter could be otherwise. But whether one accepts this thesis or not can scarcely be settled without trying to see what the thesis is. In fact, it turns out to have several forms.

First of all there is G. E. Moore's thesis[14] that no evaluative term, such as 'good', can be *defined* in non-evaluative terms. That any such attempted definition must be impossible is shown by the 'open question argument', which is that if any x is suggested as being what is good, we can always ask, without being involved in a contradiction, 'but *is* x good?' An example of this definitional fallacy would be to say that 'right' just *means* 'what God commands', for it always makes sense to ask 'but is what God commands right?' Since evaluative terms can therefore be defined, if at all, only by means of other evaluative terms, then evaluative discourse may be said to be in this sense autonomous.

A second but connected form of the thesis concerns not meaning but inference. It originates in a celebrated passage in David Hume's *A Treatise of Human Nature* (1739, bk. 3, part I, section I). The thesis, sometimes crisply expressed as a declaration that 'you cannot get an ought from an is', says that in any inference which has an evaluation as its conclusion there must be at least one evaluative statement among the premises, or else the inference is invalid. Often, of course, it appears that an evaluative conclusion is being drawn from 'facts' alone, either because the evaluative premise is suppressed, or because it is too obvious to need stating. But unless such a premise can be supplied, the conclusion contains more than is logically warranted and hence the inference is invalid. 'God made the world, therefore we ought to do as He commands' would be an example of such a fallacious inference. Compare: 'Hitler is the *führer, therefore* we ought to do as he commands.' To authorize such inferences, an additional premise must be supplied. One might note that round the corner from here there lurks a problem concerning the status of the *ultimate* premises of evaluative inference. What validates them?

This question leads to yet a third form of the autonomy thesis and one which is clearest in the work of R. M. Hare, J. P. Sartre and K. R. Popper. Its purpose is to show that our actions are in no way constrained by inclinations, customary social practices, role-expectations, authorities, gods, human nature or mindless processes. We *choose* or *decide* to act in the way we do. This is autonomy of 'the will' rather than of some form of discourse, though the two are connected in the following way. When I try to decide what I ought to do, no 'facts' can determine my decision, since that would involve me in a logical fallacy (thesis two). Only if there are rules, principles or values as criteria of relevance can the fallacy be avoided and the facts be regarded as *reasons*. But what is the status of these rules, principles or values? Must I accept *them*? On the contrary, I can always put them in question, always withdraw my commitment to them, and if I do not do so it is because I *choose* not to. I am autonomous, free and hence responsible for all that I do. There can strictly be no appeal to such excuses as 'facts forced me to ...', 'it is only human nature to ...', 'I was told to ...', or 'God says ...'. My own assent must also have been present for the action to have occurred at all.

Before seeing how this thesis affects the relation of morality to religion, however, it would be as well to elaborate a little on this third form of it, since its affirmation of individual freedom and responsibility will prove to be a crux. Three points deserve brief mention. First, 'choice' is being used here in an extended or stipulative sense in which I can be said to have 'chosen' anything if I do it at will, and hence *could* choose *not* to do it. Thus I may be said to have 'chosen' a course which in fact I have never once reflected on or compared with other, rejected, alternatives. Secondly, placing supreme value on individual freedom is apt to result in the absence of any discussion at all as to what are good reasons for choosing this or that, though surely it matters how we choose only if something other than freedom itself is at stake. Sartre, for instance, was in the absurd position of completely neglecting all ordinary desires and the institutional framework that mirrors them. But totalitarian and democratic institutions alike offer us choices: whether to struggle with the secret police or go quietly, whether to gas Jews or fight the party, and so on. If the only thing that matters is *that I choose*, then there can be no complaints or preferences here. This absurdity does not show that what is being asserted is wrong, however, but only that it is insufficient.

The third point is that this exclusive stress on individual freedom of choice seems to accompany a justificationist theory of rationality, to the following effect: a belief is not rationally held unless grounds can be given for it back as far as something that is logically un- assailable. Where choice and action are concerned, this inevitably leads to the conclusion that *ultimately* all our choices must be arbitrary, involving gratuitous commitments in favour of one way of life rather than another. But this confuses being *logically* question- able with actually having a good reason to question something. As a theory of rationality this is incoherent, as Popper and others have shown, for it counsels its own rejection. The assertion 'nothing is rationally held unless it can be justified' is not *itself* justified.

The valid point contained in this talk about freedom can, how- ever, be detached from justificationism and retained if it is put in this way: to act rationally, we do not need to have grounded every- thing on a logically unassailable foundation, but only to hold our actions open to *serious* (as opposed to merely logically possible) criticism. We are not determined in what we do, for we could always *not* do it, but why should that launch us out into anguish in advance of actually finding good reasons to question what we do? Even then, not *everything* will be in question, since we will be doubting on a basis of other things that for the moment we accept. Everything *could* be questioned, but not everything at once, and why question at all without good reason?

Religion and autonomy. It might be said that morality is a matter of God's commands for us His creatures. These commands con- stitute the moral laws by which we should be governed in all that we do. But immediately there are two objections to this, the first epistemological and the second ethical. The epistemological objec- tion concerns the difficulty of finding out what God commands. What *is* His law for us? Is it really to institute apartheid, sacrifice our son Isaac, engage in holy wars, or refuse blood transfusions, as some believe, or have believed? How do we know? The ethical objection is that even if we know, or think that we know, what God commands, why should we obey? As we have seen (thesis two), it is fallacious to argue 'God commands *x*, *therefore* I ought to do *x*'. That one has been given orders can never by itself be a sufficient reason for a responsible moral agent to do anything. To suppose that it could be was the moral error of Adolf Eichmann and others. We must, therefore, have independent moral standards by which the orders are to be judged, and hence morality must be logically *prior* to assent to God's commands, even if we know what they are.

Alternatively, however, it might be said that how one ought to conduct oneself was not so much ordered by God as shown by Him in Christ, who was the supreme exemplar and paradigm of a moral human life. But again there are epistemological and ethical objections. The epistemological objection concerns the difficulty of establishing a historically accurate narrative of the life of Christ. The search for an indisputably true account of what we are to model ourselves on has proved difficult though fascinating, and theologians are still not agreed on such crucial facts as whether Christ actually rose from the dead. And then there is the problem of finding the right theological description for the historical life.

But even if we had an account of Christ's life as a model to imitate, why should we do so? To judge such a life to be perfect *already* presupposes, as Kant pointed out, that we possess criteria by which to judge, and criteria which are valid independently of the contingency that Jesus happened most perfectly to exemplify them. Even if it were the case that only through his life were we able to realize what those criteria were, once realized they would have no logical dependence on the fact that Christ lived, or was the son of God. An atheist might assent to such criteria. In fact, however, not all of Christ's life may be so obviously deserving of imitation. Much of what he said and did seems to be intelligible only as a policy adopted in the face of an imminently expected end to the world. Stories of taking no thought for the morrow, turning the other cheek, laying up no treasure, and giving all to the poor may have a certain poetic charm, but few seriously follow them without subjecting them to interpretation. Other difficulties appear on further reflection, such as the thought that if riches are to be got rid of as being harmful, how can it be other than malicious to give them to the poor? And by now we are, of course, judging for ourselves.

There is, however, a third possible form of argument that might be used. This time the autonomy of ethics is granted, but there is nevertheless asserted to be a connection with religion in two important ways. A range of fundamental human values, such as freedom, truth, integrity and happiness, are taken for granted, so that there is no fallacious inference from the fact of God's commanding or Christ's example. Then it is asserted that religion shows us what true freedom, happiness and so on, *really are*. Religion reveals the heart's desire and discloses the way to fulfilment, lasting peace and happiness. True happiness is to be found in the worship and ultimately the company of God, while real freedom is the choice of submitting to God's will for us His creatures. Moreover, in being omniscient and omnipotent, God has such attributes as supremely fit Him to indicate the best and wisest way of life for us. Nor is this to make obedience to God's will a matter of calculating prudence, for it is not the good for *me* but for *man* that I now see. Thus religion, it might be said, articulates what in an earlier chapter we called the 'individual ideal' component in ethics.

What of social morality? Here again autonomy may be granted. Every society must, by definition, have a language and rules of behaviour, and hence must have at least *some* notion of truthfulness and justice. Moreover, the Bible itself grants that the moral law may be known apart from revelation (Romans, II, 14–15), and the Thomist doctrine of natural law concedes that this much may be discerned by the light of natural reason. Religion is not necessary to seeing that cruelty and stealing are wrong, or that truthfulness and fidelity to promises are right. It will, of course, be necessary where specifically religious duties are concerned, such as not to blaspheme, to pray regularly, and so on, but the autonomy of social morality may be taken as granted.

Yet, consistently with a recognition of such autonomy, a dependence on religion for a certain inward significance may be asserted. This would come about through the 'superimposition' of religious on moral concepts. Thus in the light of religious beliefs about man, God and the world, doing wrong is also a *sin*, life is not just enormously valuable but *sacred*, marriage is not just a matter of solemn promises and fidelity to them but a *sacrament*, overcoming one's inclinations is not just a matter of moral self-control but a form of *sacrifice*, and so on. Moreover, changes advantageous to morality may in various degrees derive from this superimposition, since morality is thereby solemnized and institutionally reinforced. Concrete models on which imagination can fasten are offered and we are constantly reminded, through the doctrine of the common fatherhood of God, of our duties concerning the welfare of others. Inward support is given to us through God's grace and through Christ's promise that he is with us always. How we act is no longer just a matter of private conscience, for we are not alone and we have a spiritual destiny. A disadvantage of this reinforcement, however, is a conservatism insensitive to greatly changing social circumstances.

This is an altogether more persuasive picture of how morality and religion might be related, but, much as we might wish to accept it, there are some important criticisms that have to be faced. In the first place, granting the autonomy of ethics serves only to shift the weight of criticism over to the *truth* of religious claims. Some of the objections to be raised here were earlier indicated in chapter four. Suffice it to say that a parallel autonomy thesis can also be presented in respect of beliefs as to matters of fact. How, then, are we to be satisfied of the truth of the claims which make possible this articulation of individual ideal and this superimposition of religious on moral concepts?

A second line of criticism arises if the demand for a substantiation of the truth-claims is seen as having failed. For, characteristically, an appeal is then made to *faith*. This, of course, is not to give grounds for belief at all, since if there were grounds then faith would be unnecessary. The consequent criticism is directed at the required *submission* of one's reason and will to God's mysterious ways and inscrutable judgements. Is this not an abdication of the individual's responsibility to judge for himself? Here, of course, is the crux, for moral responsibility requires that we judge God's will by our independent standards, and moral autonomy reduces the expression of His will to the status of advice. But to judge God is to deny God. If this is avoided by making it definitional that God is right, then judging whether *this* is 'God's will' is still a matter of our independent judgement, therefore not of faith, and therefore only contingently anything to do with God at all.

The conclusion to which we come, therefore, is in line with our former remarks on the teaching of religion in common public schools. Following Strawson, we distinguished between social morality and individual ideal. Social morality was argued to be a matter on which properly to insist in public education as being a basic condition of any tolerable form of social life. The matter of individual ideals, however, was argued to be much more a matter of personal choice, with the teacher's function being no more than that of disclosure of possible ideals.

It was also suggested, following Peters, that the fundamental formal principles of social morality are fairness and the considerations of people's interests, or good. Important among such interests would be not being hurt, being helped in need, respect for property, truthfulness and promise-keeping Often, of course, morality is given particular specification in terms of the norms constitutive of social roles, such as those of teacher, motorist, father and doctor. Learning the 'moralities' of such roles, and the more general rules that lie behind them, will be an important part of moral education.

John Hospers · *Human Conduct*

John Hospers, *Human Conduct: An Introduction to the Problems of Ethics*, Rupert Hart-Davis 1963, pp.248-250. Copyright © 1961, 1972 by Harcourt Brace Jovanovich, Inc, and reprinted with their permission

One of the strongest claims made by Christianity, however (and other religions as well), is that religious belief is indispensable to the moral life – that in the absence of religious belief human beings would have no motivation to do anything for others at all. (It is often not clear whether religious belief means specifically Christian belief or religious belief of any kind.) If this claim is true, then religious belief is justified, if not on grounds of evidence, at least on grounds of utility.

This claim, however, has been questioned by Mill in his essay 'The Utility of Religion.' Let us examine Mill's main points and then consider the general question of the relation between religion and moral practice. Mill's main points are these:

(*a*) On the one hand the periods of history in which religious belief has been most widespread have not been those which, by virtually any standard, stood highest in moral behavior. For example, in the Middle Ages many people were so concerned with religious worship that they paid little or no attention to their fellow men and allowed others to starve in the streets without having any qualms of conscience about such behavior. On the other hand, powerful moral influences have often been exerted without religion: the Greeks cultivated a high degree of honesty, justice, and temperance ('moderation in all things') without any particular religious motivation at all. Most Greeks had some religious belief, but Greek religion had almost no effect on conduct: there was no sacred book, no moral code handed down to them, no moral commands to be obeyed in the name of religion. Indeed, it is precisely because of this fact that they were free to use their own rational powers to solve moral problems. The Spartans too had a highly effective moral code, instilled not in the name of religion but of the state.

(*b*) Religious education is admittedly an important factor in the moral upbringing of many human beings. But the moral influence of early religious training owes more to its being early than to its being religious. It is true that most early training is instilled in the *name* of religion; but the training can be just as effective when it does not have that sanction, provided that it is instilled consistently and repeatedly. When a child is encouraged to put himself in the place of other individuals and develop imaginative sympathy with their problems, he is receiving his first important lesson in morality, regardless of whether he is taught in the name of religion. The specifically religious character of the training ('God commands you to do this') can scarcely have much effect upon the child: only if what God commands is also commanded by the parents and enforced by their authority is it likely to be effective; God becomes, for all practical purposes, the parents.

(*c*) In later life, moral rules tend to be effective when they are backed up by public opinion. Religion alone, without public opinion, has comparatively little effect on most people. Dueling was long practiced without many qualms of conscience, although it was always forbidden by the religious commandment against killing. Illicit sexual intercourse is still more frowned upon in women than in men, although the Biblical injunction against fornication and adultery applies equally to both sexes.

> Without the sanctions superadded by public opinion, its [religion's] own sanctions have never, save in exceptional characters or in peculiar moods of mind, exercised a very potent influence. ... If ever any people were taught that they were under a divine government, and that unfaithfulness to their religion and law would be visited from above by temporal chastisements, the Jews were so. Yet their history was a mere succession of lapses into paganism (Mill, 'The Utility of Religion').

(*d*) Those persons for whom religion *is* essential to morality are usually those who have been brought up from early childhood to believe in their inseparability. For such persons, religious belief counts as the only reason why human beings should behave morally toward one another; and if that belief were to be destroyed, they would lapse into a life of immorality. But there is no reason why the two should be instilled as inseparable. Those in whom moral beliefs were instilled *without* religion find it just as easy to behave decently toward their fellow men as those whose morality was instilled in the name of religion. And if someone whose morality depends on religious belief ever comes to doubt or reject this belief, then the morality may (and often does) go down the drain along with the religion – a result which could have been avoided by not tying morality to religion in the first place.

Wilson, Williams & Sugarman · *Introduction to Moral Education*

John Wilson, Norman Williams and Barry Sugarman, *Introduction to Moral Education*, Penguin Books 1967, pp.176-178. Copyright © The Farmington Trust 1967

We have had a great many enquiries about this Unit's attitude to religion and religious education, and many readers will no doubt be wondering how they fit into the criteria for moral education which we have outlined above: so we must give a brief account of this. I must make two points plain at the outset. First, this account cannot begin to do justice, either to any particular set of religious beliefs, or to the very complex philosophical questions that arise about the nature and verification of religious belief in general. Second, what I shall say is intended to apply to all religions or systems of metaphysical belief, not just to Christianity or any particular version thereof.

One motive for establishing this Unit was the feeling, now widely shared, that religious education alone could not provide a completely satisfactory framework for moral education. The reasons for this are obvious enough. In our society there are people of many religious creeds and of none: it would be difficult to identify a particular set of religious beliefs that could be regarded as 'established' in any but a purely political sense: and in any case, there is much uncertainty amongst religious believers both as to the interpretation of their own beliefs, and as to the way in which these should enter into anything that we might call 'religious education'.

This might lead us to suppose that our Unit is totally neutral in relation to religion and religious education; and there is a sense in which this is true. We are certainly not committed, nor should we be committed, either for or against any form of belief or disbelief, or any particular sect, church, or metaphysic. But it plainly does not follow from this that we can merely leave the whole matter on one side. For certain religions or metaphysics, like Fascism in Nazi Germany (to use a fairly controversial example), may both in theory and practice collide head-on with the criteria for moral education we have outlined in previous chapters. Here we cannot be neutral without resigning from our task altogether. Thus we cannot say, in effect, 'A morally educated person must base his moral views and actions on other people's interests, awareness of the facts etc., but of course if some religion or metaphysic says that they can base them on something quite different, *which may conflict with this*, such as what the Führer (or the Koran or the Bible or Karl Marx) says, that's perfectly all right with us.'

The sense in which we want to be neutral is something like this: We hope to have established criteria for morality which should commend themselves to anyone who will take the trouble to think about the matter intelligently: that is, criteria derived from the concept of morality, not from any partisan belief or disbelief. These criteria will almost certainly *cut across* the partisan categories in which most of us are still accustomed to think. Thus if we summarize our criteria in terms of 'rationality' ('lack of prejudice', 'awareness', etc.,) then so far as morality goes there will be more or less rational (and irrational) Christians *and* agnostics, Buddhists *and* atheists, and so forth. We are concerned only that these criteria should be preferred to any partisan set of values, whether religious or anti-religious. There will be forms of religious belief which meet our criteria adequately, and other forms which do not: but we do not expect, and certainly do not presume, that there will be any correlation between those forms which are adequate and those forms which are the particular preserve of any single faith or sect.

I do not think that this *need* generate any very violent conflict. Whatever view may be held by religious believers of such notions as 'faith', 'revelation', 'authority', 'conscience' etc., or of the logical status of their belief in general, I would hope that most believers would not regard these notions as being essentially *in opposition to* the criteria for morality that we have suggested. This for two reasons. First, many religious believers would grant that, whatever the importance of the 'faith' or 'revelation' which they have, there is still a need to work out particular moral problems by our criteria: i.e. by attending to the facts, to people's feelings, to logic and so forth. Secondly, and more importantly, a believer might want to say that his religion is justifiable and valuable partly and precisely *because* it instantiates and supports the criteria. Thus the commandment 'Love thy neighbour', which is indeed as good an injunction as any to deploy the moral skills we have commended, plainly should not conflict with anything we have said. The commandment, and the religious belief of which it is a part, may be thought justifiable precisely because it indicates the right way of going about morality; and (in general) religious revelations, commandments and authorities may be regarded as acceptable because they fit human nature and the human condition – they are not accepted arbitrarily, but because they are good sense.

Moral Education

7 · Introduction

There has been a great deal of activity and a rapid growth of research and writing in the field of moral education in recent years. This is not to say that the subject or concern is new. The question of whether virtue can be taught was discussed by Plato in the *Meno* and it is suggested by W. K. C. Guthrie that this was a lively debate at the time of Socrates.[1] Nevertheless, the attempt to think in terms of moral education being a part of mass general education is relatively new, as is any systematic attempt to see what is required and how teachers should proceed with the task.

One of the striking aspects of these recent discussions about moral education is the difference between two levels of the debate that can roughly be indicated. At what might be called the popular level there is a considerable diversity of view both about what characterizes the moral life and what can be done to develop it. The only consensus at this level of discussion is that moral matters are important in education, a view shown to be strongly held by pupils, parents and teachers in a recent Schools Council investigation.[2] There is, however, another body of opinion constituting what one might call an informed view of moral education. This view is to be found among those educationalists and others who have tried to apply some of the thinking of philosophers, psychologists (especially developmental psychologists) and sociologists to problems of moral education. These writers share the popular view that moral education is important, but they differ from the popular view in their nearness to consensus about two issues that divide broader opinion. Firstly there is general, if not universal, agreement that morality is basically a matter separable from religion, an autonomous area of thought and action with its own justification, principles and methods. This was the subject of the discussion in our second part. Secondly, there is a growing agreement among those writing directly about moral education as to those qualities that should characterize the moral life and the moral person, and agreement that certain objective criteria are justifiable and describable. We shall look at some of these conceptions and characterizations in the next chapter.

A further feature of what I have called the informed consideration of problems of moral education is that it is based upon a remarkable growth of empirical knowledge, especially about moral development, that we just did not have before, say, the time of Piaget's earlier writings. Piaget's work on moral development, published in England in 1932,[3] led to widespread further research on the questions he raised in Europe and in the United States of America. We now have an extensive body of research literature, both at the level of reports of original research and at the level of surveys and critiques of the available research.[4] Without claiming that all problems are solved, which is very far from being the case, we can at least claim that we have some factual information about the ways in which children at different ages approach notions of right and wrong, and about at least some of the factors affecting their approaches. There is thus a reasoned and evidential note struck in recent writings that contrasts with the confident, but hardly justifiable, assertions and injunctions in the teaching manuals common in the early years of this century.[5]

Following partly upon this increase in interest and research, but also because many people claimed an observable decline in moral standards and demanded that the schools do something about it, two very influential teams working full-time on problems of moral education were set up in the 1960s. A privately endowed organization, The Farmington Trust, set up a research unit at Oxford in October 1965 with a brief to study problems of moral education over a period of ten years. The team consisted of a philosopher, John Wilson, a sociologist, Barry Sugarman and a psychologist, Norman Williams, to provide the interdisciplinary approach that seemed necessary to deal with the problems involved. Later, in September 1967, another team commenced work at Oxford, this time under the auspices of the Schools Council and with the direct task of producing and testing materials on moral education for use by teachers and children in secondary schools. These materials appeared in 1972 under the title 'Lifeline'.[6] From September 1972 this team continues under its Director, Peter McPhail, with a further programme of work at Cambridge.

From a large amount of material that could have been chosen we have selected extracts grouped under four headings. Chapter eight illustrates conceptions of the morally-educated person, the idealizations that moral educators strive to realize. Chapter nine is concerned with attempts to break these idealizations down into manageable, and perhaps measurable skills, attributes and attitudes that could be meaningful and realizable objectives for a teacher. Chapter ten gives examples of the psychological considerations that have been increasingly examined in the research literature. The intention here is to show the *kind* of research that has gone on. Any claim to exhaustiveness, or even fair representativeness, would be out of place in this introductory context. Chapter eleven directs attention to the practical problems of the school and the teacher.

In most cases the writers of the extracts are relatively recent, but it must be noticed that in many cases their ideas derive from traditions of moral thinking established much earlier. We have mentioned Plato's concern with the teaching of virtue. Much of the present-day emphasis on rationality comes from Kant and the influence of the emotions has been much discussed in a tradition stemming from David Hume. Concern for consequences and their relation to people's happiness is in the utilitarian tradition of Bentham and J. S. Mill. To include extracts from these influential and important writers would inflate unduly the scope and intention of the present work; nevertheless, the attention of readers is drawn to the historical roots of much that appears here.[7]

8 · The Characteristics of the Morally Educated Person

Before we can educate anyone in the area of morality we need to know what it is that we are aiming at. What is it, in other words, to be a morally educated person? A survey conducted by one of the editors invited fifty-seven teachers to indicate the characteristics they would expect to find in a morally educated school-leaver. The characteristics given ranged very widely indeed but the main interest attaches to the five characteristics mentioned with by far the greatest frequency. These were:

1. Thoughtfulness, consideration or respect towards others;
2. Honesty, integrity and truthfulness;
3. Responsibility;
4. Possession of individual principles;
5. Tolerance.

Such a small survey has little significance in itself, but it accords very well with the main characteristics mentioned repeatedly in the moral education literature. These are altruism, autonomy, responsibility and rationality, and the way these characteristics are viewed is shown typically by William Kay in his book *Moral Development*, when he says:

The morally mature person must be rational; he must be altruistic; he must be responsible; and as the term autonomy implies he must be morally independent. Here one has four primary moral attitudes all of which in a fully developed form mark the morally mature. It may be argued by some that a rationally moral man is morally mature. But is he, if he is not altruistic? Again others may say that an altruistic, responsible man is morally mature. And, again it must be asked, 'Is he, if he is not reasonable?' Indeed it is clear that moral maturity is not only indexed by rationality, altruism, responsibility and moral independence but consists of their co-existence in a developed form.[1]

The word 'altruism' as used by these writers does not usually mean concern for others *as opposed* to concern for oneself, but rather concern for others *as well as* oneself. Sometimes other words with similar connotations are used. 'Respect for persons' is a widely used phrase.[2] Some religious writers, like Joseph Fletcher or Jacques Maritain, are particularly likely to talk of 'love' or 'agape'. There are many different emphases, but at least there is agreement that it would be nonsense to call someone moral who had no positive concern for others. It is in this sense that we can talk of altruism as a basic and necessary characteristic of the moral person.

Autonomy refers to the now widely accepted view that morality must in some sense involve the independent choice of free agents. Mere conformity, or mere obedience to authority, while perhaps being a stage on the way to becoming moral, or a stage of a lower or inferior morality, is no longer considered an appropriate characteristic of a fully moral person. This does not, of course, mean that moral persons do not conform or do not obey authorities; it only means that they require adequate reasons for conforming and obeying, seeing no virtue in conformity or obedience for their own sakes.

Jean Piaget was much concerned to trace the development of autonomous morality from the earlier heteronomous or authority based morality. Our two brief extracts show Piaget relating the notion of autonomy to a fully-developed notion of justice. The extract from the writing of Norman Bull shows a more recent description of autonomy with comments on slightly differing meanings of this ideal.

It is to be noticed that Piaget refers to 'a whole set of complementary and coherent ideas which characterize the rational mentality' and Bull refers to rational procedures like 'applying one's own moral principles to particular situations'. It is largely because autonomy would be anarchy without reason that many of our writers emphasize rationality as a basic characteristic of the morally educated. This is to be seen especially in the extract from Professor Hirst's paper where the 'uncompromising' rationality is seen as their distinguishing feature. The idea that only in subjection to reason, of which one is part author, can one be both free and yet subject to moral law, derives mainly from the work of the eighteenth-century German philosopher, Immanuel Kant, and to this extent a Kantian tradition is very influential in modern writers or moral education.[3]

There is, however, another influential tradition that emphasizes the importance of love or sympathy; the importance, that is, of some affective concern for other human beings. This is related to, indeed sometimes opposed to, reason in various ways in different writers. Jacques Maritain, in our extract, emphasizes love as against knowledge, and has interesting things to say about how one comes to be the loving person it is necessary to be to be moral. Joseph Fletcher, who would also see the moral person as essentially one who loves, opposes such a conception to that of one who simply follows a code. Love works variously in different situations, hence the advocacy of 'situation ethics', whereas 'code ethics' is rigid, making no allowances for the operation of love. Erich Fromm also sees the moral person as one possessing a capacity for love and sympathy, but he sees at the same time the moral person as possessing a capacity for reason. Fromm does not make one or the other, love or reason, dependent upon the other, but rather sees the healthy human situation as requiring both of these in conjunction with the ability to create or produce.

While being careful not to imagine a non-existent consensus, we do find some measure of agreement among these writers that the morally educated person must be able to reason and to attach importance to the findings of his reason in an autonomous way, that he has some kind of love, respect or concern for other people and that he acts responsibly according to principles based on these considerations. A person having these characteristics to a fully-developed degree is described by Peck and Havighurst in their picture of the Rational-Altruistic type, which is for them the highest form of moral development.

There are references in some of the extracts of this chapter to *how* the desired characteristics are to be brought about. For example, Piaget mentions his finding that relationship with peers is more important than relationship with adults in developing autonomy. For the purpose of this chapter, however, these references are by the way; our main concern here is to illustrate what the writers have in mind when they think of a fully-developed moral person.

This is a chapter of ideal conceptions, towards which educators might strive.

Jean Piaget · *The Moral Judgment of the Child*

Jean Piaget, *The Moral Judgment of the Child*, Routledge & Kegan Paul 1932, pp.195-6, 324

Our study of the rules of a game led us to the conclusion that there exist two types of respect, and consequently two moralities – a morality of constraint or of heteronomy, and a morality of cooperation or of autonomy. We became familiar in the course of the last chapter with certain aspects of the first. The second, which will occupy us now, is unfortunately much more difficult to study; for while the first can be formulated in rules and thus lends itself to interrogation, the second must be sought chiefly among the more intimate impulses of the mind or in social attitudes that do not easily admit of definition in conversations held with the children. We have established its juridical aspect, so to speak, in studying the social play of children between 10 and 12. We must now go further, and penetrate into the child's actual consciousness. And this is where things begin to be complicated.

But if the affective aspect of cooperation and reciprocity eludes interrogation, there is one notion, probably the most rational of all moral notions, which seems to be the direct result of cooperation and of which the analysis can be attempted without encountering too much difficulty – we mean the notion of justice. It will therefore be on this point that most of our efforts will be directed.

The conclusion which we shall finally reach is that the sense of justice, though naturally capable of being reinforced by the precepts and the practical example of the adult, is largely independent of these influences, and requires nothing more for its development than the mutual respect and solidarity which holds among children themselves. It is often at the expense of the adult and not because of him that the notions of just and unjust find their way into the youthful mind. In contrast to a given rule, which from the first has been imposed upon the child from outside and which for many years he has failed to understand, such as the rule of not telling lies, the rule of justice is a sort of immanent condition of social relationships or a law governing their equilibrium. And as the solidarity between children grows we shall find this notion of justice gradually emerging in almost complete autonomy.

In conclusion, then, we find in the domain of justice, as in the other two domains already dealt with, that opposition of two moralities to which we have so often drawn the reader's attention. The ethics of authority, which is that of duty and obedience, leads, in the domain of justice, to the confusion of what is just with the content of established law and to the acceptance of expiatory punishment. The ethics of mutual respect, which is that of good (as opposed to duty), and of autonomy, leads, in the domain of justice, to the development of equality, which is the idea at the bottom of distributive justice and of reciprocity. Solidarity between equals appears once more as the source of a whole set of complementary and coherent moral ideas which characterize the *rational* mentality.

Norman Bull · *Moral Education*

Norman Bull, *Moral Education*, Routledge & Kegan Paul 1969, pp.51-52

Autonomy

The fourth and highest stage in the development of moral judgement is that of autonomy, self-rule, when the rules governing moral behaviour come from within the individual. The controls of the stages of heteronomy and socionomy are from without, although both stages are accompanied by an increasing inner development without which autonomy could not be achieved. In the stage of autonomy the controls are internalised; it is, therefore, to this stage that the term 'moral' applies in all its fullness.

1   Autonomy as the ideal

We must, however, at once ask whether it is legitimate to hold autonomy to be the ideal of moral progress. Such a conviction may itself be regarded as a subjective value judgement. By no means all human societies have held autonomy to be the moral ideal. Some educationists and some educational institutions, in practice even if not in theory, are dominated by the heteronomy of authoritarianism – as are other social and religious institutions. Many, again, would hold conformity to the social code to be the end of education. Such viewpoints may become even more strongly held in reaction to a society that becomes increasingly fluid and permissive in its morality. But the question remains as to whether merely habitual conformity, however firmly imposed, is adequate to a rapidly changing democratic society in which traditional values are weakened by the impact of new knowledge and new attitudes.

There is a broad distinction to be observed between 'shame' and 'guilt' societies. The sense of guilt dominates those societies in which emphasis is laid upon individual responsibility, accompanied by a sense of sin which deepens personal unworthiness. Autonomous conscience – in the shape of the guilt-ridden super-ego – becomes the supreme value. Such societies are typically those affected by the Protestant Reformation. Morality, in such societies, is inner-directed. In shame societies, by contrast, morality is other-directed. The individual sees himself, not in the light of his own inner conscience, but as he appears in the eyes of others. Shame takes the place of guilt.

Some American thinkers see such 'other-directed' anxiety developing as the moral control in traditionally Protestant societies. In our own society the permissiveness, strongly apparent in elements of the younger generation, may be seen as the lack of a sense of guilt in areas where it was, in the traditional puritan code, the supreme control – notably in sexual relationships. Since, however, conscience can only be derived from society, we may see here the failure of the older generation to inculcate such a sense of guilt. Such a failure must stem from refusal to impose the traditional heteronomy; and here the influence of psychology has been profound. No longer is the natural egocentricity of the child seen as original sin, to be beaten down through repressive conditioning, denial of natural instinctive tendencies and breaking of the will. Every biological constituent of the individual has a purpose; all must be recognised and accepted. From them flow both virtue and vice. For moral maturity, therefore, we must, in the dictum of Hadfield, 'know ourselves, accept ourselves, be ourselves'.[4] Hence the search of the young, characterised by much sincerity, for a new basis for genuine personal relationships.

It remains true, however, that, even without deliberate moral education, the normal child naturally develops a moral self through the process of identification; and hence, among other results, the inner conflict that is so characteristic of man. We find ample evidence of a sense of guilt from our probing of areas of deep moral concern. But we shall also observe the struggle to adapt deep-rooted moral principles to personal relationships in concrete, moral situations.

Paul Hirst · *The Foundations of Moral Judgment*

From Paul Hirst, 'The Foundations of Moral Judgment', *Spectrum* I, 2, 1969

What, then, is the basis on which moral principles are distinguished from all others? The answer lies, I think, in their uncompromising rational character. Man's search for what is right has, I suggest, always been a search for objective reasons for his actions, rather than an appeal to tradition, intuition, power or even revelation. That a principle is backed by tradition, intuition, power or revelation does not make it a moral principle. Only if it is rationally justifiable is it that. Of course, authority, power, tradition, even personal intuition, *may* be on the side of morality but none of these things makes the principle moral. Only a grounding in the foundation principles of reasoning about actions will suffice.

But what are these foundation principles that characterize morality? It will possibly help in picking these out if we first look at the equivalent position in science. In this latter area anything that is ultimately to count as a reason for what is claimed must be an observable state of affairs. It is a foundation principle of the scientific pursuit that truth rests on observation. If this principle is rejected, there simply cannot be scientific reasoning or scientific knowledge. The principle, therefore, sets out what a scientific reason is. But what of reasons for actions? In his book *Ethics and Education*, Professor R. S. Peters picks out a number of fundamental principles that govern reasons in this area. We cannot, for instance, have reasons for our actions unless we only treat people differently if there are relevant differences between them. It would be nonsense to claim reasons for different treatment for identical cases. In addition, the notion of reasons for actions is redundant unless there is a presumption of freedom of action which reasons can properly influence. Again, it is the consideration of people's interests that provides the content of moral debate; without this there would be no area of morality. Armed with these and other fundamental principles, together with the facts of human life, people's wants, the physical environment and so on, reasons can be produced for and against different kinds of actions; there can develop on this basis that body of more detailed principles and rules that govern the moral life.

But even if it is accepted that there could be a coherent account of moral principles along these lines there remains one great difficulty to this whole approach that situationists have usually taken to be insuperable. If we work from general principles to particular cases, isn't the result repeatedly action that is manifestly grossly wrong? If in all circumstances I stick to the principle of truth-telling, for instance, before long I shall cause quite unnecessary suffering and harm. Clearly the principle of truth-telling frequently conflicts with another principle, that of not causing unnecessary suffering. Stick to one of these principles and one must go against the other. How, then, can principles be any more than useful general guides if in practice they are frequently broken? How can they possibly determine the morally right thing to do?

The first thing that must be said, I think, is that in spite of these difficulties, truth-telling remains a principle that can and clearly does determine what is right in the vast majority of cases. But what is much more important, it is I think a great mistake to assume that principles are no good if they sometimes clash so that only one can be satisfied. Moral principles aren't like scientific laws where a counter instance shows the law false. Whatever clashes there may be, it is by the moral principles we bring to the situation alone that we even begin to know what the moral issue is. What principles do is state one moral consideration for all situations, they do not assert that this is the only or even the major consideration. Of course there are clashes in these considerations in complex cases. But no principle is rendered unimportant or ineffective because another is more important in some context. Clearly the logic of particular judgments in the light of principles is difficult to analyse and no really satisfactory account of this seems to have been given as yet. Still, nothing is to be gained by denying the central role in this that moral principles play, for without these we only give up the very concern for morality itself.

Jacques Maritain · *Education at the Crossroads*

Jacques Maritain, *Education at the Crossroads*, Yale University Press, New Haven 1943, pp.95-97

Now, since we are dealing with morality and moral teaching, we must not overlook the practical truth which is of the greatest moment in this regard: as to the actual uprightness of the will and human conduct, knowledge and sound teaching are necessary but are surely not enough. In order for us rightly to judge what to do in a particular case, our reason itself depends on the uprightness of our will, and on the decisive movement of our very freedom. The melancholy saying of Aristotle, contrasting with the Socratic doctrine that virtue is only knowledge, is to be recalled in this connection: 'To know,' he said, 'does little, or even nothing, for virtue.'

What does a great deal for virtue is love: because the basic hindrance to moral life is egoism, and the chief yearning of moral life liberation from oneself; and only love, being the gift of oneself, is able to remove this hindrance and to bring this yearning to fulfillment. But love itself is surrounded by our central egoism, and in perpetual danger of becoming entangled in and recaptured by it, whether this egoism makes the ones we love a prey to our devouring self-love or merges them in the ruthless self-love of the group, so as to exclude all other men from our love. Love does not regard ideas or abstractions or possibilities, love regards existing persons. God is the only person whom human love can fly to and settle in, so as to embrace also all other persons and be freed from egotistic self-love.

Love, human love as well as divine love, is not a matter of training or learning, for it is a gift; the love of God is a gift of nature and of grace: that is why it can be the first precept. How could we be commanded to put into action a power which we have not received or may not first receive? There are no human methods or techniques of getting or developing charity, any more than any other kind of love. There is nevertheless education in this matter: an education which is provided by trial and suffering, as well as by the human help and instruction of those whose moral authority is recognized by our conscience.

Here the educational sphere involved is first of all the family.

Is not family love the primary pattern of any love uniting a community of men? Is not fraternal love the very name of that neighborly love which is but one with the love of God? No matter what deficiencies the family group may present in certain particular cases, no matter what trouble and disintegration the economic and social conditions of our day have brought to family life, the nature of things cannot be changed. And it is in the nature of things that the vitality and virtues of love develop first in the family. Not only the examples of the parents, and the rules of conduct which they inculcate, and the religious habits and inspiration which they further, and the memories of their own lineage which they convey, in short the educational work which they directly perform, but also, in a more general way, the common experiences and common trials, endeavors, sufferings, and hopes, and the daily labor of family life, and the daily love which grows up in the midst of cuffs and kisses, constitute the normal fabric where the feelings and the will of the child are naturally shaped. The society made up by his parents, his brothers and sisters, is the primary human society and human environment in which, consciously and subconsciously, he becomes acquainted with love and from which he receives his ethical nourishment. Here both conflicts and harmonies have educational value; a boy who has experienced common life with his sisters, a girl who has done so with her brothers, have gained unawares invaluable and irreplaceable moral advance as regards the relationship between the sexes. Over and above all, family love and brotherly love create in the heart of the child that hidden recess of tenderness and repose the memory of which man so badly needs, and in which, perhaps after years of bitterness, he will immerse himself anew each time a natural trend to goodness and peace awakens him.

Joseph Fletcher · *Situation Ethics*

Joseph Fletcher, *Situation Ethics*, SCM Press 1966, pp.29-30, 30-31

There are various names for this approach: situationism, contextualism, occasionalism, circumstantialism, even actualism. These labels indicate, of course, that the core of the ethic they describe is a healthy and primary awareness that 'circumstances alter cases'

– i.e., that in actual problems of conscience the situational variables are to be weighed as heavily as the normative or 'general' constants.

The situational factors are so primary that we may even say 'circumstances alter rules and principles.' It is said that when Gertrude Stein lay dying she declared, 'It is better to ask questions than to give answers, even good answers.' This is the temper of situation ethics. It is empirical, fact-minded, data conscious, inquiring. It is antimoralistic as well as antilegalistic, for it is sensitive to variety and complexity. It is neither simplistic nor perfectionist. It is 'casuistry' (case-based) in a constructive and nonpejorative sense of the word. We should perhaps call it 'neocasuistry.' Like classical casuistry, it is case-focused and concrete, concerned to bring Christian imperatives into practical operation. But unlike classical casuistry, this neocasuistry repudiates any attempt to anticipate or prescribe real-life decisions in their existential particularity. It works with two guidelines from Paul: 'The written code kills, but the Spirit gives life' (II Cor. 3:6), and 'For the whole law is fulfilled in one word, "You shall love your neighbour as yourself"' (Gal. 5:14).

As we shall see, *Christian* situation ethics has only one norm or principle or law (call it what you will) that is binding and unexceptionable, always good and right regardless of the circumstances. That is 'love' – the *agapē* of the summary commandment to love God and the neighbor. Everything else without exception, all laws and rules and principles and ideals and norms, are only *contingent*, only valid *if they happen* to serve love in any situation. Christian situation ethics is not a system or program of living according to a code, but an effort to relate love to a world of relativities through a casuistry obedient to love. It is the strategy of love. This strategy denies that there are, as Sophocles thought, any unwritten immutable laws of heaven, agreeing with Bultmann that all such notions are idolatrous and a demonic pretension.

In non-Christian situation ethics some other highest good or *summum bonum* will, of course, take love's place as the one and only standard – such as self-realization in the ethics of Aristotle. But the *Christian* is neighbor-centred first and last. Love is for people, not for principles; i.e., it is personal – and therefore when the impersonal universal conflicts with the personal particular, the latter prevails in situation ethics. Because of its mediating position, prepared to act on moral laws or in spite of them, the antinomians will call situationists soft legalists, and legalists will call them cryptoantinomians.

Erich Fromm · *The Sane Society*

Erich Fromm, *The Sane Society*, Routledge & Kegan Paul 1956, and Holt, Rinehart & Winston, Inc, NY, pp.69, 172-173. Copyright © 1955 by Erich Fromm. Reproduced by arrangement with the publishers

Summing up, it can be said that the concept of mental health follows from the very conditions of human existence, and it is the same for man in all ages and all cultures. *Mental health is characterized by the ability to love and to create, by the emergence from incestuous ties to clan and soil, by a sense of identity based on one's experience of self as the subject and agent of one's powers, by the grasp of reality inside and outside of ourselves, that is, by the development of objectivity and reason.*

Ethics, at least in the meaning of the Greco-Judaeo-Christian tradition, is inseparable from reason. Ethical behavior is based on the faculty of making value judgments on the basis of reason; it means deciding between good and evil, and to act upon the decision. Use of reason presupposes the presence of self; so does ethical judgment and action. Furthermore, ethics, whether it is that of monotheistic religion or that of secular humanism, is based on the principle that no institution and no thing is higher than any human individual; that the aim of life is to unfold man's love and reason and that every other human activity has to be subordinated to this aim. How then can ethics be a significant part of a life in which the individual becomes an automaton, in which he serves the big It? Furthermore, how can conscience develop when the principle of life is conformity? Conscience, by its very nature is nonconforming; it must be able to say no, when everybody else says yes; in order to say this 'no' it must be certain in the rightness of the judgment on which the no is based. To the degree to which a person conforms he cannot hear the voice of his conscience, much less act upon it. Conscience exists only when man experiences himself as a man, not as a thing, as a commodity. Concerning *things* which are exchanged on the market there exists another quasi ethical code, that of *fairness*. The question is, whether they are exchanged at a fair price, no tricks and no force interfering with the fairness of the bargain; this fairness, not good and evil, is the ethical principle of the market and it is the ethical principle governing the life of the marketing personality.

This principle of fairness, no doubt, makes for a certain type of ethical behavior. You do not lie, cheat or use force – you even give the other person a chance – if you act according to the code of fairness. But to love your neighbor, to feel one with him, to devote your life to the aim of developing your spiritual powers, is not part of the fairness ethics. We live in a paradoxical situation: we practice fairness ethics, and profess Christian ethics.

Peck & Havighurst · *The Psychology of Character Development*

Robert F. Peck and Robert J. Havighurst, *The Psychology of Character Development*, Wiley & Sons, NY 1960, pp.8-9

The Rational-Altruistic type describes the highest level of moral maturity. Such a person not only has a stable set of moral principles by which he judges and directs his own action; he objectively assesses the results of an act in a given situation, and approves it on the grounds of whether or not it serves others as well as himself. (He may do this either consciously or unconsciously; the issue is not the consciousness, but the *quality* of the judgment.) In the ideal case he is dependably honest, responsible, loyal, etc., because he sees such behavior is for everyone's well-being. He is 'rational' because he assesses each new action and its effects realistically, in the light of internalized moral principles derived from social experience; and he is 'altruistic,' because he is ultimately interested in the welfare of others, as well as himself. He is not interested in pursuing a principle for its own sake, without regard to its human effects. He has a strong, firm conscience or superego, but he tests, modifies, and applies its directives in order to achieve the ultimate purpose of the rules it contains.

He observes situations accurately, sees implications beyond the immediate, and can experiment mentally to decide on the most moral course of action. He recognizes objectively what other people want and how they feel. He is able to feel as they do, or know how he would feel in their position, without losing perspective by completely identifying with them.

He is as much concerned with assuring the well-being of others as with assuring his own. He is capable of self-sacrifice, but only if it genuinely helps others, not for neurotic self-satisfaction. He enjoys seeing others live a full life, and his efforts to aid them are based on what they need and want. His motives are not primarily to win personal gratification, using others as a means to this end.

He wants to work constructively in some area and produce results useful to everyone. He sees his relations with others as a pleasant, cooperative effort toward mutual goals, whether vocational, social, or recreational. As an adult, he assumes an appropriate share of responsibility in his role as member of a family, community, nation, and the human race. His moral horizon embraces all mankind, as his behavior demonstrates. He is honest with all, kind to all, and respects the integrity of every human being.

He is actively *for* his principles, neither a passive conformist nor an intolerant 'reformer.' He does not interfere with others' constructive activity; but he uses voice and action to prevent anyone from acting destructively.

He reacts with emotion appropriate to the occasion. This does not mean he is unemotional, for he is enthusiastic about promoting what is good, and aroused to prevent what is bad. He knows himself, and faces his own reactions honestly. He does what is morally right because he wants to, not because it is 'the thing to do.'

His behavior is both spontaneous and rationally oriented. He accepts responsibility for his own acts, and blame if it is deserved. He judges other people's discrete actions without making a blanket approval or condemnation of the person as a whole. He knows what is good for himself and others, and acts accordingly. He is consistent in principle, but not rigidly ritualistic. He assesses each situation in its own terms, but follows his principles in deciding what to do. He has no logic-tight compartments in his thinking.

His public and private values are just about identical. He sees himself as he is, works for deeper perception and understanding, and respects his own capacities as he does other men's. He feels no irrational anxiety or guilt. If he errs, he feels guilty; but his response is to take steps to rectify the error. If he succeeds, he no longer feels guilty. He justifies his actions by their moral effect, not by rationalization or defensive misperception. Such a person, it was proposed in this study, is moral to the highest degree. He is also mature, emotionally 'well-adjusted,' and using his constructive capacities to the fullest.

9 · Necessary Skills and Attitudes

The extracts in the previous chapter were concerned with ideal conceptions of the moral person wherein we claimed to see at least some measure of agreement about what the morally educated person should be like. This chapter illustrates writers on moral education attempting to move from highly general aims and characterizations to more specifically stated skills, attitudes or other behaviours that might serve as realistically achievable objectives or direction indicators. This is the kind of move familiar in other areas of curriculum development, but not always so common in connection with moral education, partly because of the difficulty of the required analysis, but partly also because of a reluctance to see moral character as analysable into smaller elements that can be taught in a specific manner. There has been a tendency to see virtue as 'caught' in some holistic form from those already virtuous, rather than as 'taught' by some who claim to know the particular skills and how to teach them. There is, of course, no sharp dividing line between general aims and more specific objectives. Some of our writers seem closer to a discussion of general aims, but some become very specific as to the skills, attitudes, habits or dispositions we should try to engender in pupils we are trying to educate morally.

Peter McPhail, Director of the Schools Council Moral Education Project, gives a crisp statement of the objectives of moral education as he sees it when he writes:

'Moral education is basically concerned with helping us all to find out what others feel and need, and to consider what others feel and need when we act. To become good at this we must:

1. Develop our ability to receive messages which others send to us – the words, the actions and the cues, verbal and non-verbal;

2. Learn to interpret such messages in terms of what they tell us about the initiator's feelings and interests;
3. Become proficient at deciding what we should do, what we should say, in order to help the other; and
4. Become skilled at conveying our help in clear, unambivalent messages which the other will find it easy to interpret correctly.[1]

Here is clearly an attempt to translate general terms and phrases like 'altruism' and 'concern for others' into something specifically teachable. We might feel that the analysis is still not precise enough, or that its emphasis is one-sided, but at least it is undeniable that it moves from the area of ideal aim to something more manageable in terms of a teacher's endeavours. Of course the skills and attitudes analysed out of the general aims and characterizations must not only be *necessary*, but collectively they must be *sufficient* for morality.

John Wilson's list of moral components aimed to serve a research purpose. If one could determine the necessary components of morality one could start on a number of tasks that would be difficult if not impossible without such a 'phenomenological description'. Such tasks would include the devising of tests to see which of the components given pupils have or do not have, investigating likely methods of bringing about the particular skills or attitudes, and examining particular school organizations and procedures as to their connections with the acquisition of any of the components. Teachers who can accept the given description could also use it as a teaching guide, or even as an assessment guide for indicating successes and failures in their attempts to educate morally.[2] It must be noted that while John Wilson's description includes components like EMP which are close to Peter McPhail's concerns, it also heavily emphasizes the importance of rationality and indicates several ways in which reason would have to be used by the moral person.

William Kay draws attention to the place of attitudes in morality, and argues that one of the main jobs of the educator is to bring about the formation or change of certain attitudes. Such a view raises many problems. Considered in one way the deliberate changing of pupils' attitudes looks somehow reprehensible – indoctrinating rather than educating.[3] On the other hand we certainly *do* want pupils to have a favourable attitude towards, say, reason and concern for others. Much would hinge on what one considered an attitude to be, and to what extent an attitude embodied beliefs that were at least available to rational criticism. We do know enough to realize that some techniques of attitude-changing would themselves be held by many to be of dubious moral standing. In other words, to note that attitudes are necessarily involved in morality does not of itself lead to the conclusion that moral education is solely, or even mainly, a process of attitude change. Further, we would require more of the methods than that they were 'adequate to the work', if this is taken simply to mean that they *do* change attitudes.

Norman Bull is concerned to analyse the necessary objectives where personal autonomy is emphasized as an aim. He says at the end of our extract, 'given the goal of personal autonomy, both the content and the methodology of moral learning can be patterned in its light'. One important point to note in Bull's account, emphasized also by others, is that close connections, indeed possibly necessary connections, exist between autonomy and reason. Reason and autonomy are not separate but rather inter-connected aims of moral education and the development of one involves the development of the other. 'The supreme characteristic of such personal autonomy is that its authority is reason'.

Bull goes on to point out authoritarianism, punitive physical discipline and indoctrination as 'enemies' of reason and autonomy. This is an important consideration for teachers and parents who still regard moral behaviour as simple conformity, since when the reason of an older child starts to question conformity it is often one of these three 'enemies' that is brought to bear to enforce or achieve the conformity. The effect of this, if successful, is that the child becomes 'stuck' at what Piaget would call the heteronomous stage of morality, unable to pass on to the more mature autonomous stage. Evidence that this in fact happens very often is revealed in the work of Lawrence Kohlberg, which we consider in the next chapter.

The remainder of our extract from Bull is concerned with moving from the general notions of reason and autonomy to the kinds of knowledge, habits,[4] dispositions, concepts and emotions that would characterize reason and autonomy and provide the teacher with more specific objectives. We should note the similarity between this and moves in other curriculum areas; e.g. moving from a general notion of mathematical understanding towards the kind of skills, concepts and dispositions that would both mark out mathematical understanding and provide directions in which to work; or moving from a general wish that children should gain some religious understanding towards some specific characterization of the knowledge and concepts distinctive of such an understanding.

It is in a long tradition of moral education to see it as the development of character,[5] and the nature of character is explored by Peck and Havighurst in our last extract of this chapter. There are several points of interest to note about this extract. For example there is the insistence on the idea that character traits discernible at early ages persist through later ages. This is noteworthy because the idea is somewhat at odds with the general importance attached to changing developmental stages by most other writers. We cannot discuss this at length but one point is worth making. Peck and Havighurst did study the *same* children over a lengthy period of time, whereas Piaget, Kohlberg and other developmentalists appear to have studied *different* children at different ages and to have based their conclusions about stages of development upon these observations. This would obviously confuse comparisons about the persistent stability or otherwise of character patterns through age changes. If Peck and Havighurst are right, then the importance of education in the early years of childhood is highlighted.

Notice, too, that Peck and Havighurst link themselves with a Freudian, or depth-psychology, tradition by the use of concepts like 'ego-strength' and 'superego-strength'. One must beware, however, of reading too much Freudian psychology into the use of these terms. Peck and Havighurst see superego strength as the 'degree to which behavior is effectively guided in accord with a set of inner moral principles, whatever those principles may be', and the use here of a word like 'principles' has much more of a rational and conscious connotation than the irrational, unconscious and punitive idea of Freud's original description of the superego.[6] Taken in conjunction with Peck and Havighurst's account of the rational-altruistic ideal we have to assume that the use of the term 'superego strength' refers to something more like strength of conviction about one's principles, a concept much more attached to reason than the original concept of Freud.

The attachment to rationality on the part of these writers is emphasized by their concern that children can become 'stuck' at inferior levels of moral thinking, and that only those 'who show a significant degree of rational altruism ... are able to question life intelligently ... and meet unforeseen situations with effective morality'.

Objectives and direction indicators are not spelled out quite so systematically in this extract as in some others we have noted. They are derivable, however, from the considerations of the aspects of personality that appear to be related to mature character development, and to the prerequisites that seem to be connected with these. For example ego-strength, it is claimed, relates positively to mature character and ego-strength is itself dependent upon characteristics like intelligence, observation, appraisal of self and others (as in McPhail's work), mature emotions and consistency. Obviously none of this is without problems, but it can be seen how a chart of possible objectives or direction indicators could be plotted on the basis of Peck and Havighurst's general characterizations in our last chapter and their further analysis in this.

What stands out in these extracts taken collectively is above all the complexity and range of the qualities and characteristics moral educators must seek to achieve in their pupils. These are not only cognitive but affective and attitudinal in kind. Awareness of their nature leads on to two further problems: firstly the extent of our empirical knowledge regarding the development of these qualities, which we examine in the next chapter, and then the steps that can be practically taken in classroom or home to achieve the objectives of moral education or to move children as far as possible in the direction shown to be desirable, which is the subject of our last chapter.

Wilson, Williams & Sugarman · *Introduction to Moral Education*

John Wilson, Norman Williams and Barry Sugarman, *Introduction to Moral Education*, Penguin Books 1967, pp.192-195. Copyright © The Farmington Trust 1967

A. *A List of Moral Components*

What we need in order to make further progress is something like a phenomenological description of morality, which can be broken down into a number of components, each of which has some chance of being assessed in neutral terms. We have made some progress towards doing this, and the following scheme – though it is both vague and logically shaky – may be of interest. We have used the first few letters of a number of classical Greek words to give names to our components:

(*a*) PHIL refers to the degree to which one can identify with other people, in the sense of being such that other people's feelings and interests actually count or weigh with one, or are accepted as of equal validity to one's own. Different PHIL ratings might refer to the degree to which people are able to identify, and also to the range of this ability. Thus some people may identify very highly with, say, other gang-members, and not at all with old ladies: other people may identify very poorly with those of another class or colour, and so forth. (The degree with which one *ought* to identify in particular situations is of course in question here: but the general principle is that one ought to identify sufficiently to think and act in such a way as always to take their interests into account, regarding them as on an equality with oneself.) Like the other components, this is a matter of whether, in principle, one accepts others as equals: not a matter of how far one loves them, feels for them, etc.

(*b*) EMP refers to awareness or insight into one's own and other people's feelings: i.e., the ability to know what those feelings are and describe them correctly. A distinction might be drawn between self-awareness (AUTEMP) and awareness of others (ALLEMP). EMP does not of course logically imply PHIL, though as a matter of psychological fact it may be that one cannot develop in such a way as to have much EMP without also having PHIL. (Thus one can imagine a tyrant who, having EMP, could manipulate others cleverly, without regarding them as equals: but how many such cases exist in practice is a matter for further research.)

(*c*) GIG refers to the mastery of factual knowledge. To make correct moral decisions, PHIL and EMP are not sufficient: one also needs to have a reasonable idea of what consequences one's actions will have, and this is not entirely a matter of EMP. Thus a person might have enough EMP to know that negroes felt pain as much as white people did, and enough PHIL for this to count with him in making moral choices: but, through sheer ignorance rather than lack of EMP, believe that (say) because negroes have less nerve-endings or thicker skulls they do not get hurt so easily. Similarly Marie Antoinette ('let them eat cake') *may* have lacked GIG rather than EMP or PHIL.

(*d*) DIK refers to the rational formulation of EMP and GIG, on the basis of PHIL, into a set of rules or moral principles to which the individual commits himself, by the use of such universalizing words as 'good', 'right', etc., where these rules relate to other people's interests. There may be people, good at PHIL, EMP and GIG, who nevertheless do not put all these together to make a set of consistent and action-guiding *principles*, or who draw their moral (or pseudo-moral) principles irrationally from elsewhere.

(*e*) PHRON refers to the rational formulation of rules and principles (whether we call them moral or not) relating to one's own life and interests. Thus a drug addict or a suicide makes decisions which may affect virtually no one's interests but his own. There are, I think, reasons for saying that these choices are in some sense 'irrational', 'mentally unhealthy', or whatever. Such a person would be lacking in PHRON rather than in DIK. For PHRON, EMP (or at least AUTEMP) and GIG would be logically necessary. Whether PHIL is necessary – whether people can get to be aware of their own feelings, or even of factual consequences, without identifying with other people – is, as a *psychological* question, quite open. But logically they are distinct.

(*f*) KRAT refers to the ability to translate DIK or PHRON principles into action: to live up to one's moral or prudential principles. (One could distinguish between DIKRAT and PHRONKRAT if required. A person might be very conscientious towards other people but show a good deal of 'akrasia' or weakness of will about himself.) In talking of KRAT one is of course talking of the person who has genuinely decided on a principle, whether moral or prudential, but who is in some sense compelled to act otherwise: the model case is the addict.

Thus a typically 'morally educated' person would act as follows: he is driving a car, for instance. He identifies with other people sufficiently for their sufferings or inconvenience to count with him (PHIL). He knows how aggravating it is if a road-hog crowds one into the side of the road, or if one is held up by an unnecessarily slow driver (EMP). He knows that if, say, he drives his car at a steady 30 m.p.h. on a crowded main road, most people will want to pass him, because most cars cruise at more than 30 m.p.h. (GIG). Putting these together, he formulates and commits himself to a rule ('It is not right to drive at only 30 under these circumstances [sc. either for me or for anyone else]'), or ('One shouldn't crowd people into the side of the road') (DIK). He is then capable of acting on this principle, not carried away by fear of going too fast, or a desire to be obstructive or anything of that sort, and increases his speed (KRAT). Some average of these might perhaps be made to give a general 'moral education' rating (ARI).

Though this framework is certainly extremely crude, and may have important logical gaps, I quote it here chiefly in order to show the general direction of our thinking, which is (it seems to me) the direction that any such large-scale enquiry which is not based on partisan values must take. It should not be beyond our powers to devise some means of assessing the ratings of these various components. We should then be in a position to do a number of interesting things; for instance:

  (i) One could detect just which components were missing in certain classes or groups of people e.g. delinquents, teenagers, etc., or particular sub-groups of these: and conversely with groups that might have a high ARI rating.

 (ii) One could detect what measures increased what ratings (e.g. it is a reasonable guess that the use of films with discussions, etc. would increase EMP).

(iii) One could make a more intelligent guess about what sorts of things schools ought to try, once one knows more precisely where the weak components are.

It goes without saying that the general findings of psychology and sociology would give us at least a clear lead as to the causes of high or low ratings and there would be interesting comparisons with social class, I.Q. and many other things.

William Kay · *Moral Development*

William Kay, *Moral Development*, Allen & Unwin 1968, pp.240-243

An Analysis in Terms of Attitudes

Both the developmental and the attitudinal models are therefore required if we are to understand moral development more clearly. But before concluding it is necessary to clarify still further.

If one speaks of moral development in terms of intellectual development the position is quite clear. Because there are different levels of development, conduct and thought appropriate to each stage can be clearly defined. How then is morality to be understood in terms of attitudes? The above arguments are convincing but they leave one with a hazy notion of morality. It is rather like saying that a house is made of bricks. It may be true, but this provides one with a very imperfect image of the building in question!

In its simplest form morality can now be considered as a series of stages in development, each level of which is characterized by a dominant attitude. At the level of authoritarian morality for example a positive attitude to authority figures dominates. Later, at the level of social morality a positive attitude to one's peer society dominates. Thus at every stage this complex of attitudes precipitates one which dominates and so induces conduct of a specific kind.

Of course this is an over simplification. A dominant religious attitude, for example, can be more clearly defined. As an attitude, it may be related to a whole series of referents. Thus one in whom the religious sanction is operating can have positive attitudes towards God, the Bible, a Church, a particular religious leader, or a religious code and each of these can dominate at different times. Equally, one in whom an authoritarian sanction operates will have positive attitudes to parents, teachers, policemen or any other authority figure in his social environment.

Yet in essence there appears to be a series of displacing attitudes. They rearrange themselves according to circumstances, but at any one moment a dominant attitude dictates the quality of conduct. Now these it will be observed can also be understood in terms of a developmental scheme. Thus for the moment morality, as understood under the model of attitudes, still fits neatly into the more readily recognized form of individual development. Yet these amoral, authoritarian, social and personal attitudes do not exhaust the content of morality. It would be extravagant to say that they are the least important, but they certainly must be subordinated to those moral attitudes which are of supreme importance. Now what are these further moral attitudes which are so supremely important?

If we briefly recall the evidence provided above to show the different dimensions of moral development, it will be remembered that there were certain features of moral maturity which emerged with startling clarity. The morally mature person must be rational; he must be altruistic; he must be responsible; and as the term autonomy implies he must be morally independent. Here one has four primary moral attitudes all of which in a fully developed form mark the morally mature. It may be argued by some that a ration-

ally moral man is morally mature. But is he, if he is not altruistic?
Again others may say that an altruistic, responsible man is morally
mature. And again it must be asked, 'Is he, if he is not reasonable?'
Indeed it is clear that moral maturity is not only indexed by rationality, altruism, responsibility and moral independence but consists
of their co-existence in a developed form.

What picture now emerges of morality in terms of attitudes?
Simply this; there appears to be a developmental series of displacing attitudes which mark the different levels of moral maturity.
Co-existing with these are the four primary moral attitudes which
slowly emerge as the moral agent matures. (See Fig. 4.)

His rationality and altruism etc. may have initially to operate
within the limits of earlier moralities and his moral independence
be circumscribed by them. Yet these slowly emerge and finally
mark the morally mature.

Peck and Havighurst it will be remembered found that those
adolescents who finally reached the highest level of rational/
altruism in morality had displayed these attitudes in their childhood. Even in the pre-teen years, they had shown a tendency to
respond to people with love and to moral problems with reason.

Thus co-existing with the displacing series of moral attitudes
one finds an emerging complex of attitudes which slowly mature
into genuine morality. This is interesting because in the maturing
of these primary attitudes one has a clear illustration of the kind
of development described by Isaacs and Fleming. It is a constant
growth characterized by increasing complexity and understanding
with no critical phase to distinguish qualitatively different levels
of growth. There will undoubtedly be critical moments. Rationality
cannot but be affected by those crises in intellectual development
outlined above. Moral independence cannot help being influenced
by the pubescent tendency to become independent of authority.
Altruism is certainly affected, as Swainson has shown, by the ideal-
ism of adolescence. Yet the growth of these primary attitudes is not
inevitable, nor staggered into phases, nor entirely controlled by
genetic factors, for even rationality in morals does not depend
upon the level of intellectual development but is rather the ability
to submit moral problems to the requirements of reason.

These primary attitudes will be more adequately defined in the
companion volume. For the moment it should be sufficient to say
that altruism is essentially that attitude which reveals a concern
for people rather than things and places the needs of others equal

Fig. 4 MORAL DEVELOPMENT IN TERMS OF ATTITUDES

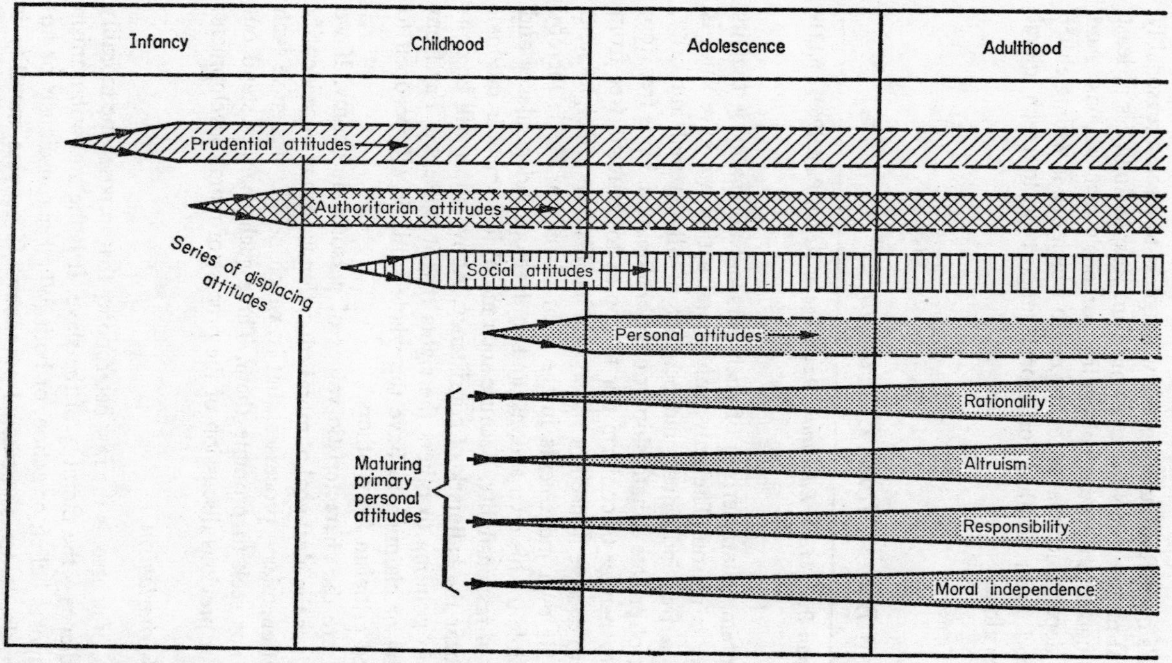

N.B. 1. These are generic terms referring to groups of attitudes, not specific attitudes.

2. The direction and duration of the broken lines as well as the relationship between the displacing series of attitudes is subject to individual personal variations.

3. For a clear analysis of personal attitudes see K. M. Evans, *Attitudes and Interests in Education*, Routledge & Kegan Paul 1965.

with one's own. Rationality is the willingness to discuss reasonably the moral requirements imposed on man. Responsibility is at least the willingness to accept culpability for one's own actions. And moral independence marks the degree to which one is willing either to depend upon another for moral support or to reach moral decisions alone.

Norman Bull · *Moral Education*

Norman Bull, *Moral Education*, Routledge & Kegan Paul 1969, pp.121-129

The supreme characteristic of such personal autonomy is that its authority is reason. The only truly moral action, we have said, is that of a free individual, independent of all external authority, whether of private dictatorship or of public opinion. He is free, too, in having neither to conform nor to appear to conform, free from having to deceive himself or others. He has his own principles, and makes his own judgements in the light of reason. He is thereby responsible for his own actions, and so develops independence and a sense of responsibility. Because such moral judgement is rational, it will bear the hallmark of consistency. Above all, it will be consistent in granting to others the rights that it possesses. Far from assuming or claiming to have the whole truth, it will be open to reasoned criticism from others.

Such are the characteristic values of personal autonomy. If we accept it as the ideal goal of moral education we can at once identify its chief enemies – processes, that is, which neither recognise such values nor seek to promote them. Three such enemies stand out from our previous discussion of the process of moral development.

1 Authoritarianism

First, of course, is the raw heteronomy that imposes the morality of obedience – the morality of the slave. It is the authoritarianism that imposes belief, or action, or both. Whether consciously or unconsciously, it denies personal autonomy. If genuine morality is the action of a free individual, such heteronomy is truly immoral.

We have seen throughout that heteronomy is essential if there is to be development towards autonomy. But this is the reasoned heteronomy that is never imposed as an end in itself. It sees itself as a means to the true end – the free, morally responsible individual. It thus seeks to make itself unnecessary. But heteronomy imposed as an end in itself is authoritarianism. It demands obedience rather than understanding; fulfilment of the law rather than concern with motives; acceptance of authority rather than self-rule. Its greatest ally is punishment. Its greatest enemy is questioning and the discussion that is simply the application of reason to moral concerns, for both presuppose autonomy. It promotes hypocrisy rather than integrity; and a rigidity in moral judgement that we have seen to subordinate persons to rules. Nor must we forget that such authoritarianism not only prevents co-operation and all the moral sentiments that flow from interpersonal relationships. It also tends to defeat its own ends; the child will lie in order to avoid the inevitable punishment.

True heteronomy is rational, in seeking to reason morality. Authority thereby attaches to the principle, not to the adult who asserts it. There is therefore, all the difference in the world between being authoritative and being authoritarian. If moral principles are reasoned, the child can accept them as being reasonable. Such reasoned authority promotes understanding and therefore autonomy. Authoritarianism, being essentially irrational, promotes neither.

2 Physical discipline

Closely allied with authoritarianism, secondly, is the type of upbringing that we have described as physical discipline. It is the aggression, physical or verbal, that is the direct imposition of adult power, and that ensures and enforces obedience. It is irrational, in that the child learns nothing – save to avoid that particular offence or, alternatively, detection. It is, moreover, inevitably impulsive and inconsistent. The result is the child without moral concepts or skills who is at the mercy of adult whims and physical power. Above all, he is morally dependent upon external controls. Such an upbringing must be the enemy of personal autonomy; at the very least impeding progress towards it, if not actually making it impossible.

The contrast is with the psychological discipline that reasons morality with the child; that builds up moral concepts from particular situations; that makes motivation the heart of all morality; that encourages individual judgement and gives moral responsibility

– and all this within a warm personal relationship that promotes active sympathy and all the moral emotions flowing from it. Such an upbringing promotes a personal autonomy that is not only reasoned, but also altruistic in its concern for the dignity and equality and rights of others.

3 Indoctrination

A third enemy of personal autonomy must be the deliberate process of indoctrination that seeks to impose upon the young child beliefs and teachings that are not founded upon, nor can ever be open to, the processes of reason. Such indoctrination is most obviously characteristic of some forms of religious upbringing. Moreover, as we have seen, the transcendental religious tradition holds that morality, too, must be similarly a matter of indoctrination. The basis of all such education is authority, whether human or – immensely more powerful – divine, and not reason. Democracy rejects such indoctrination, based upon unsubstantiated beliefs, in politics. It is coming to be seriously questioned in religion and morality, too. In particular, as we have discussed at length, the tying of social morality to religious beliefs has been a leading cause of the contemporary moral confusion.

Indoctrination denies the values that we have seen to be characteristic of personal autonomy. In terms of moral education, it could only be harmful, dangerous and, at worst, self-defeating. As a subtle form of authoritarianism, it not only denies the individual his rights as a person and as a rational being. It also exposes him to the possibility of moral breakdown if and when reason asserts itself and cracks open the flimsy foundations upon which values had been built. Morality must be reasoned, and seen to be reasonable, if it is to have sure foundations.

The Practice of Morality

If personal autonomy is the ideal goal of moral education, and reasoning is one of its chief characteristics, there must be a body of knowledge involved in moral education. Thus, Aristotle distinguishes between two kinds of virtue – intellectual and moral; and adds the practical point that, since the intellectual derives mainly from teaching, time and experience are involved. 'Moral goodness, on the other hand, is the child of habit, from which it got its very name, ethics being derived from *ethos*, "habit" ...' (*Ethics*, II.1, tr. Thomson). It is the habitual and continuous doing of right actions that builds up the disposition to act rightly; so that the set of habits derived from education in childhood make 'all the difference in the world' (op. cit.).

The practice of virtuous action therefore involves three conditions: conscious knowledge of it, deliberate willing of it 'for its own sake', and an 'unchangeable disposition to act in the right way' (op. cit., II.4). Moral education must clearly be concerned with all three

1 Knowledge

We have found ample evidence of the vital role played by heteronomy in the development of moral judgement. Its true function, we have concluded, is to provide knowledge of social morality, which, if reasoned, can become progressively interiorised. The individual acts within the limits of his moral awareness. The greater, therefore, his moral understanding, the greater is his potentiality for moral conduct. There is, then, an important place for moral knowledge in the process of moral action. The child needs to learn how he ought to act.

Such moral learning assumes some level of intelligence. But we have also seen that, while intelligence must have a key place in moral judgement, it is by no means the only factor involved; and that, indeed, higher intelligence may in fact facilitate more clever and subtle forms of misconduct.

Again, strongly positive association between moral knowledge and moral conduct could scarcely be proved. The offences of delinquents have not generally been found to be attributable to ignorance of moral laws. Most of us, at one time or another, offend against known moral obligations, as feelings of guilt amply indicate. The motives are various: to win esteem, to avoid disapproval, to secure attention, to prove independence, to retaliate, not to mention sheer sloth and bad temper. Complete consistency in moral conduct is therefore rare, so that conduct could not be wholly and infallibly predicted. But, we have agreed, while there is specifically in moral conduct, especially in immature children and unintegrated adults, there is also that generality which alone makes it possible to speak of anyone as having a definable 'character'.

We have, further, distinguished between the cognitive and emotional aspects of moral judgement, a distinction broadly parallelling that of Aristotle between intellectual and moral virtue. Since moral concepts are strongly toned by emotion, the distinction is academic rather than realistic. Moral knowledge relates to the cognitive; and hence the fact that knowledge of the good cannot be guaranteed to be translated automatically into conduct. Such implementation of moral knowledge depends upon the orectic, non-cognitive aspects of the personality. The issue is decided by the will, the functioning of the organised self, made up of set dispositions.

2 Habit

Moral education, therefore, must be as much concerned with building up dispositions as with transmitting moral knowledge. Aristotle sees the moral virtues as being attitudes built up by repeated moral actions. They are, therefore, the fruit of habit. 'So men become builders by building, harp-players by playing the harp. By a similar process we become just by performing just actions, temperate by performing temperate actions, brave by performing brave actions' (op. cit. II.1). Moral skills, like any others, are learnt by their habitual practice.

The child is told that a certain action should, or should not, be done; and far more effectively if the wisdom or folly of the action concerned is reasoned. Thereafter, on the occasion of any similar incident, only a reminder is normally necessary to recall the moral issue involved. So good habits are built up.

The value of such habits is threefold. First, they do away with the necessity for making endless moral judgements. By becoming habitual, second nature, and more or less automatic, they by-pass many areas that would involve constant decision-making. Secondly, they build up recognisable attitudes. Many habits concern relationships with others, and so play a real part in moral conduct. Habits of kindness and courtesy, for example, shape and express attitudes towards others. Thirdly, by coping with less important and more peripheral concerns, habits leave the individual free to concentrate upon more crucial moral areas, where judgements must be conscious, deliberate and concerned.

3 Disposition

Good habits, therefore, are not the heart of morality, useful and important as they are. Good habits are valuable precisely because they have become second nature. But they are therefore limited precisely because they are not motivated by 'deliberate willing' of action 'for its own sake', nor by 'unchangeable disposition'. Virtues, says Aristotle, are not inborn capacities for feeling, nor are they the feelings themselves. They are 'states of mind in virtue of which we are well or ill disposed in respect of the feelings concerned' (op. cit., II.5). Morality cannot be founded upon transient and, possibly, ambivalent feelings. Its only solid foundation must be deep, unchanging personal attitudes.

Here, then, is the third vital concern of moral education. Moral knowledge is vital; but it may not be acted upon. The practice of good habits helps to develop moral skills; but intimate relationships between persons involve more than moral craft. If we may again cite the adolescent's conflict between the fixed principle of truth-telling and felt obligations of friendship and love, neither knowledge nor habit nor skill are wholly adequate in reaching a decision. It is the very fact of caring for others that creates the conflict. True morality, we have said, subordinates rules to persons. It involves, that is to say, all the orectic, non-cognitive sentiments that flow between persons. Hence the vital place in moral education of the shaping of attitudes towards others.

Developmental Moral Education

Since our whole concern has been with the development of moral judgement in the child, it will be obvious that moral education must be closely geared to it. It would be as foolish to advance too far beyond the child's developmental stage as to lag too far behind it. But there are three factors that may usefully be stressed in thinking, finally, of developmental factors in the principles that must lie behind moral education.

1 Concepts

Moral thinking, like religious thinking, is simply the application of normal thought processes to a particular area of life. It must, therefore, be closely linked to the child's stage of mental development – and limited, therefore, to it. Hence, too, the place of non-moral knowledge that we have instanced by the law of cause and effect, and the crucial awareness of motivation. Conceptual development must therefore be a constant concern of moral education.

We may illustrate, negatively, from the traditional dogma of original sin. If this is interpreted as a purely religious belief, it has no relevance to moral conduct as such. But in so far as it has been taken to be manifested in moral conduct, it has ignored the normal development of the child, and not least of mental concepts. We have commented upon the enormities of cruelty to children that have flowed from this rigid dogma. Its ignorance of child egocentricity resulted in punishment of the child for 'selfishness', before he had developed concepts of others, of their separate concerns, interests and roles. Its ignorance of the child's inability to distinguish between wish and reality, flowing from the same egocentricity, resulted in punishment for 'lying' when the child was romancing. Our analysis of lying has shown how much development is required before the child can come to conceive of lying as deliberate deceit. The same dogma, too, held it necessary to break the 'self-will' of the child – that is, to break down, rather than to build up, the essential concept of self.

A positive, and crucial, example, secondly, is the concept of a person. We have said that all morality consists of relationships between persons; that its three concerns are, therefore, self, others and the relationships between them; and that the heart of morality is therefore respect for persons. The child from an early age grows in awareness of the separate identity of others, and so develops the concept of a person. But while this concept does not have to be learnt as such, it does have to be built up by moral education in terms of knowledge, habits and attitudes. To illustrate again from the lying situation, much development is necessary before the child can come to see lies as piercing the very heart of personal relationships. The ultimate aim must be to build up respect for the self-respect of others. Such a development has its basic foundation in the concept of what it is to be a person, and therefore of how to treat other persons. But if, as we have suggested, the true function of religion in the moral sphere is to motivate rather than to dictate conduct, the concept of the value of personality may be transmuted into a concept of the sacredness of personality.

2 Emotions

The key place of orectic, non-cognitive factors in moral judgement has been stressed throughout. Not least among them are the instinctive emotions. When uncontrolled and disordered, they can overwhelm reason, distort motivation, twist memory, and, of course, promote rash and impulsive conduct. But all thinking is emotionally toned. Concepts are derived from perception. Sensations arise spontaneously, but emotions are associated with perception of objects and situations. Hence the natural human process of evaluating such experience, and the emotional toning of mental concepts.

Moral education is, then, no less concerned with emotions. Negatively, there is the need for control of emotions that harm accepted social morality. This may be achieved by their suppression, especially in early stages of development; by fuller awareness of obligations to other persons; by development of the ego-ideal, and the force of self-respect; by the formation of good habits; and by their sublimation.

Positively, moral education must have as its ideal the development of worthy emotions towards both self and others. Here, too, its concern is with developmental factors, given the link between concepts and emotions. Only as concepts grow can appropriate emotions be experienced.

3 Developmental goals

All such moral education must have developmental goals. It must, that is to say, be essentially forward-looking. Its aim being personal autonomy, it must always have that end in view in its concern with the development of moral concepts, emotions and skills.

When the child is held in the controls of heteronomy, for example, it is no function of moral education to cement him more firmly in its grip. Certainly it can seek to show the need for rules through the process of reasoning; showing, for example, how every human society has its wisdom – rulers, that is, for measuring and guiding the conduct of people towards each other. But the whole purpose of imposing discipline from without is the development of self-discipline within. Hence, for example, the constant need to give the child such responsibility as he can cope with; for only so can a sense of responsibility and self-discipline develop.

Again, when a sense of justice begins to develop with the raw reciprocity of tit-for-tat, the child's development would be impeded and hindered by concentration upon the Iron Rule of 'eye for eye, tooth for tooth'. Learning would be far more valuably centred upon higher levels of reciprocity – and not least the universal Golden

Rule – as the child now develops awareness of mutual relationships with his peers.

All moral education must thus be closely geared to the overall development of the child. We can usefully think in terms of 'readiness' for moral education, in order to emphasise the vital necessity for it to be determined, at each stage, by the child's capacities and needs. Too much and too soon would be as ineffective, if not harmful, as too little and too late. Respect for self and respect for others can only be learned within the limits of the child's developmental capacities. But, given the goal of personal autonomy, both the content and the methodology of moral learning can be patterned in its light.

Peck & Havighurst · *The Psychology of Character Development*

Robert F. Peck and Robert J. Havighurst, *The Psychology of Character Development*, Wiley & Sons, NY 1960, pp.166-170

The Nature of Character

Judging from the present research, it appears possible and useful to define 'basic character' in a series of five types, arranged on an ascending scale of psychological and moral maturity:

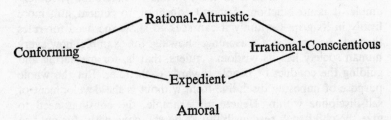

These 'types' are merely a descriptive device. It was found, as anticipated, that no one was entirely of one type. All the subjects proved to be complex mixtures of motives. Nonetheless, when the *dominant* type in each individual's profile was used to classify him at the appropriate point on the ascending scale of Maturity of Character, it turned out that the subjects who fell in each type group showed some highly significant psychological features in common, and equally important differences from the subjects of the types above and below them on the scale.

The Psychogenesis of Character

'Character' can be regarded as a special aspect of personality; or, otherwise stated, as a function of certain personality characteristics. In this research, six aspects of personality were found to be relevant: Moral Stability, Ego Strength, Superego Strength, Spontaneity, Friendliness, and a Hostility-Guilt Complex. *Moral Stability* is composed of such things as overt conformity to the expectations of mother, age mates of the opposite sex, and the community at large; stable, controlled overt behavior of a pleasantly toned kind; and a wide range of moral horizon. It is more a descriptive than an explanatory, motivational dimension. *Ego Strength* subsumes the perceptual capacities of intelligence, observation, and insight; realism in appraising self and others. It also includes psychological autonomy, maturity of emotional reaction, and internal consistency – or integration – of the personality system. *Superego Strength* measures the degree to which behavior is effectively guided in accord with a set of inner moral principles, whatever those principles may be. *Spontaneity* includes spontaneity, as such, and also such characteristics as empathy, a lack of guilt about overt behavior, and good feelings for father and for same-sex peers. *Friendliness* is a measure of a generalized, inner attitude toward other people. The *Hostility-Guilt Complex* consists of hostile feelings toward mother and toward opposite-sex peers, overt rejection of father's standards, and chronic guilt feelings about one's inner impulses.

In general, moral stability, ego strength, and superego strength all correlated very significantly with the Maturity of Character scale, and with moral reputation attributed by both teachers and age mates. Spontaneity showed a curvilinear relationship with character. Spontaneity tended to be highest among subjects of either very good or very poor character; it was lowest among the Irrational-Conscientious, the Conformers, and even the Expedient adolescents, in the middle range. Friendliness was significantly related to the Maturity of Character scale, although not to moral reputation with age mates and teachers. The Hostility-Guilt Complex was negatively related to good character.

The adolescents who showed the most notably Amoral tendencies had a distinctive personality pattern: extremely low in moral stability, ego strength, and superego strength, and, with one exception, an actively hostile attitude. Several were extremely spontaneous; but others were actually somewhat constricted and restrained. All of the highly Amoral subjects, except the one friendly 'moral weakling,' had intense cases of the hostility-guilt conflict, although the subjects with composite profiles of equal Conforming-Expedient-Amoral scores were more free of this complex. All in all, the poor character of these people could easily be understood. They hate life. They have chaotic perceptions, extreme, inappropriate emotionality, ineffective superegos, and generally disorganized, internally contradictory, often impulse-ridden personalities. They have neither the internal incentive nor the capacity to conduct themselves in a stably ethical manner. The one partial exception was a boy who 'meant well' but was too passively dependent on others' good will, and too inadequate in his personality, to conduct his own life dependably.

These adolescents with a large Amoral component in their characters might be described in neo-analytic terms as heavily fixated at the early 'oral' stage of psychological development. They demonstrate a profound lack of what Erikson has called 'basic trust'[7] and also lack the perceptual and judgmental ego powers which are necessary to achieve what both Erikson and Piaget have referred to as 'psychological autonomy.' It is not much use appealing to their 'reason,' for they are largely incapable of ruling their own behavior according to intelligent reasoning. They are very much at the mercy, too often, of violent hungers, hates, and other passions which can overwhelm what 'good sense' they may at other times demonstrate. Remedial treatment for such children requires firm outside control and guidance, at the start, as Bettelheim[8] and Redl[9] have empirically demonstrated.

The subjects with dominant or near-dominant Expedient motives show low to very low moral stability and below-average to very weak ego strength. They range from a little above average to very weak in superego strength, and also in spontaneity. These self-centered 'operators' are by no means just gaily impulsive. On the contrary, with the exception of two rather passively self-indulgent boys, these adolescents show a great deal of strained self-control. Except for one of the boys just mentioned, all the Expedient subjects are actively hostile in their underlying attitude toward life, most of them to an extreme degree.

The unspoken attitude of these children might be summed up as 'you have to look out for yourself; if you don't nobody else is going to look out for you.' Psychogenetically, their orientation is not much past the late 'oral' stage. They are self-centeredly preoccupied with *getting*. At the same time, they show a chronic sense of frustration; they never get 'enough,' or not enough to make them view the world as a trustworthy, rewarding place. They have developed sufficient ego identity and enough realism to recognize the need to go along with society's rules, when they have to, but they have not internalized these rules very much; not to the point where any of them could be said to have strong moral convictions or principles. They are more autonomous than the Amoral subjects, but not any more than the Conformers. Some of them show a little more initiative, in Erikson's sense; but even here they tend to be driven from within by irrational hungers that ordinary acquisitions or human response cannot satisfy. All in all, the subjects at this level show a narcissistic, childlike orientation toward life that years of experience through childhood and adolescence have not appreciably altered.

The modal pattern in the Conforming group is one of definite moral stability which is produced much more by habituated super-ego dictates than by reasoned use of ego powers. Indeed, these subjects tend to have below-average ego strength. They show a built-in, restrictive inner control, however, which keeps them firmly in line with the conventions of their world. Some of them are very friendly and good natured in their general attitude; some distinctly are not. In either case, how they feel personally, influences their behavior much less than what they believe others expect of them – and, indeed, what they rather blindly expect of themselves, in terms of the social rules they have unquestioningly incorporated. Even at seventeen, these are 'good children' of the unthinkingly submissive kind, little more developed in their psychological autonomy or use of reason than in middle childhood. They have mastered and passed the developmental tasks of the 'anal' stage – except, perhaps, for their underdeveloped autonomy – but they have not met and resolved the issues of the 'genital' stage. They may consciously rebel, sometimes, at direct dictation by adults; but they need and seek to be surrounded by a familiar world that reinforces their belief in the rightness of the authoritative 'answers' that have been trained into them without their own participating thought.

The Irrational-Conscientious subjects show only differences of degree, in the characteristics measured, from the Conformers. They, too, have relatively underdeveloped ego powers, but they have even more powerful, dominant superegos. They are covertly hostile, but too restrained to allow themselves to show it in any way that would violate the moral conventions they have learned to observe.

The most highly Rational-Altruistic group tend to show the highest degree of moral stability of all, but not by unreasoning imitation or habituation. They have highly developed ego powers which they use to probe and solve ethical problems. Often, their reasoning is not made conscious nor is it always verbalized; but that does not necessarily decrease the quality of their judgment. They have moderate to strong superego principles. These are not compartmentalized from their reasoning, however, and they do not blindly dictate stereotyped behavior. These principles of conscience are held open to examination and redirection, to suit changing circumstances.

As an integral part of their personalities, too, these subjects show a very decided friendliness of outlook, and notably lack the hostility-guilt complex. They can therefore afford to be thoroughly spontaneous, and they are. The nature of their impulses is in comfortable accord with their ethical principles and with the ethical needs of society.

Of all the adolescents studied, only these last are still growing, psychologically, and still open to further growth. The other three-quarters of the research population appear to be fixated at immature levels of development, and in the ordinary course of events may remain permanently 'stuck' with childlike ways of viewing and meeting life. The quarter, or so, who show a significant degree of rational altruism are almost the only ones who are able to question life intelligently, question their own preconceptions, and thus be able to grow in moral wisdom and meet unforeseen situations with effective morality. They show the characters of Freud's 'genital' type; and of Erikson's person who has firm identity, good capacity for human intimacy, and a creative, generative orientation. They likewise fit Fromm's 'productive orientation,' and Riesman's 'autonomous character.'

10 · Some Psychological and Developmental Considerations

In the previous chapters concerned with moral education we have looked at considerations that might broadly be called philosophical, in so far as we have been concerned with ideal conceptions of the moral life and the aims and objectives that might be derived from them. Much of the literature of moral education, however, is not concerned with philosophical or ethical considerations as such, but rather with empirical matters of direct and systematic observation. By far the greatest amount of such literature has been written from the viewpoint and methodological stance of psychology, and this chapter will deal mainly with this; but another and increasingly influential area of empirical enquiry is that of sociology, and some mention must be made of this.

Sociological enquiry can help the moral educator in a number of ways, but two important approaches must be picked out. Firstly, it is by means of sociological enquiries and surveys that we find out what moral views are actually held by children, young people, parents and teachers. These views, on careful investigation, do not always turn out to be those attributed to such groups of people by, say, newspapers and television. At least two such surveys, for example, have shown great concern about moral matters on the part of young people, which runs counter to much popular assertion that the majority of young people seem at least amoral.[1]

There is another, and perhaps more positive, contribution that the sociologist can and does make. This is to accept some account of what the fully developed moral person should be like in terms of a certain kind of behaviour, and then, as Barry Sugarman puts it: 'Given that we are interested in this kind of behaviour, the sociologist's function is to discuss how different kinds of social factors or preconditions tend to make it more or less common.'[2] The sociologist will thus examine the larger society and culture, as well as the social structure of the school, and be concerned with concepts like social class and the norms and standards of homes and families and other kinds of small social groups. Some interesting work has already been done in these areas of investigation, but there is little doubt that this is still a rich area for further enquiry.[3]

Psychologists have investigated aspects of moral behaviour for a long time and we cannot cover anything like all aspects of this work.[4] There are, however, a number of matters of considerable and perennial importance that we illustrate by the extracts of this chapter.

Morality has provided continued interest to development psychologists. Sigmund Freud, for example, suggested at least two theories connected with character development. Firstly the theory that certain character traits in adult life were consequent upon distortions of normal libido development through the oral, anal and genital stages; and secondly the theory of the development of the super-ego or conscience through the internalization of parental authority. These theories have been so influential and widespread, especially in literature and drama, that they are part of the quasi-mythology of modern times. There has not been an accompanying direct influence on moral education, however, and the influence is seen more indirectly through the work of Peck and Havighurst, for example, or through the work of innovators in the Freudian tradition, like Erikson and Fromm.[5]

A much more direct influence, by now almost classical, is that of Jean Piaget, and we include a masterly summary of Piaget's work on moral judgment by John H. Flavell, one of the most thorough of Piaget's many commentators. Piaget was concerned to investigate the development of moral judgment, first in connection with children's changing respect for rules and then in connection with their changing conceptions of justice. The general thesis that he derived from his questioning of children of different ages described the progression from early ideas of right and wrong based on adult constraint to a more autonomous morality involving notions of equity and reciprocity. This developmental description is now widely accepted in its general terms, if not in its detail or in its causal account, and has encouraged and provoked a large number of further researches both replicative and of a more sophisticated kind.

The most important of these is probably the work of Lawrence Kohlberg in the United States. Kohlberg's investigations, described in a number of recent works,[6] are both more sophisticated in conception and more wide ranging in the cultural backgrounds studied than the original work of Piaget. Our extract shows the basic account of the stages of development explored and hypothesized by Kohlberg. This work was based largely on a group of Chicago boys and girls, but similar, though not identical results were derived from populations studied in places like Taiwan and Turkey. This cross-cultural reference is important if the sequential changes noted are to indicate anything more than the changed conceptions of right and wrong through which children pass in any given society.

One important point about Kohlberg's findings must be made. This is that not all stages are achieved by all people. For example, in the graphs given by Kohlberg we can see that only something like five or six per cent of the sixteen year-old age group reached the highest level of moral development in the Chicago study. In other groups studied the percentage was lower still. We must note, then, that the highest stage is an ideal, presumably not achieved at present by most human beings. We must also note that the ideal, if justifiable, and in some sense at least realizable, points to the need for improved methods of moral education to help larger numbers of people towards such achievement.

A similar conclusion is reached by a further look at the work of Peck and Havighurst, already met in our earlier chapters on moral education. Here again we see stages set up as a developmental hierarchy, though we must remember that Peck and Havighurst also insist on the relative permanence of certain character traits. The number of young people reaching or achieving the highest level is again a very small proportion of the group studied.

There is no fundamental disagreement among the three developmental accounts here given, though there is considerable difference of perspective and detail. Basically an autonomous morality of individual principles is held to be the highest form of morality, but early stages of more or less sophisticated conformity are indicated, through which some but by no means all people pass. There also appears agreement that all of this is preceded by a period of amorality.

Our next extract focuses more directly on a problem already discussed by Peck and Havighurst as providing criteria for describing their stages, the problem of motivation. The difficulty is easily stated: getting somebody to understand what it *is* to be moral is not the same as getting him to *want* to do the moral thing. There are, however, a number of complications to this problem. For example, we would not be satisfied that we had overcome the problem of motivation simply because we had got pupils to want to perform certain actions considered as moral *by others*. As Peck and Havighurst show, there is a developmental hierarchy of motivation as well as of judgment: people can want to act in certain ways for bad, good and better reasons. It is not just a question, then, of getting children motivated, but of getting them *appropriately* motivated. If we agree with the ideal of a rational autonomous morality, then we want people to come to want for themselves to do what their own moral reasoning and principles lead them to see as right. Peter McPhail argues that this will only be the case if such behaviour is rewarding in some sense. He seems dismissive of the idea that reasoning out what is right is sufficiently motivating in itself. Yet some moral philosophers, notably Kant, have argued strongly that doing something *because* it is seen as a moral duty is the only true moral action. To do something for other kinds of satisfactions like those listed by McPhail would be falling short of being moral, however convenient and socially pleasant or cohesive it might be. McPhail and others take the view that this would be a grossly unrealistic view for the moral educator to take; 'there is no reason by rejecting natural self-benefit motivation in moral education to make our task more difficult'. Some might say that the reason for being at least a bit dubious about such motivation is that there is a long tradition of considering 'self-benefit' and morality to be somewhat opposed. Kantians would say that duty is still duty even when it is not self-rewarding, and the force of this is difficult to resist. There are, therefore, obvious dangers in influencing the affective dispositions of pupils unless we also strongly assist the development of those powers of reason that alone make autonomy meaningful.

McPhail mentions the development of conscience in his article, and our final extract in this chapter deals with one view of the development of conscience. If we consider conscience to be some aspect of our thought and feeling which makes us feel uncomfortable when we contemplate certain actions, then it is important to realize that there are several ways of conceiving of what it is that produces such discomfort.

We have already mentioned Freud's account of the super-ego which provides one description of the early formation of conscience. Eysenck's account, the subject of our extract, is a different way of describing the formation of a conscience but, since the conscience is produced by conditioning, it would be just as non-rational in its effect as the super-ego as originally conceived by Freud. Also, because (*a*) we know that people vary as to their conditionability, and (*b*) we know that conditionability is susceptible to change by drug treatment, the way is open to the manipulative social conditioning of human beings by other human beings. It would be possible to view moral education as no more than this, hence the importance of the work and hypotheses of people like Eysenck and the similar, though theoretically different, work of Skinner.[7]

Fortunately for those of us who would see this kind of approach as dealing with morality only at the level of conformity, and not at the more desirable level of autonomy, conscience *can* be viewed in another way. That is, we might admit to qualms of conscience brought about by the non-rational modes of introjection or conditioning described by Freud or Eysenck, but argue that the rational moral educator will endeavour to supplant these primitive and punitive feelings by a concern for *conscious* altruism based on reason. A fully moral person would then ignore these feelings and heed rather the feelings of discomfort he gets when he *knows* he has not done what his *reason and principles* tell him he should have done. A rational conscience, in other words, can and should supplant a primitive and non-rational conscience.

J. H. Flavell · *The Developmental Psychology of Jean Piaget*

J. H. Flavell, *The Developmental Psychology of Jean Piaget*, pp.290-297, published by Van Nostrand Reinhold Company, copyright 1963 by Litton Educational Publishing Inc

Moral Judgment

The Moral Judgment of the Child is concerned, as its title says, with the child's moral *judgments*, i.e., his ideas and attitudes about rules, justice, ethical behavior, and so on. Although it does here and there deal with questions of moral behavior as well, it treats these as secondary and subsidiary to those of moral judgment. Although this work is not a direct, fifth-volume sequel to the other four, there is, nevertheless, considerable continuity. Piaget makes ample use of his earlier insights in the design and interpretation of the research in this area. As a case in point, he identifies a *moral realism* in children which directly parallels the *intellectual realism* described earlier. The book consists of four long chapters: the first three experimental and theoretical and the fourth purely theoretical. Research findings are, as usual, interpreted in terms of developmental stages. It should be noted, however, that Piaget is exceedingly cautious and guarded about how the term *stage* should be construed in this area. He indicates again and again that individual differences in moral judgment are enormous at every age level studied, that his stages are thereby so overlapping as to be almost (but not quite) reducible to agenetic types, that similar studies carried out on populations of children different from his would likely yield different developmental patterns, and so on.

The book commences with an interesting investigation of children's attitudes and behavior with respect to the rules of a game, namely, the game of marbles as played by children in French Switzerland. The inquiry consists of two parts. The first part is designed to find out the extent to which the child conforms to rules of the marble game in his actual playing behavior. The experimenter gives the child some marbles and, feigning ignorance of the game,[8] asks the child to show him how to play it. With the youngest children this procedure was supplemented by watching them play the game together. The second part of the inquiry aims at the child's verbally expressed understanding of the nature of rules, his attitudes towards them, and so on. The experimenter begins by asking if the child could make up a new rule for the marble game and, if so, whether other children would agree to it, whether it would be 'fair', etc. He then asks about the history and origins of rules: whether people have always played the game by present rules, and how the rules originated.

As to the child's behavioral conformity to the rules, the stages appeared to be as follows. In stage 1 the child uses the marbles simply as free-play materials, without any attempt to adapt to social rules. At most, the child develops private rituals of play which might be called *motor rules*. Stage 2 (about 3-5 years) begins when the child imitates aspects of the rule-regulated play behavior of his elders. However, it is clear that the child assimilates what he sees to private, egocentric schemas; confident that he is playing by the older children's rules, he nonetheless plays in an idiosyncratic, socially isolated manner, unintentionally flouting the rules at every turn. From about 7-8 years on, the child begins to play the game in a genuinely social way, in accordance with a mutually agreed upon set of rules. But until about age 11-12, this grasp of and conformity to the rules is still vague and approximative (stage 3). From 11-12 on, however, they are completely understood and obeyed to the letter by all (stage 4); moveover, the act of codifying rules now seems to have a positive fascination for the child, e.g., he is constantly engaged in revising the statutes to cover new and unforeseen contingencies.

For the child's verbalized notions about rules, Piaget found three stages. Stage 1 corresponds to the stage 1 in behavioral conformity to rules: rules are simply not part of his life space. Stage 2 is more interesting. Here, the child regards the rules of the game as eternal and unchangeable, stemming from parental or divine authority; suggested changes in the rules are usually resisted; the new rules 'are not fair', even if others agree to abide by them. But there is a curious hiatus between theory and practice in this stage. While regarding the rules as sacred and inviolable in his conscious thought, he unwittingly breaks them at every turn in his actual behavior (the stage 2 in the practice of rules). In stage 3 (about 10-11), the child evidences quite different attitudes and beliefs with respect to rules. Rules may always be changed, provided only that others agree to abide by them. Rules are neither God-given nor eternal; children of long ago were probably the first marble players, and the rules have undoubtedly evolved and changed considerably since then. And, as we have seen, this relativistic attitude towards rules in theory is accompanied by scrupulous adherence to rules in practice – just the reverse of the situation in stage 3.

A second series of experiments bear on developmental changes in attitudes towards actions more specifically moral than conformity to the rules of a game. In one group of studies the subject was presented with a number of stories in which a child performs some morality-relevant act under a specified set of circumstances. The subject was then to judge the relative culpability of the various acts, giving the reasons for his judgment. The results can be summarized as follows. Although individual differences were substantial as usual, the younger children tended to regard as most immoral those acts which had the most serious objective consequences, with no consideration of subjective antecedents (motives, etc.) in the wrongdoer. Thus, the child who breaks fifteen cups through an accident he could not have avoided was judged 'naughtier' than one who accidentally breaks a single cup while engaged in deliberate malfeasance. Similarly, a child who steals a roll to give to a poor and hungry friend was judged guiltier than one who steals a (less costly) piece of ribbon for herself. The older children (particularly from 9-10 years on) were more inclined to take into account the motives behind the wrongful act and weigh moral responsibility accordingly.

Other investigations in this series deal with the child's ideas about and attitudes towards the telling of lies. The results parallel those for clumsiness and stealing and can be summarized as follows. First, the youngest children define a lie simply as 'naughty words', i.e., lying is rather like swearing. A little later, it is defined as an untrue statement of any kind, with or without intention to deceive. And finally, it is restricted exclusively to untruths with intent to deceive. Second, younger children regard a lie as culpable in the degree that it deviates from the truth, regardless of the intent of the teller. Thus, a tall tale innocently told by a young child is worse than a more believable untruth told with deliberate intent to deceive, just as the bigger theft with altruistic motives was worse than the smaller one with selfish motives. Again, the older children tend to evaluate guilt in terms of the motives involved. Third, younger children judge a lie which *fails* to deceive (usually because it is so 'big', so unbelievable) as 'naughtier' than one which succeeds; for them, it is the exposure of the untruth which is reprehensible. With older children, on the other hand, the lie which succeeds in its deceitful intent is worse. Fourth, as with clumsiness, an unintentional falsehood with serious objective consequences is judged worse by the younger subjects than a deliberate lie which happens not to result in anything serious. Again, older children reverse this evaluation. Fifth, younger children are inclined to say that a lie is bad because one is punished for it; older children think it is bad *per se*, whether one gets punished or not, because it violates mutual trust, makes good relations with others impossible, etc. And finally, younger children tend for various reasons to believe that a lie told to an adult is worse than one told to a peer, while older children see them as equally blameworthy.

The third chapter of the book⁹ deals with the child's conception of justice. There is a lot of theory and research in this long (135 pages) and meaty chapter, but at least its main points can be summarized. Ideas about how various misdeeds ought to be punished (what Piaget calls the problem of *retributive justice*) constitutes the first topic. Piaget distinguishes two broad classes of punishment. The first is *expiatory punishment*: the wrongdoer should suffer, expiate by means of, a punishment which is painful in proportion to the seriousness of the offense but need in no way be related to the offense. The second is *punishment by reciprocity*: the emphasis here is not so much on inflicting severe punishment for expiation's sake but in bringing home to the offender in the most direct possible way the nature and consequences of his breach of relations with others by setting a punishment which is logically related to the offense. Suppose the offense consists of a child failing to bring home food for supper, having been told to do so (*ibid.*, pp. 200-201). To spank the offender, deny him some privilege, etc., would be classed as expiatory punishment. Punishments by reciprocity might include giving the child less supper than usual (since he failed to bring home the food) or refusing to do him a favor (since he refused to do you one). The point here is to 'make the punishment fit the crime' in some intrinsic way so that the transgressor will better understand the implications of what he has done. Piaget posed hypothetical misdeeds of this kind and had the children choose, from several different suggested punishments, the one they thought was 'best' or 'fairest' for the case at hand. There was at least a tendency for the younger children to favor expiatory punishments (and usually the more severe the better) with the older children electing punishments of the reciprocity type. Furthermore, the older children were less inclined to think that direct and severe punishment itself, without explanation and discussion of why the act was wrong, would be an effective deterrent to future wrongdoing.

Two other investigations described in this chapter are worth relating. In the first, Piaget found that the younger children were more prone than the older ones to believe in what he calls *immanent justice*: the idea that Nature herself will punish misdeeds, e.g., a boy running away from a policeman (he had been caught stealing apples) crosses a river on a rotten bridge and the bridge breaks (*because* he had just done wrong; ordinarily it would not have broken). The second investigation consisted of various studies of *distributive justice*, i.e., how punishments and rewards should be distributed to members of a group. These interesting studies seemed to point to the existence of three rough stages. In the first (prior to age 7-8), the child is inclined to regard as 'just' or 'fair' whatever rewards or punishments the authority figure decides to dispense, even if it involves unequal punishment for the same crime, the granting of special privileges to favored individuals, and so forth. In stage 2 (about 7-8 to 11-12 years), the child is a rabid egalitarian: all *must* be treated equally, no matter what the circumstances. In stage 3 (from 11-12 or so), the child tempers equality with equity – a kind of relativistic egalitarianism in which strict equality will sometimes be winked at in favor of a higher justice. The subtle difference between stages 2 and 3 can be illustrated by responses to the following story:

> *Story II*. One Thursday afternoon, a mother asked her little girl and boy to help her about the house, because she was tired. The girl was to dry the plates and the boy was to fetch in some wood. But the little boy (or girl) went and played in the street. So the mother asked the other one to do all the work. What did he say? (*ibid.*, p. 276).

The stage-2 response is simply to assert the basic unfairness of the request and advocate noncompliance. The stage-3 response grants the basic inequity but suggests compliance anyhow, out of wish to help the mother, not to make her suffer in the service of principle, and so on. Similarly, equity may preclude hitting back a small child who has hit you first, whereas equality demands an eye for an eye with no exceptions.

The changing concept of justice is also expressed in children's reactions to this vignette:

> One afternoon, on a holiday, a mother had taken her children for a walk along the Rhône. At four o'clock she gave each of them a roll. They all began to eat their rolls except the youngest, who was careless and let his fall into the water. What will the mother do? Will she give him another one? What will the older ones say? (*ibid.*, p. 267).

Here is a judgment which is both pre-equality and pre-equity, with punishment at all costs winning the day:

PAIL (7): '*He shouldn't be given another. He didn't need to let it drop.*—And what would the older ones have said if the little boy had been given another roll? – *That it wasn't fair: "He's let it drop into the water and you go and give him another one."* – Was it right to give him another one? – *No. He hadn't been good*' (*ibid.*, pp. 268-269).

And here is a case in which a conception of justice founded on strict equality prevails (with possibly a hint of equity):

MEL (13), G.: '*They should have divided up what the other children had left and given some to the little chap. –* Was it fair to give him any more? – *Yes, but the child ought to have been more careful. –* What does "fair" mean? – *It means equality among everyone*' (*ibid.*, p. 270).

A number of the oldest children also reached an essentially egalitarian conclusion (the child ought to be given a second roll), but by means of a more subtle and mature line of reasoning involving considerations of equity. These subjects carefully distinguished between the loss of the roll as a disembodied and abstract bit of wrongdoing and the same event as it occurred in its living context, with extenuating circumstances (the wrongdoer is young and irresponsible, etc.):

CAMP (11), G.: '*The little boy ought to have taken care. But then he was a little boy, so they might give him a little piece more. –* What did the others say? – *They were jealous and said that they ought to be given a little piece more too. But the little one deserved to be given a little piece more. The older ones ought to have understood. –* Do you think it was fair to give him some more? – . . . *Of course! It was a shame for the little one. When you are little you don't understand what you are doing*' (*ibid.*, p. 271).

Throughout these three chapters, and especially in the final chapter, Piaget interjects what amounts to a theory of the development of moral judgment. In brief, it is this. There appear to be two moralities in childhood, at least within the culture from which Piaget's subjects were drawn. The developmentally earlier one is a *morality of constraint*, formed in the context of the unilateral relations between child as inferior and adult as superior. The child adapts to the prohibitions and sanctions handed down from on high by reifying them (a *moral realism* akin to the *intellectual realism* studied earlier) into moral absolutes – simple 'givens' which are unquestioned and sacred, in theory if not in practice. Hence, the child views wrongdoing in objective rather than subjective terms, is confined to the letter rather than the spirit of the law, and is incapable of seeing morality-relevant acts either in terms of the inner motives of the actor or in terms of the social-interpersonal meaning of the act itself (i.e., as a breach of solidarity and mutual trust between group members). For a morality of constraint, it must be the overt consequences alone which count in assessing the wrongfulness of acts (untruths, clumsiness, and the like), not the inner intentions and motives involved. Similarly, justice reduces simply to whatever the authority commands, rather than being seen as an equitable distribution of sanctions and rewards, these sanctions and rewards meaningfully related to the acts which engendered them.

With developments, this morality of constraint is at least partially replaced by a *morality of cooperation*, formed out of the reciprocal relationships among status peers and based on mutual, rather than unilateral, respect. With a growing understanding of the role of motives in the actions of self and others and of the social implications of antisocial behavior, the child comes to the basic *raison d'être* of morality and begins to conceive (if not always to follow in practice) moral action as an autonomous good, essential to the intact functioning of any social unit. With this orientation, rules become rational conventions which serve orderly group action rather than arbitrary and untouchable dicta; malfeasance is judged by motivational as well as objective criteria; and justice, now placed in a social context, is seen in terms of equality and equity.

It is clear that the mechanism which Piaget holds responsible for the development of a rational morality is exactly the same as that which he thinks engenders rationality in general, and therein lies the important theoretical tie between this and the preceding four books (*ibid.*, pp. 406-411).[10] Both morality and logic are fired in the crucible of the spontaneous give and take, the interplay of thought and action, which takes place in peer-peer interactions. The prescripts, logical and moral, which parents and other adults impose upon the young and egocentric mind are compliantly accepted but at the same time simplified and distorted. It is only through a sharing of perspectives with equals – at first other children, and later, as the child grows up, adults – that a genuine logic and morality can replace an egocentric, logical, and moral realism. It might also be mentioned that even in these early days Piaget had developed strong opinions about how to educate children, based on just these conceptions (*ibid.*, pp. 411-414). For example, he believed that schools should foster and encourage group projects in which children could freely exchange ideas on a common intellectual task close to their own interests. As he himself acknowledged, his philosophy of education is closely aligned in this respect with that of Dewey and other progressivists.

Lawrence Kohlberg · *Children's Orientations Toward a Moral Order*

From Lawrence Kohlberg, 'The Development of Children's Orientations Toward a Moral Order I. Sequence in the Development of Moral Thought', *Vita Humana*, vol.6, no.1-2, 1963[11]

The Isolation of Six Stages of Development in Moral Thought

Our developmental analysis of moral judgment is based upon data obtained from a core group of 72 boys living in Chicago suburban areas. The boys were of three age groups: 10, 13, and 16. Half of each group was upper-middle class; half, lower to lower-middle class. For reasons to be discussed in the sequel to this paper, half of each group consisted of popular boys (according to classroom sociometric tests), while half consisted of socially isolated boys. All the groups were comparable in I.Q.

We have also used our procedures with a group of 24 delinquents aged 16, a group of 24 six-year-olds, and a group of 50 boys and girls aged 13 residing outside of Boston.

The basic data were two-hour tape-recorded interviews focussed upon hypothetical moral dilemmas. Both the content and method of the interviews were inspired by the work of *Piaget* (1932). The ten situations used were ones in which acts of obedience to legal-social rules or to the commands of authority conflicted with the human needs or welfare of other individuals. The child was asked to choose whether one should perform the obedience-serving act or the need-serving act and was then asked a series of questions probing the thinking underlying his choice.

Our analysis of results commenced with a consideration of the action alternatives selected by the children. These analyses turned out to shed little light on moral development. Age trends toward choice in favor of human needs, such as might be expected from *Piaget's* (1932) theory, did not appear. The child's reason for his choice and his way of defining the conflict situations did turn out to be developmentally meaningful, however.

As an example, one choice dilemma was the following:

Joe's father promised he could go to camp if he earned the $50 for it, and then changed his mind and asked Joe to give him the money he had earned. Joe lied and said he had only earned $10 and went to camp using the other $40 he had made. Before he went, he told his younger brother Alex about the money and about lying to their father. Should Alex tell their father?

Danny, a working class 10-year-old of I.Q. 98 replied: 'In one way it would be right to tell on his brother or his father might get mad at him and spank him. In another way it would be right to keep quiet or his brother might beat him up.'

Obviously whether Danny chooses to fulfill his 'obligation' to adult authority or to peer loyalty will depend on which action he perceives as leading to the greater punishment. What interests us most, however, is the fact that Danny does not appear to have a conception of moral obligation. His judgments are predictions; they are not expressions of moral praise, indignation, or obligation. From one to the next of the situations presented to him, Danny was not consistently 'authoritarian' or 'humanistic' in his choices, but he was consistent in choosing in terms of the physical consequences involved.

A careful consideration of individual cases eventually led us to define six developmental types of value-orientation. A Weberian ideal-typological procedure was used to achieve a combination of empirical consistency and logical consistency in defining the types. The six developmental types were grouped into three moral levels and labelled as follows:

Level I. Pre-Moral Level

Type 1. Punishment and obedience orientation.
Type 2. Naive instrumental hedonism.

Level II. Morality of Conventional Role-Conformity

Type 3. Good-boy morality of maintaining good relations, approval of others.

Type 4. Authority maintaining morality.

Level III. Morality of Self-Accepted Moral Principles

Type 5. Morality of contract and of democratically accepted law.

Type 6. Morality of individual principles of conscience.

These types will be described in more detail in subsequent sections of this paper. The typology rests upon 30 different general aspects of morality which the children brought into their thinking. One such aspect was the child's use of the concept of rights, another his orientation toward punitive justice, a third his consideration of intentions as opposed to consequences of action, etc. Each aspect was conceived as a dimension defined by a six-level scale, with each level of the scale corresponding to one of the six types of morality just listed.

A 'motivational' aspect of morality was defined by the motive mentioned by the subject in justifying moral action. Six levels of motive were isolated, each congruent with one of the developmental types. They were as follows:

1. Punishment by another.
2. Manipulation of goods, rewards by another.
3. Disapproval by others.
4. Censure by legitimate authorities followed by guilt feelings.
5. Community respect and disrespect.
6. Self-condemnation.

These motives fall into three major levels. The first two represent on the verbal level what *McDougall* (1905)[12] termed 'the stage in which the operation of the instinctive impulses is modified by the influence of rewards and punishments'. The second two correspond to *McDougall's* second stage 'in which conduct is controlled in the main by anticipation of social praise and blame'. The fifth, and especially the sixth, correspond to *McDougall's* third and 'highest stage in which conduct is regulated by an ideal that enables a man to act in the way that seems to him right regardless of the praise or blame of his immediate social environment'.

A more cognitive aspect of morality, conceptions of rights, was defined in terms of the following levels:

1. No real conception of a right. 'Having a right' to do something equated with 'being right', obeying authority.

2. Rights are factual ownership rights. Everyone has a right to do what they want with themselves and their possessions, even though this conflicts with rights of others.

3. Same as the second level concept but qualified by the belief that one has no right to do evil.

4. Recognition that a right is a claim, a legitimate exception, as to the actions of others. In general, it is an earned claim, e.g., for payment for work.

5. A conception of unearned, universal individual or human rights in addition to rights linked to a role or status.

6. In addition to level 5 conceptions, a notion of respecting the individual life and personality of the other.

Each of the 50 to 150 moral ideas or statements expressed by a child in the course of an interview could be assigned to one of 180 cells (30 dimensions $\times$ 6 levels per dimension) in the classification system. This classification yielded scores for each boy on each of the six types of thought based on the percentage of all his statements which were of the given type. Judges were able to assign responses to the moral levels with an adequate degree of agreement, expressed by product moment correlations between judges ranging from .68 to .84.

In spite of the variety of aspects of morality tapped by the 30 dimensions, there appeared to be considerable individual consistency in level of thought. Thus 15 boys in our original group of 72 were classified (in terms of their moral response) as falling in the first of our six types. On the average, 45% of the thinking of these 15 boys could be characterized as Type 1.

The differences between our age groups offer evidence concerning the developmental nature of the typology. The age trends for usage of the six types of thought are presented in figure 1.

It is evident that our first two types of thought decrease with age, our next two types increase until age 13 and then stabilize, and our last two types increase until age 16. Analyses of variance of the percentage usage for each type of thought by the 10-, 13-, and 16-year-old groups were carried out.[13] The differences between the three age groups in usage of all types of thought but one (Type 3) were found to be significant beyond the .01 level.

If our stages of moral thinking are to be taken as supporting the developmental view of moralization, evidence not only of age trends, but of sequentiality is required. While the age trends indicate that some modes of thought are generally more difficult or advanced than other modes of thought, they do not demonstrate that attainment of each mode of thought is prerequisite to the attainment of the next higher in a hypothetical sequence ...

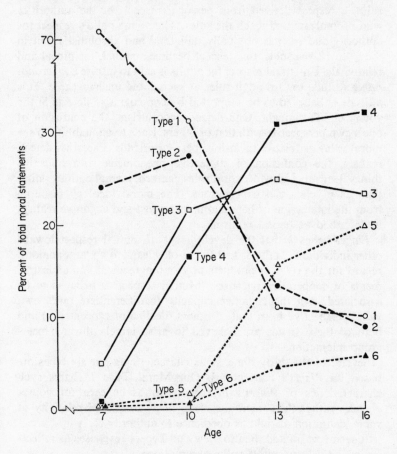

Fig. 1. Use of six types of moral judgments at four ages.

The First Two Stages Compared with Piaget's Stages

Our proposed sequence of stages must have logical as well as empirical support. In characterizing our stages, we shall attempt a logical justification of their location in the hierarchy and at the same time, a comparison of our stages and concepts with *Piaget's* (1932) theory of developmental stages of moral judgment.

Piaget (1932) starts from a conception of morality as respect for rules, a respect derived from personal respect for the authorities who promulgate and teach the rules. The young child's respect for authority and rules is originally unilateral and absolutistic, but in the 8- to 12-year-olds, this respect becomes mutual, reciprocal and relativistic. Unilateral respect for adults is said to inspire a *heteronomous* attitude toward adult rules as sacred and unchangeable. This attitude is believed to be supported by two cognitive defects in the young child's thought. One defect, egocentrism, the confusion of one's own perspective with that of others, leads to an inability to see moral value as relative to various persons or ends. The other defect, realism, the confusion of subjective phenomena with objective things, leads to a view of moral rules as fixed, eternal entities rather than as psychosocial expectations. The moral ideology resulting from the interaction of heteronomous respect and cognitive realism is described as 'moral realism'.

Piaget believes that the development of mutual respect toward other individuals in the 8- to 12-year-olds leads to an 'autonomous' regard for the rules as products of group agreement and as instruments of cooperative purposes. 'Mutual respect' is believed to be associated with the cognitive capacity to differentiate one's own value perspective from that of others (decline of egocentrism) and both of these trends are believed to arise largely through peer-group interaction.

Several of the thirty dimensions characterizing our six types are based on *Piaget's* conceptions. Our Moral Type 1 shares such characteristics of *Piaget's* heteronomous as concern for consequences rather than intentions, lack of awareness of relativity of value, definition of right as obedience to authority ...

It seems warranted then to view our Type 1 responses as reflecting cognitively primitive value assumptions.

Type 1 value assumptions, furthermore, are externalized from the motivational point of view, as indicated by definitions of right and wrong in terms of punishment and conformity to power-figures. As an example, Tommy defines the druggist's wrong in terms of a prediction with regard to punishment, and in terms of conformity to the wishes of important persons.[14]

Such an interpretation of Tommy's responses as involving external motives is open to question, however. *Piaget* would see these responses as reflecting the young child's deep respect for authority and rules. *Piaget* sees the young child's morality as externally oriented only in a cognitive sense, not in a motivational sense. According to *Piaget*, the strong emotional respect the young child feels for authority and rules makes him feel unable to judge for himself, and forces him to rely on external adult sanctions and commands to define what is right and wrong. In the *Piaget* view, the child is oriented to punishment only because punishment is a cue to what is disapproved by adults or by the 'sacred World-Order'.

In contrast to *Piaget's* interpretation, it has seemed to us simpler to start with the assumption that the Type 1 definition of wrong in terms of punishment reflects a realistic-hedonistic desire to avoid punishment, rather than a deep reverence for the adult 'World-Order'. The children of 10 and older who represent Type 1 morality did not in fact seem to show strong respect for adult authority ...

We have concluded that it is possible to interpret all our observations with regard to 'moral realism' without invoking *Piaget's* notion of the child's sense of the sacredness of authority and rules. This conclusion is consistent with the findings of other studies of *Piaget's* moral judgment dimensions, as is documented elsewhere (*Kohlberg*, 1963).[15]

Regardless of the validity of *Piaget's* interpretation of 'moral realism', *Piaget's* assumption that the young child feels a strong idealized moral respect for adult authority requires direct investigation. *Piaget* shares this assumption with psychoanalysts, and some form of the assumption seems critical for widely accepted notions as to the early childhood origins of adult neurotic guilt. In collaboration with *B. Brener*, we attempted a direct study of the validity of the *Piaget* assumption of 'heteronomous respect' to explain the moral judgments of children aged four to eight. Earlier work with children of six and seven indicated that these children defined right and wrong mainly by reference to punishment when faced with simplified versions of our moral dilemmas. Did this indicate a basically 'hedonistic' view of right or wrong or did it rather reflect a lack of cognitive resources in answering 'why' questions in the context of a concern for conformity to sacred authority (*Piaget's* view)?

To investigate this issue, 96 children, aged 4, 5, and 7 were confronted with doll-enactments of stories in which disobedience to a rule (or adult) was followed by reward, and other stories in which obedience to a rule was followed by punishment. One such story was of a boy who was ordered to watch a baby on a couch while his mother left the house. The boy in the story proceeded to run out of the house and play outside. The *S* was asked to complete the story. The *S* was told that the mother returned and gave the disobedient boy some candy. *S* was then asked whether the child-doll had done good or bad, and a series of related questions.

In general, the 4-year-olds defined the story act as good or bad according to the reward or punishment rather than according to the rule or adult command. The older children showed considerable conflict, some of the 7-year-olds defining right and wrong in terms of the rule and showing concern about the 'injustice' of punishing good and rewarding evil. These older children, however, still explained the rightness and wrongness of the act in relation to sanctions, but took a long-range or probabilistic view of this relation. Disobedience might have been rewarded in that situation, the children said, but in general it would still lead to punishment.

These results, while not consistent with *Piaget's* assumptions, should not be used to conclude that the moral decisions of 4–5-year-olds are based on crafty hedonism. Only as children reach a level of cognitive development at which the meaning of moral concepts can be differentiated from punishment can they attain either a definite hedonism or a degree of disinterested respect for authority.

The emergence of individualistic hedonism out of such growing cognitive differentiation is suggested by the responses which fall in our Type 2. Just as our first stage of morality coincides descriptively with *Piaget's* 'heteronomous stage' but differs from it in interpretation, so our second stage coincides descriptively with *Piaget's* autonomous stage but differs from it in interpretation. Like *Piaget* and others, we found an increase in the use of reciprocity (exchange and retaliation) as a basis for choice and judgment in the years six to ten, though not thereafter. We also found age increases in notions of relativism of value, and in egalitarian denial of the moral superiority of authorities.

These reactions were common enough and well enough associated in our 10-year-olds to help define our Type 2 ...

The advance in cognitive differentiation of this type of response over that of Type 1 seems evident. It seems clear that such definition of value in terms of ego-need and reciprocity of needs is in a sense internal; i.e., it is not simply a reflection of direct teaching by others. It reflects rather Type 2's increasing awareness of its own ego-interests and of the exchange of ego-interests underlying much of social organization.

It also seems evident, however, that the Type 2 modes of thought are far from constituting an adequate or mature basis for morality. We find in a number of our older delinquent boys that further intellectual development seems to carry this Type 2 morality to the cynicism which is its logical endpoint ...

From a developmental view, then, the Type 2 morality of need and reciprocity reflects both cognitive advance and a firmer internal basis of judgments than does the Type 1 morality. It does not, however, give rise to any of the characteristics usually attributed to moral judgment, or to a sense of obligation. While possessing the basic attributes stressed by *Piaget* as characterizing the stage of moral autonomy, this type of thought is not based on mutual (or any other type) moral respect (as *Piaget* had hypothesized).

The Intermediate Stages of Moral Development

It is clear that Type 1 and Type 2 children do not express attitudes toward 'the good' and 'the right' like those we take for granted in adults and which we often regard as moral cliches or stereotypes. These stereotypes first appear in our Type 3 and Type 4 pre-adolescents, whose verbal judgments and decisions are defined in terms of a concept of a morally good person (the implication of labelling Type 3 as a 'good boy' morality) ...

In terms of motivation, this second level is one in which conduct is controlled in the main by anticipation of praise and blame. Praise and blame are, of course, effective reinforcers even in the child's earliest years. In these early years, however, disapproval is but one of the many unpleasant external consequences of action that are to be avoided. In contrast, our Type 3 and Type 4 pre-adolescents attempt to make decisions and define what is good for themselves by *anticipating* possible disapproval in thought and imagination and by holding up approval as a final internal goal. Furthermore, the pre-adolescent is bothered only by disapproval if the disapproval is expressed by legitimate authorities ...

To summarize, we have mentioned the following 'cognitive' characteristics of moral definitions at our second level:

a) Moral stereotyping. Definition of the good in terms of kinds of persons and a definition of persons and roles in terms of moral virtues.

b) Intentionalism. Judgments of moral worth based on intentions.

c) Positive, active and empathic moral definition. Duty and moral goodness defined in terms going beyond mere obedience to an actual service to other persons or institutions, or to a concern about the feelings of others.

On the motivational side we have mentioned:

d) Sensitivity to and self-guidance by anticipated approval or disapproval.

e) Identification with authority and its goals.

All of these characteristics imply that moral judgments at this level are based on *role-taking*, on taking the perspective of the other person with legitimate *expectations* in the situation, as these expectations form part of a *moral order*.

For children dominantly Type 3, this order and its associated role-taking is mainly based on 'natural' or familistic types of affection and sympathy, as our examples have suggested. For children of Type 4, the moral order is seen as a matter of rules; and role-taking is based on 'justice', on regard for the rights and expectations of both rule-enforcers and other rule-obeyers. The distinction between Type 3 and Type 4 styles of role-taking in moral judgment may be illustrated by two explanations as to the wrong of stealing from a store. Carol (13, I.Q. 108, lower-middle class, Type 3) says:

'The person who owns that store would think you didn't come from a good family, people would think you came from a family that didn't care about what you did.'

James (13, I.Q. 111, lower-middle class, Type 4) says:

'You'd be mad, too, if you worked for something and someone just came along and stole it.'

Both Carol and James define the wrong of stealing by putting themselves in the role of the victim. James, however, expresses the 'moral indignation' of the victim, his sense that the rights of a community member have been violated, rather than expressing merely the owner's disapproval of the thief as a bad and unloved person. In both, Type 3 and Type 4, regard for rules is based upon regard for an organized social order. For Type 3, this order is defined primarily by the relations of good or 'natural' selves; for

Type 4 it is rather defined by rights, assigned duties, and rules.

Moral Orientation at the Third Developmental Level

It is often assumed by psychologists that moral conflicts are conflicts between community standards and egoistic impulses. If this were true, it seems likely that the Type 3 and 4 moral orientations would persist throughout life. The story situations we used, however, placed in conflict two standards or values simultaneously accepted by large portions of the community. Many of the children at stages 3 and 4 went to great lengths to redefine our situations in such a way as to deny the existence of such conflicts between accepted norms, no matter how glaringly this conflict was presented. Both types of children took the role of the authority figure in defining right and wrong, tending to insist that the authority figure would adjust the rule in the interests of the various individuals involved.

In contrast, children of Types 5 and 6 accept the possibility of conflict between norms, and they attempt something like a 'rational' decision between conflicting norms. This is most clear in our Type 6 children who attempt to choose in terms of moral principles rather than moral rules. Conventional examples of moral principles are the Golden Rule, the utilitarian principle (the greatest good for the greatest number) and Kant's categorical imperative. A moral principle is an obligatory or ideal rule of choice between legitimate alternatives, rather than a concrete prescription of action. Philosophically such principles are designed to abstract the basic element that exists in various concrete rules, and to form an axiomatic basis for justifying or formulating concrete rules.[16] Moral principles, of course, are not legally or socially prescribed or sanctioned, they are social ideals rather than social realities.

An example of the use of the utilitarian maxim as a moral principle is provided by Tony (age 16, I.Q. 115, upper-middle class). He is replying to a situation involving a choice of leaving or staying at a civilian air-defense post after a heavy bombing raid may have endangered one's family:

'If he leaves, he is putting the safety of the few over the safety of many. I don't think it matters that it's his loved ones, because people in the burning buildings are someone's loved ones too. Even though maybe he'd be miserable the rest of his life, he shouldn't put the few over the many.'

Tony says that leaving the post is wrong, not because of the actual consequences, but because he evaluated the situation wrongly, and 'put the few over the many'. This is not merely a matter of utilitarian economics but of the requirement of justice that all lives be treated as of equal value.

Moral principles are principles of 'conscience', and Type 6 children tend to define moral decisions in these terms. When Type 6 children are asked 'What is conscience?', they tend to answer that conscience is a choosing and self-judging function, rather than a feeling of guilt or dread.

A more easily attained 'rationality' in moral choice than that of Type 6 is embodied in the Type 5 orientation of social contract legalism. Type 5 defines right and wrong in terms of legal or institutional rules which are seen as having a rational basis, rather than as being morally sacred. Laws are seen as maximizing social utility or welfare, or as being necessary for institutional functioning. It is recognized that laws are in a sense arbitrary, that there are many possible laws and that the laws are sometimes unjust. Nevertheless, the law is in general the criterion of right because of the need for agreement.

While Type 5 relies heavily on the law for definitions of right and wrong, it recognizes the possibility of conflict between what is rationally 'right' for the individual actor, and what is legally or rationally right for the society. George (16, upper-middle class, I.Q. 118) gives a fairly typical response to the questions as to whether the husband was wrong to steal the drug for his dying wife:

'I don't think so, since it says the druggist had a right to set the price since he discovered it. I can't say he'd actually be right; I suppose anyone would do it for his wife though. He'd prefer to go to jail than have his wife die. In my eyes he'd have just cause to do it, but in the law's eyes he'd be wrong. I can't say more than that as to whether it was right or not.'

(Should the judge punish the husband if he stole the drug?)

'It's the judge's duty to the law to send him to jail, no matter what the circumstances. The laws are made by the people and the judge is elected on the basis that he's agreed to carry out the law.'

George's belief is that the judge must punish even though the judge may not think the act is wrong. This is quite consistent with his belief that the act was individually 'just', but legally wrong. It reflects a typical distinction made at this level between individual person and social role, a distinction which contrasts with the earlier fusion of person and role into moral stereotypes. The judge's role is seen as a defined position with a set of agreed-upon rules which the role-occupant contractually accepts on entering office. At the level of definition of role-obligation, then, contract replaces earlier notions of helping the role-partner, just as legality replaces respect for social authority in defining more general norms.

All these aspects of a Type 5 orientation seem to be, in part, reactions to a cognitive advance in social concepts to what *Inhelder and Piaget* (1958)[17] describe as the level of formal operations. Such a cognitive advance permits a view of normative judgment as deriving from a formal system derived from a set of agreed-upon assumptions. Any given set of norms or roles is then seen as one of many possibilities, so that the major requirement of normative definition becomes that of clarity and consistency.

Peck & Havighurst · *The Psychology of Character Development*

Robert F. Peck and Robert J. Havighurst, *The Psychology of Character Development*, Wiley & Sons, NY 1960, pp.3-8

Developmental Levels of Character: A Theory

In an attempt to answer the first question, 'What is character?', a set of five character types was defined, each conceived as the representative of a successful stage in the psychosocial development of the individual:

Character Type	Developmental Period
Amoral	Infancy
Expedient	Early Childhood
Conforming	
Irrational-Conscientious	Later Childhood
Rational-Altruistic	Adolescence and Adulthood

This set of character-types was intended to: (1) be defined and labeled in terms of the control system the individual uses to adapt his search for satisfaction to the requirements of the social world;

(2) include all the possible modes of adaptation; (3) be defined in terms of motivation (so long as it achieves behavioral expression); (4) represent both operational patterns of behavior, and the stage in psychosocial development to which each pattern presumably is most appropriate.

Since few people are so completely all of a piece that they have only one kind of motivation at all times, it is more accurate to think of the five motivation patterns, or 'character types,' as *components* of character. Indeed, that is the way they were treated throughout most of the research. However, for purposes of exposition, it is convenient to define them in terms of five pure 'ideal types.' This serves an additional purpose in thinking about the motivation patterns as an ascending developmental sequence, from childlike reasons to mature reasons for behaving morally. Consequently, while these five 'main motives' are henceforth treated as *components* of moral character, the term 'character type' is used in defining and discussing them.

The first 'pure' character type represents the absence of any self-imposed control, or any concern for adaptation to the moral requirements of social living. The last four represent the four kinds of reasons why a person may behave according to the moral standards of his society. (At least, it seemed that these four modes of adaptation to society covered the gamut; this may or may not hold true when other people have had an opportunity to reflect on the problem.) Names were selected for the types which would, as far as possible, indicate the chief dynamics operating in each. This becomes a little unwieldy at points, but it may have the virtue of conveying the central concept in quick, brief fashion.

The definition of each type was phrased in terms of a hypothetical individual whose character structure would be a 'pure' example of the type. Actually, one would expect to find only rarely a person who operated so exclusively in one way as to constitute a pure type. In practice, what was assessed was the relative proportion of each person's dynamic structure which belonged in each of the five type categories. It was found that one component often tended to predominate and make the person a reasonably clear-cut example of one particular character type. In every case, however, there always were some times when the person acted according to other type patterns.

Amoral

This type corresponds to what is often called clinically the 'psychopathic personality.' Such a person follows his whims and impulses, without regard for how this affects other people. He considers himself the center of the universe, and sees other people or objects as means to direct self-gratification. If his basic emotional attitudes are mainly hostile, he is apt to be found committing delinquent or criminal acts. If he has a positive, pleasant view of others, he is more apt to be known as 'charming but irresponsible.' He may form temporary alliances with people, but will abandon them the minute he sees a richer source of gratification.

He has no internalized moral principles, no conscience or superego. He feels no need to control his personal impulses, and exhibits no control. His impulses may or may not be actively *immoral*, antisocial, or destructive in intent; but in any case he disregards the moral connotations and consequences of his behavior.

In a real way, this is a picture of an infant, in its first year. Adults who show such a pattern are spoken of clinically as fixated at an infantile level. To the best of our knowledge, they act so because they have never learned to accept prohibitions or sanctions from others. The percentage of near-complete psychopaths in our society is probably small. More often, a tendency of this sort may be present to some degree, partially repressed or suppressed, within a person who is otherwise responsive to social demands.

Expedient

A person of this type is primarily self-centered, and considers other people's welfare and reactions only in order to gain his personal ends. He tends to get what he wants with a minimum of giving in return. He behaves in ways his society defines as moral, only so long as it suits his purpose. For instance, he may act in 'honest' ways to keep an advantageous reputation. If he can gain more by being dishonest, particularly if he can avoid detection and censure, he does so. He is not particularly concerned about other people's welfare, except as he may observe it in order to obtain their approval. Like the amoralist, he regards himself as the only person who is really important; but he is more aware of the advantage of conforming to social requirements in the short run, in order to achieve long-run advantages. Hence, his outward behavior may often be honest or responsible, in the main, as far as others can see. The key to his low-level morality is his 'me-first' attitude in a critical situation, where an unmoral act may bring advantages that outweigh any disapproval.

A clue to his basic motivation, despite any outward conformity to social patterns, is that in the long run he may be inconsistent in living up to moral principles. He may or may not have a well-organized, rational system of personal values, firm self-control, and realistic perception of how to get what he wants; but he has no internalized moral principles, no conscience or superego.

Such a motivation-behavior pattern is characteristic of many very young children, who have learned to respect the reward-punishment power of adults, and to behave correctly whenever an adult is around. External sanctions are always necessary, however, to guide and control their behavior, and keep it moral. In the absence of such controls, they immediately relapse into doing what they please, even if this involves shoving other children around, taking what they want or otherwise gratifying their self-centered desires.

Conforming

This kind of person has one general, internalized principle: to do what others do, and what they say one 'should' do. He wants to and does conform to all the rules of his group. He wants to do what others do, and his only anxiety is for possible disapproval.

The conformist is seen most often, perhaps, in stable folk societies. He learns, more by habit than by awareness of moral cause and effect, to behave in each specific situation in a certain prescribed way. He is kind and loyal to his family and tribe, because he is rewarded for acting in such a way on this occasion, punished for transgressing the rule on that occasion. He may learn that he should be polite and considerate of male relatives on his mother's side, but is freely permitted to insult and take advantage of men from his father's family. He has no generalized principles about being 'honest' toward everyone. He follows a system of literal rules, specific for each occasion, with no necessary overall consistency as to the degree of morality in different situations.

A convenient way to distinguish this type may be to ask whether the person feels bad when he breaks a rule, out of *shame* or *guilt*. We define shame as fear of disapproval by others. Thus, a person who acts morally because he would be ashamed if others found him violating the moral rules is controlling himself according to external sanctions: a violation is not wrong in itself, nor because of its effects, but because other people say it is wrong and their approval is at stake. This is a childlike attitude, uppermost in Piaget's heteronomous period, no doubt. It differs from the Expedient approach in that social conformity is accepted as good for its own sake. A Conformist may frequently ignore chances for personal advantage, if they require departure from the prescribed rules of conduct.

In a sense, such a person might be said to have a crude conscience, since he may feel very uncomfortable about departing from the rules. However, he does not follow them for a moral purpose, that is, because he is concerned about the effect of his behavior on other people. He defines 'right' as acting by the rules. If this sometimes hurts others, he feels no moral responsibility, no guilt. Further, he has no abstract principles of honesty, responsibility, loyalty, etc. The rules he lives by may call for kindness to some people, cruelty to others. This does not concern him.

This kind of pattern is visible in middle and late childhood. It may be an alternative solution to the problem of living in society, parallel with the Irrational-Conscientious kind of orientation. Both types ultimately spring from and depend on external rules and sanctions to make their behavior consonant with a code of morality.

Irrational-Conscientious

This is the person who judges a given act according to his own internal standard of right and wrong. In the adolescent or adult of this type, conformity to the group code is not the issue. Rather, it is conformity to a code he has internalized and believes in. If he approves of an act he sees as honest, he carries it out whether or not the people around him approve. He appeals to an abstract principle of honesty, applying it as he interprets it to any situation where it seems relevant. If he fails to live up to his own idea of what is moral, we call his anxiety 'guilt.' It is a feeling of having violated one's own integrity.

The irrational component is visible in the individual's customary rigidity in applying a preconceived principle, somewhat in the manner of the Conformist. An act is 'good' or 'bad' to him because he defines it as such, not necessarily because it has positive or negative effects on others. This is the 'blind,' rigid superego at work. It is characteristic of children who have accepted and internalized the parental rules, but who have not attained awareness that the rules are man-made and intended to serve a human, functional purpose. Consequently, they may be so rigidly 'moral' that they sometimes act to the detriment of others. This would seem to be an alternative form of childlike morality, occurring at the same developmental level as the Conforming type, and thus parallel with it as far as concerns any measure of the maturity of character development.

On the positive side, this may be reasonably effective in insuring outwardly moral behavior at all times. We assume this strong, blind conscience to be 'the heir of the parental superegos.' If the parents' code fits in well with a moral code which has been produced in the society by long, empirical testing of what is good for people, then it probably contains few seriously destructive elements. This would not be true, of course, of the Irrational-Conscientious child of a criminal subgroup in a society, if such a combination could exist.[18]

Peter McPhail · *The Motivation of Moral Behaviour*

Peter McPhail, 'The Motivation of Moral Behaviour', *Moral Education*, vol.2, no.2, Pergamon Press 1970, pp.99-106

In this paper I consider why individuals feel inclined, disposed, moved or impelled to treat others morally in the sense that they take others' feelings, interests and needs into consideration when acting. In more general terms I suggest some answers to the question 'What can incline an individual to adopt a considerate style of life?' The discussion is about causes – explanations for acting, and not about reasons – justifications for acting.

The problem of motivation is central to moral education because unless we know what motivates boys and girls to behave morally we cannot be sure of designing materials or approaches which will improve their treatment of other people. First, we must develop materials and approaches which make looking for answers to the question 'What ought I to do?' attractive, and second, the materials and approaches must themselves motivate schoolchildren to translate their autonomous answers into moral behaviour because they incorporate situations and stimuli which are known to dispose the children to treat people better. Many arguments about how to educate morally are really arguments about motivation. The familiar question 'Can morality survive without religion?' is of this kind. The questioner is asking 'Does religious belief provide an essential and unique kind of motivation for moral behaviour?' or, more moderately, 'Does religious belief provide stronger motivation for moral behaviour than that which can be gained in any other way?' While this paper is not primarily concerned with considering these questions I hope that it may encourage others to do so.

Failure to face the central motivational problem of moral education has at least three basic causes: first is the inability or reluctance to see that motivation is a problem; second is ignorance of the modern psychological work which has been done on human motivation; and third is the fact that there has not been a reputable large-scale study on children's and adolescents' motivation for behaving morally. Those doing research on moral development have tended to concentrate on moral concept formation and the arguments which children advance for saying that something is 'right' or 'wrong'; arguments which all too often have the air of being second-hand and imperfectly understood statements produced for the occasion. They tell us little or nothing about how the child feels like behaving, or is likely to behave.

It is easy not to recognise the motivational problems if, like many otherwise sophisticated people, you do not move from the 'just ought' kind of moral thought. When such people say that something 'ought' to be done they frequently assume that, if the moral reasoning leading to a decision about what should be done is sound, you, the listener, the rational man, will, because you are rational, be motivated to do whatever it is. However, even personal recognition that something ought to be done and the intellectual conviction that one ought to do it, do not necessarily provide most of us with the impetus to act in the approved way. All of us need help and practice to develop the ability to reason morally, to make sound moral judgements, to reach moral decisions, but in the last resort whether we act morally will depend on the extent to which we are motivated to do so – to put our judgement and decisions to work. The Pauline difficulty – 'The good that I would I do not but the evil which I would not that I do' is real and contemporary. Effective moral education must give people the power to do good – that is to say at least the power not to do evil and at best the cheerful inclination to behave morally. Let us therefore consider kinds of motivation for considerate action.

Most of us feel moved to treat people with consideration for their needs, interests and feelings when we like them, and a likeable person is one whom it is rewarding to be with. We like someone and feel moved to treat him with consideration when he gives certain verbal and non-verbal cues which we find rewarding in themselves, or interpret as indicating that having a relationship with him would be rewarding in some way, for example in confirming our self-image. We are social beings who need other people so that the basic motivation to like and be liked exists for the majority of us and can be used to increase our ability to understand others and to meet their needs as well as to make ourselves more attractive to them. It follows that we can regard the four abilities listed below either as being facets of a morality of communication, or as notes on what makes A attractive to B. It is an empirical fact that boys and girls like to develop these abilities and enjoy using material which helps them to do so.

The abilities are:

(1) *Reception Ability* meaning the ability to remain 'switched on' to the right wave-length, to listen, to look, to receive the message sent by others.

(2) *Interpretative Ability* meaning the ability to interpret correctly the message which another person is sending, what he really means, what he really wants.

(3) *Response Ability* meaning the ability to decide on and adopt appropriate reactions. It involves evaluation as well as psychological know-how.

(4) *Message Ability* meaning the ability to translate appropriate reactions into clearly transmitted unambivalent messages.

The study of these abilities provides almost infinite scope for the analysis, practice and discussion of interpersonal communication and it is worth stressing that the moral treatment of others involves not only motivation and decision but also the ability to communicate effectively. 'Do I really understand what "A" is saying?' and 'Do I give "A" the impression which I intend to give?' are key questions in this connexion.

The following diagram illustrates the situation where 'B' likes 'A' and is motivated to be considerate to him.

Most of us also feel moved to treat an individual with consideration when he has already treated us well by doing something for us. A similar diagram to that already used can illustrate this. The difference is that 'A' has actually said and done things which were rewarding to 'B' and were intended to be so. Whether two individuals feel moved to treat each other well depends to a consider-

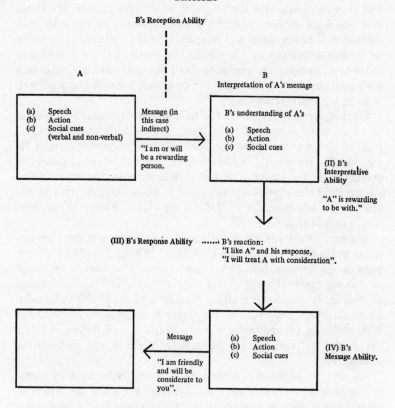

DIAGRAM

N.B. Initially A may say nothing and do very little, but by his appearance and animate presence give sufficient cues to convince B that he will be rewarding in interaction.

able extent on their mutual ability to get on the same wave-length, to receive and interpret accurately each other's messages. To relate effectively 'A' and 'B' should be able to handle each other's styles of interaction, which seems an obvious thing to say but which nevertheless has profound significance in moral education and for the treatment of a whole range of social problems including mental illness and prejudice.

Adolescents especially have to find out what 'works' socially and morally, what confers adult status, and therefore feel the need to make 'social experiments' – to try out various courses of action so that they can learn from the feedback which they receive. It follows that one form of motivation for treating another person with consideration is to see what will happen. It is true that the inclination to try out behaviour is not specifically moral, but on a trial and error basis persons are generally likely to settle for treating others with consideration rather than the converse, because the feedback is so much more rewarding.

Further, we may feel moved to behave morally towards someone in anticipation of general social approval but without the expectation of specific rewarding feedback from a particular person or persons. We learn early in life the kind of action which is generally commended, and commendation is pleasant. In the case of the young child the appeal for approval is naive, blatant, and if approval does not immediately follow, the child may cry in desperation 'Look how good I am!'

We may also be inclined to treat people with consideration because neglecting to do so has unpleasant results. Possibly we have been conditioned to fear punishment or to avoid hostile reactions so that we 'treat with kid gloves' any who are likely to be punitive or hostile. It of course matters morally and psychologically why we treat others well, but in this paper I am primarily concerned with outlining the causes of moral behaviour and prefer to leave the reader to consider for himself their value and dangers as implements.

We may be disposed to treat a person morally because by doing so, we have learned that we not only 'earn' his gratitude, which is pleasant, but also gain a measure of practical control over him. He owes us something, and we can to some extent decide how and when he will pay. Being an individual means being able to control, modify or influence one's environment. Where the means of exercising healthy control, meaning control which is neither hurtful to others nor immoderate to the extent that it denies the other's individuality – his opportunity to modify his environment – is denied to an individual or is inadequate due to perverse environmental influences, then that individual often seeks pathological control over others. The 'considerateness' of the neurotic is rare. When it is apparent it can almost invariably be understood as an attempt to curry favour with, and gain control over, some 'useful' person.

Perhaps a further word on pathological, abnormal feedback is in order here if only because it underlines the importance of the questions about reasons – justifications for acting with which we are not at present concerned. We feel moved to treat people with consideration when they reward us in our own way – not necessarily by treating us with consideration in the usually accepted sense. To take a sick example, the masochist may treat with 'consideration' the person who whips him. In a completely sick, masochistic relationship 'treating with consideration' might itself be interpreted by the participants as meaning whipping. Can we then make the evaluative comment that 'treating with consideration' ought to mean treating a person with respect for his 'true interest' as far as we can identify it? If we do so everything depends on the criteria of 'true interest' which we adopt. In practice, how we identify another's 'true interest' depends of course on what we as individuals are, including the state of our mental health. We can assert and argue, if not prove, that a person will benefit when we treat him in a particular way. What we have a moral obligation to do is to state our criteria of judgment, evaluate the evidence and keep the debate open. Few person-destructive identifications of 'true interest' survive such treatment.

Some motivation for treating others with consideration for their needs, interests and feelings is in part dependent on immediate feedback and in part on internal (though not necessarily innate) factors. A good example is provided by a dangerous rescue situation when 'A' shall we say, rescues 'B' from the sea. 'A' is a good swimmer but even for him what he is attempting is dangerous. Initially he may 'internally' feel the challenge and the excitement of the situation from the external-cues which he picks up. He feels the positive attraction of risk-taking, of mild fear, of which there is copious psychological evidence from experimental and field-study work. The sensations when he plunges into the sea may reinforce these feelings. 'A' may also have compassionate feelings towards the potential victim, feelings of affiliation, of identification even, which will be reinforced by interaction during and after the rescue. He may, or may not, enjoy the general approval of what he is doing, and finally, he may have thought that he ought to attempt rescue. The point which is most frequently missed when we discuss rescue operations is the internal one. Perhaps people are reluctant to accept that a life-boatman, for example, can in part be motivated by the positive attraction of danger because they do not feel so motivated themselves in that situation, or think that by suggesting such motivation they are detracting from the bravery of a courageous man.

Most of us will admit that 'atmosphere' is important and affects the way in which we behave towards one another. This applies to the atmosphere between people which is generated by interaction or lack of interaction. It also applies to the atmosphere which is created by the towns, the houses, we live in; the music we listen to, the pictures we look at, by all our aesthetic experiences. Our perception of the world around us is now well enough understood in terms of the cues which we receive, the physiological changes which follow experience, the feelings which accompany these changes and the influence of feelings on behaviour, on our treatment of others, for us to do far more to create an environment which facilitates treating others with consideration than we at present attempt. It is a fact that we tend to treat people better when we ourselves feel 'good'.

We may feel moved to treat another person with consideration because treating someone in this way confirms the picture we have of ourselves – our ideal self or ego-ideal. We are so motivated because we enjoy 'living with ourselves' when we behave in such a way: indeed we may only be able to accept ourselves if we do live in that way. In a sense the reward here is internal and would apply even if no one else were to know of our action, though it is often through interaction, from rewarding feedback, that individuals come to select an ideal model or hero as a self-image, and are first rewarded for behaving in the ideal's way.

Another form of motivation for moral behaviour, and even more particularly for launching an intellectual assault on a moral problem, is that which depends on the rewardingness of exercising intellectual ability. Intellectuals derive satisfaction from intellectual activity, from problem solving, from finding the best available solution, and sometimes even from applying it. This satisfaction is not divorced from ego-ideal motivation and again can be developed or strengthened in interaction. However, the important thing to note is that feeling moved can be the result of intellectual conviction. Indeed really believing that I ought to behave in a certain way is very likely to motivate me to some extent to behave in that way. 'Feeling moved' is not divorced from reason and the circularity of 'reason or belief – feeling reason or belief' – is well established. What we have to guard against is assuming:

(1) that such motivation will necessarily of itself give us enough drive to behave normally, and

(2) that everyone is capable of experiencing it.

People disagree about whether every man possesses an active conscience which motivates him to treat others with consideration by 'whispering' words of approval or disapproval about his proposed actions. Lancelot Gobbo claimed experience of such a 'voice' – 'My conscience hanging about the neck of my heart says to me . . .' but represented 'it' as carrying on a dialogue with a fiend who also advised him, sometimes the more persuasively. 'The fiend gives the more friendly counsel . . .' Freud 'gave' man a super-ego – a regulative prescriptive force – motivating him and controlling through a censor even the thoughts which were allowed to emerge into the conscious mind. During sleep the censor might, like Cerberus, fed on drugged cakes, become drowsy, though even then 'wicked' thoughts have to disguise themselves in order to flit past. Perhaps Freud's most valuable theoretical contribution in this area was to suggest that the super-ego (the conscience) is the product of a person's early upbringing so that its strictness or relative leniency can be explained with reference to social learning, albeit social learning which is almost exclusively ascribed to mother-child interaction. C. S. Lewis is one of those who claim that everyone has an active conscience which passes on God's advice and warnings, but it is hard to accept this in the face of people's varying statements about their divergent feelings on contemplating the same course of action. It appears most acceptable to think of 'conscience' as a product of early negative and positive conditioning and of being for many, but not for all, an important motivating force. The majority of people who talk about their experience of conscience stress its negative force of disapproval, its apparent dependence on Freudian taboos, which may be why Lancelot Gobbo thought conscience less persuasive than his fiend who offered a more positively attractive course of action. When a colonel was supposedly asked by his priest whether he entertained wicked thoughts he replied: 'No, but by Jove, they entertain me!' – a sad comment on our morality – so often negative and exclusively sexual. Conscience may not make cowards of us all but many suffer its pangs.

It is often argued that we treat another person with consideration because we feel 'natural love' or affection for him, and early in this paper I suggested that the social being man needs other people so that the basic motivation to like and be liked exists. The tendency to feel 'natural love' certainly seems widespread in man and not always to depend on the ability of the other person to respond, though affection for other people is neither equally distributed amongst the population nor in any society equally applied to all others. Without considering the factors relevant to the development of hostility or prejudice one can say that adults generally feel moved to help the young, the helpless and the 'beautiful'. They may not feel the same way about foreigners or some other group. There is, I believe, a distinction between this 'natural love' and liking a particular person which was discussed earlier in that the love, the affection, is dependent in a much more general way on the cues which other people give, less on the cues which a particular individual gives and which may indicate that to have more to do with him will be rewarding. To give an example, including animals other than man, young creatures give cues such as a round appearance and an uncertain gait which give rise to considerate or at least non-aggressive behaviour in adults. (One cannot however take this example as expressing a general truth. For instance, individual lesser black backed gulls also need cues from chicks which mark them out as their own chicks before they will feed them rather than eat them.) The works of Kropotkin and others nevertheless suggests that amongst the more intelligent species, animals tend to help others of the same species. Healthy rats have been seen to help old, blind rats, leading them by the ear. Amongst chimpanzees there is a tendency to help strangers, the diseased and the old, at least when they approach as supplicants. There is a danger which results from this line of thought, namely that we may assume that it is instinctive to help others, that it is a universal tendency or disposition in man. Helping others, even amongst animals other than man, need not be the result of a drive (if this term has any value) but rather of social learning. The key question is 'What do people learn to do in our society?'

We sometimes talk as if religious motivation for moral action were *sui generis* when in fact it includes a variety of elements. Certain of these elements are specifically religious in origin, others are not. For example, both religious and non-religious people may treat others with consideration in the attempt to imitate the behaviour of an ideal person, hero or model. Such a model provides an ego-ideal for those who follow him – his followers feel moved or impelled to act as he acted or acts. The uniqueness and power of the Christ model to motivate presumably lies not only in Christ's performances as a man, but also in his influence as the accepted 'son of God' – a specifically religious idea. To behave like someone you greatly admire is highly rewarding and motivates for further action. To behave like Christ has for his followers exceptional motivational power because it means for them behaving in accord with the absolute, eternal standard which gives feelings of achievement and security and the hope of salvation not only in this world but also in the next – another specifically religious idea. During some periods in the Church's history, fear of eternal punishment for unchristlike behaviour has been a strong motivating force, again a specifically religious idea dependent on the belief in personal immortality. It is of course true that following earthly leaders or models sometimes has mystical and religious elements. The followers may accept the leader as an absolute authority, they may be willing to suffer and to die for him, for their 'saviour'. Many of Hitler's supporters were in this position. Leaders frequently promise both that their followers will be rewarded and that their enemies will be punished, in which case the followers will only be selectively motivated to treat others with consideration. The danger of accepting a leader is that you may accept the 'wrong' one. Further, even the Christian who, most would admit, has taken a 'good' ideal is not absolved from thinking about the right course of action. Christ provided an example of the way in which his followers should relate to people, of how to treat individuals as ends in themselves. What he did not do was to give to those who follow him specific solutions to the moral problems which they face today and many of which did not exist in Palestine in the first century A.D. All I am really saying here is that motivation is not enough. Though the 'style' of a 'good' man who is highly motivating will reduce to a minimum the number of moral calculations which he has to make, the more complicated the moral problem or dilemma the more he will have to rely on reason, on moral calculation for its solution. Taking a leader is often more a matter of emotional need than of reason, so that men accept leadership which meets their current deficiency, for example the opportunity to be violent regardless of the consequences for others. There is evidence that old style hero-worship is in decline amongst young people and that a less idealistic identification with boys and girls from their own background who have been highly successful both materially and in imposing their image on the public has taken its place. Either way, identification makes adolescents feel less lonely in a complex, impersonal and sometimes frightening world; but the dangers are obvious, especially for moral education because individuals without moral education, may also be directed at changing society.

A brief consideration of charity, Christian love or *agape* highlights two points which are of importance in the debate about the uniqueness or special strength of religious motivation. Agape is a way of treating people rather than a way of feeling about them. Nevertheless it has its emotive aspect. First the Christian claims he is 'moved' by the 'spirit' of Christ because Christ is, in Christian terminology, 'in him' meaning that he is moved in the same way as Christ, by feeling as Christ. Is this close identification rather than imitation a uniquely religious experience? Second, the Christian asserts that he is filled with wonder by the 'fact of Christ' (and perhaps also by the world which God has created) so that he realizes that the will of God for the world is Jesus Christ and that *agape* is the whole godly trend of things, the only way in which life will work, will make sense. Is this 'wonder' a specifically religious feeling?

Finally I would like to make five points which seem to emerge from a consideration of the motivation for moral behaviour. First, feeling is no substitute for reasoning; but reasoning, without feeling disposed to do something about it, is only of academic value. Effective moral education must therefore motivate, must incorporate what we know about motivation in its methods. Second, feeling and reason are not necessarily in conflict – I can be morally educated by my emotions, I simply must not assume that I will be. The fact that what is in my interest is generally in others' interest helps, but does not absolve me from applying the test of reason. Third, there is no reason by rejecting natural self-benefit motivation in moral education to make our task more difficult. Fourth, it is unlikely that the motivation for moral action is ever unitary; we should accept a variety of motives. Fifth, there is every hope for improving personal morality if we are also devoted to improving society. In a healthy society the motivation to treat others with consideration for their needs, interests and feelings far outweighs that to be hostile to others. Habit is a great, perhaps the greatest, motivational force. If we educate children in the considerate style of life they will be considerate even to those who are not considerate to them – the habit will be very hard to break.

H. J. Eysenck · *Crime and Personality*

H. J. Eysenck, *Crime and Personality*, Routledge & Kegan Paul 1964, pp.105-110 and Houghton Mifflin Company, Mass.

We may illustrate the way in which we consider conditioning to work in the production of a conscience by looking briefly at a very famous experiment carried out by Professor J. B. Watson, one of the originators of the behaviourist school of psychological thought shortly after the first World War. He was concerned not with criminal behaviour but rather with the genesis of neurotic disorders, particularly the unreasoning fears or phobias which are so frequently found in neurotics. His hypothesis was that these neurotic fears are essentially conditioned fear reactions and he attempted to demonstrate it in the following manner. He selected a boy eleven months of age, called Albert; little Albert was particularly fond of white rats and often played with them. Watson tried in inculcate in Albert a pathological fear of rats. He proceeded to do this by standing behind Albert with a metal bar in one hand and a hammer in the other. Whenever Albert reached out for the rats to play with them, Watson would hit the bar with the hammer. In this situation, the rat constitutes the conditioned stimulus, very much as the bell does in Pavlov's experiments with the salivating dogs; the very loud noise produced by the hammer striking the bar constitutes the unconditioned stimulus which produces a reaction of fear, withdrawal, whimpering and crying. By always associating the conditioned and the unconditioned stimulus over a given period of time, Watson argued that in due course he would produce a fear reaction to the conditioned stimulus when presented alone. This is precisely what happened. He found that after a few pairings of the two stimuli Albert would begin to cringe when the rats were introduced, would try to crawl away, cry, and show all the signs of a strong fear of these animals. This fear response persisted for a long period of time and even extended, as we would have expected it to, on the principle of stimulus generalisation discussed earlier, to other furry objects, such as rabbits and a teddy bear. Thus Watson showed that, through a simple process of Pavlovian conditioning, he could produce a strong phobic reaction in little Albert. Before we go on to show how

Albert's phobic reaction may be extinguished, let us see for the moment how much light this experiment sheds on the possible growth of a conscience.

Consider the case of the very young child. He has to learn a great number of different things, by means of trial-and-error. As we have pointed out before, there is no real difficulty in accounting for this, because all correct responses tend to be rewarded immediately and incorrect ones, not being rewarded, will tend to drop out; gradually his performance will improve, and he will learn whatever he wishes to. But there are also many other behaviour patterns which he has to acquire, not so much because he wants to, but because society insists that he should. He has to keep clean, he has to learn to use the toilet, he has to refrain from overt aggressive and sexual impulses, and so on. The list of these socially required activities is almost endless. Clearly, learning, as defined earlier, does not come into this very much, because the child is not usually rewarded for carrying out these activities: quite the contrary. He is rewarded, in a sense, for not carrying them out, because in that case carrying them out is what he wishes to do. If somebody annoys him, he wants to punch him in the nose; if he feels like it, he wants to defecate and urinate wherever he happens to be without interrupting his game to go to the toilet. In other words, reinforcement follows immediately upon his disregard of these social mores, the patterns of behaviour which are desirable from the point of view of society. How, then, can the individual ever become socialised?

Suppose now that our little boy misbehaves. Immediately his mother will give him a smack, or stand him in the corner, or send him off to his room, or inflict one of the many punishments which have become customary with parents over the centuries. In this case, the particular asocial or antisocial activity in which he has been indulging is immediately followed by a strong, pain-producing stimulus and we have exactly the same situation as we had in the case of little Albert. The conditioned stimulus is a particular kind of activity in which the child has been indulging; the unconditioned stimulus is the slap, or whatever constitutes the punishment in this case, and the response is the pain and fear produced in the young child. By analogy with the experience of little Albert, we would expect conditioning to take place, so that from then on this particular type of activity would be followed by a conditioned fear response. After a few repetitions, this fear response should be sufficiently strong to keep the child from indulging in that type of activity again, just as little Albert was prevented from indulging in his customary play with the white rats.

There are, of course, many such activities which are punished; exactly the same situation hardly ever recurs twice. Nevertheless, we would expect a fairly general reaction of fear and autonomic 'unpleasure' to become associated with all antisocial activities, because of the process of stimulus generalisation which we have referred to so many times before. In fact, stimulus generalisation would be expected to be enhanced considerably by the process of 'naming', which parents usually indulge in. Every time the little child misbehaves, its misbehaviour is labelled 'bad', 'naughty', 'wicked', or whatever the term chosen by the parents might be. Through this verbal labelling the child is helped in the generalisation process and finally groups all these activities together by association as being potentially dangerous, punishment-producing, and particularly as being productive of conditioned anxiety and fear responses. Thus our little child grows up, gradually acquiring a repertoire of conditioned fear responses to a wide set of different behaviour patterns, all of which have one thing in common – that they are disapproved of by parents and teachers, siblings and peers, and that they have, in the past, frequently been associated with punishment and, therefore, with the consequent autonomic upheaval.

What will happen when the child is in a situation where temptation is strong to do one of these forbidden things? The answer is, of course, that he will tend to go and do it. But as he approaches the object arousing the temptation, there should also be a strong upsurge of the conditioned emotional reaction, the fear or anxiety which has become conditioned to his approach to such an object under such circumstances. The strength of this fear-anxiety reaction should be sufficient to deter him from pursuing his antisocial activities any further. If it is indeed strong enough, then he will desist; if it is not, he will carry on, in spite of the increasing strength of the fear-anxiety response. It will be seen, therefore, that whether he does or does not behave in a socially approved manner depends essentially on the strength of the temptation and on the strength of the conditioned avoidance reaction which has been built into him, as it were, through a process of training or conditioning.

Some people doubt whether autonomic reactions of this kind

can indeed be strong enough to have this effect. The empirical evidence suggests that autonomic reactions of anxiety and fear are very powerful indeed. It is well known that many neurotics suffering from anxiety, from phobic fears, and from reactive depression, all of which are conditioned responses of this type, prefer to commit suicide rather than go on living with these fears and anxieties. There is little doubt, therefore, that they are very strong deterrents and that they possess to the full the strength needed to fulfill their hypothetical function in our scheme. Other critics feel that, while this may be true of some special groups of people who happen to be suffering from neurotic disorders, a normal person does not have these conditioned reactions. This also is untrue, as can be shown by experiments in the laboratory. Here let me appeal, for the sake of illustration, to a very simple game which can be bought in most British toyshops. The game is called 'Contraband' and it consists of a number of cards on which are shown pictures of cameras, jewels, watches, and other precious articles, as well as the monetary value of these articles. Every player is dealt a number of these cards and one player is appointed as the Customs Inspector. The essence of the game is that each person hands on to the next person one card, and that he has to declare the value of this card to the Customs Inspector. The Inspector can accept the declaration or, if he suspects that the declaration is under-valued, he can demand to see the card. If the card has been correctly declared, the Customs official is penalised; if it has been incorrectly declared, the player who has made the declaration is penalised. It pays the player, when handing over a valuable card, to declare something less valuable, and, of course, the Customs official must be on the alert and try to detect this.

There is clearly nothing immoral or illegal about declaring the wrong value for a card; in fact, the whole game is built on the principle that the players should try to do this. However, most people, having been brought up to regard lying, cheating and trickery as being bad, find it extremely difficult to adopt a different point of view in respect to this game. There is one card in particular, the Crown Jewels, the most valuable of all, which is almost never correctly declared because it would cost the player too much. Yet very few people indeed are able to remain calm and give the wrong declaration for the Crown Jewels. The majority blush, stammer, look away from the Customs official, and in other ways betray the autonomic upheaval caused in them by this playful lying.

Most people will know that trying to smuggle something through the Customs in earnest gives rise to even greater autonomic upheavals, and indeed, most people will be familiar, from their ordinary life experiences, with the anxiety and fear reactions occasioned by behaviour which, while not strictly illegal, is counter to the mores of the society and to the rules by which the individual has been brought up. It so happens that I was brought up in a country where the cutting of potatoes with a knife is discouraged. Even now, when I live in a country where it is quite the customary thing to do, I still feel a slight pang of guilt and anxiety whenever I cut a potato with a knife. This is the lasting effect of early conditioning!

Anecdotal accounts of this kind clearly have no scientific value. However, instead of relying on simple observation of the autonomic effect, let us substitute some electronic recording device, a polygraph, say, which records the electrical conductivity of the skin, heart rate, pulse, blood volume, breathing, and other autonomic reactions. Let us now ask a given individual a number of questions and instruct him to lie in some of his answers. Will it be possible to discriminate the lie responses from the true responses by simply looking at the pattern of autonomic reaction? The answer is that it can be done and, indeed, this is the basis of the 'lie-detector'. Though not infallible, this device tends to give the right answer, at least nine times out of ten, when used by a skilled practitioner. It tends to fail – when it does fail at all – because an individual gets away with a lie because he does not react emotionally to it, so that no particularly suspicious record is obtained of his autonomic behaviour. This is often the case with psychopaths and other individuals who, according to our hypothesis, would be precisely the ones in whom conditioning of the social responses has not yet taken place. There is a good deal of evidence of this kind to suggest that autonomic responses, conditioned according to ordinary Pavlovian conditioning, form the basis of what we would normally call our conscience. Conscience is indeed a conditioned reflex!

11 · The Tasks of the School and the Teacher

Schools and teachers are not, of course, the only agencies concerned with moral education. Parents exercise considerable moral influence within the family and it has sometimes been argued that the family is the proper source of moral education rather than the school. This argument was considered by Emile Durkheim in his classic work on moral education published in 1925.[1] He certainly agreed that moral education started in the family, but he saw this as having severe limitations and leaving much for the school still to do:

> By virtue of its natural warmth, the family setting is especially likely to give birth to the first altruistic inclinations, the first feelings of solidarity; but the morality practiced in this setting is above all a matter of emotion and sentiment. The abstract idea of duty is less important here than sympathy, than the spontaneous impulses of the heart.
>
> ... But meanwhile the child must learn respect for the rule; he must learn to do his duty because it is his duty, because he feels obliged to do so even though the task may not seem an easy one. Such an apprenticeship, which can only be quite incomplete in the family, must devolve upon the school.[2]

Although modern writers on moral education might not agree with Durkheim's specification of the tasks, they would nevertheless agree with the argument that the school does have important work to do in moral education, a view that seems shared by teachers, parents and the pupils themselves.[3] An important development of the early 1970s is that specific practical guidance about moral education in schools is beginning to appear again. Not the over-confident and non-evidential assertions of the early college manuals, but carefully researched proposals by people who have themselves engaged in philosophical and empirical investigations *before* venturing their practical guidance.

We shall consider, for example, proposals for practical work in schools from the Schools Council Project in Moral Education;[4] the materials and strategy of the Schools Council Humanities Project, which whilst not overtly a moral education project will undoubtedly contribute much to the development of the skills and attitudes needed to be moral;[5] a book on *Practical Methods of Moral Education* by the Director of the Farmington Trust Research Unit;[6] and an interesting and unusual account of an actual classroom experiment in moral education.[7] Each of these is difficult to characterize and illustrate by means of extracts and we shall, instead, describe this work briefly in what follows. Two extracts from other sources are included to make two specific points and to remind readers of the range of diverse activities that is being considered.

Firstly we show John Wilson's preliminary listing of matters of context and content that appear relevant to moral education. Notice here the width and range of teaching and social management shown by such a list. Properly considered moral education is a large and complex task, and Wilson reminds us admirably of this.

Secondly we include an excerpt from Archambault's interesting paper, partly because of his emphasis on moral education as to do with the development of a certain kind of understanding and which fails if such understanding is not achieved; and partly because of his reminder that certain aspects of a normal intellectual curriculum like history, literature and science, can all be seen with a moral dimension. In the case of literature and history we can see that the very imaginative skill necessary to make sense of such studies is also the skill necessary to understand other people, which we need to do in order to be moral. The connection is thus plain. One is less convinced about the transferability of the integrity held to be necessary for science. We might agree that science *should* be taught with concern for the human consequences of scientific and technical innovation, but that is not quite the same thing.

The Schools Council Moral Education Project materials became available in 1972. They include a substantial book, *Moral Education in the Secondary School*, and a programme of materials for use in schools under the headings: In other people's shoes, Proving the rule?, and What would you have done? Another book, *Our School*, discusses the nature of democracy and the problems connected with introducing democratic organization into secondary schools. There is also excellent advice about how to develop the work in further directions. The basic book outlines the philosophy and approach of the project team, some of which we have already encountered in earlier chapters, and gives direct and practical suggestions for the use of the materials. There is little doubt that this is a major contribution to moral education, blending sound and sensible theory with direct and down-to-earth advice and guidance. It should perhaps be emphasized that the materials are not merely a series of school textbooks, but rather stimulus materials that need very active pupil and teacher participation in discussion, role-playing, dramatic work and other activities. It should also be noted, by contrast with the other Schools Council Project to be discussed, that the Moral Education Project does not expect teachers to be neutral, though they do say that 'a teacher should not inhibit discovery by saying too much, too soon, too often.'[8]

The Schools Council *Humanities* Project (it is important not to confuse these very different projects) was directed by Lawrence Stenhouse and published its materials and guidebook in 1970. The material is produced to help pupils discuss controversial issues and to increase their understanding of such issues. Since the topics are heavily value-laden, like War and Society, Education, or Sex and the Family, it is apparent that moral debate will frequently enter into the work. The Project advocates a distinctive strategy in that the teaching is expected to proceed in discussion groups with the teacher adopting the role of a neutral chairman, the role specifically rejected by the Moral Education Project. Unlike Mcphail, Stenhouse believes that the understanding of the pupil will be best advanced if the teacher deliberately withholds his own opinions regarding the controversial issues under discussion. The intention is that the pupil will not be influenced by views backed by the authority of the teacher, but will be helped by the teacher to develop his own powers of thought and enquiry. In so far as we are hoping to develop autonomous moral thinking the intention is clearly commendable. Whether 'neutrality' is the best label for the procedural technique is perhaps questionable. Nevertheless, again we have here a direct technique, backed by a distinctive philosophy and research, and also supported by extensive materials, guides and training programmes. It must be repeated that the Project team makes no claims that this is a moral education project. However, if it is successful in helping pupils towards autonomous, rational and imaginative choices of belief and action it will go far in the direction set by the ideals and objectives of our earlier chapters.

John Wilson has been insistent that there must be a great deal of preliminary work of an empirical and philosophical kind before practical advice can be given that will be anything more than mere opinion. In his book *Practical Methods of Moral Education*, he claims to 'use an already established set of aims, clearly stated and broken down into as much detail as possible, on which to base a consideration of certain methods which are in effect logically required by these aims.'⁹ The aims and objectives are those we have already shown in an earlier chapter, and Wilson derives from these four broad areas which form the four main parts of his book: Moral Thinking, Language and Communication, Rules and Contracts, and The School Community. Although in each of these four cases many practical suggestions are made, the author is always at great pains to show *why* the particular suggestion is of importance and how it is logically necessitated by a conception of what it is to be moral. For example, in the part of the book concerned with language and communication there is an extremely helpful section on discussion methods of teaching. Wilson rightly sees discussion as vitally necessary to the development of children's rational thought and therefore something to be treated with system and care: 'it is too important for the development of rationality in general (not just morality) to be left in a muddle.'¹⁰

What Wilson prescribes for discussion is somewhat similar to the suggestions of the Humanities Project, but with a rather more flexible strategy. Long lists of suggestions are given for rules and procedures, with very concrete advice on methods of developing the required skills and attitudes in pupils. Indeed, all four parts of the book have this blend of the justificatory and the practical which one hopes will characterize all writing on moral education in the 1970s and thereafter.

A. J. Grainger's work in a Leicestershire High School differs from other work and advice discussed here because it is an exception to the general point made earlier about the indirect influence of Freudian and Neo-Freudian thought on moral education.

Grainger says of his own work: 'I have drawn freely on Freudians (and Neo-Freudians) and Jungians, and also on some psycho-analytic writers who will not be pigeon-holed.'

In his book *The Bullring*, Grainger does not prescribe or advise, but describes what he did, why he did it and what seemed to come out of it. The Bullring is a kind of free-discussion lesson in which pupils sit with the teacher in a ring facing one another. The participants are free to say what they like, the name 'Bullring' being the nickname given by pupils to the process whereby a speaker and the person spoken to were exposed and alone like the matador and the bull. There is, however, a task as well as free-dom. The task is for pupils to study their own behaviour as it occurs, and the teacher's specific task is to help the pupils to do this. The rationale stems from the work of the Tavistock Institute of Human Relations and in particular to the work of W. R. Bion.[11] It is important to notice that the group does not meet to study or work at any other problem than that of their own be-haviour. The teacher draws on his own experiences of depth-psychology and his own experience of group-dynamics to help give interpretations of children's behaviour. All this is fully illustrated with many dialogues and descriptions.

In one chapter Grainger relates what he does to the outlined components of morality as suggested by Wilson. The work of the Bullring seems to contribute substantially to the development of PHIL and EMP, but perhaps its major importance lies in the fact that a quite different approach to education, formerly only used with adults, has made an effective appearance in schools. The work of group dynamics is brought together with the insights of depth psychology in a practical, though by no means easy, tech-nique.

Collectively this work on practical moral education in the schools is impressive and exciting. There is little excuse for any teacher genuinely seeking guidance not being able to find advice about what to do which is informed, intelligent and grounded in bases that are carefully researched. This is not to say, of course, that all the work is done. We still need a great deal more research: into the methodology of the various aspects of moral education, into the social arrangements in schools that are most conducive to moral development, and into the most appropriate ways of assessing the success of moral education. There are difficult problems attached to the quantification of the kind of objectives we are concerned about in moral education, yet it would seem important, now that there is growing consensus about what we are after, that we should in some way be able to measure our achievements in this field of education as in others.

Wilson, Williams & Sugarman · *Introduction to Moral Education*

John Wilson, Norman Williams and Barry Sugarman, *Introduction to Moral Education*, Penguin Books, 1967, pp.409-413. Copyright © The Farmington Trust 1967

Some Practical Suggestions

1. CONTEXT

(i) Making sure that the concept of moral education is properly understood, and that the task of moral education is responsibly undertaken.

(ii) Making whatever basic arrangements are necessary to bring the pupils into communication with the educators.

(iii) Making sure that the 'ground rules' of the institution are (*a*) based on the right *sort* of criteria (even if there is uncertainty about the facts), and

(*b*) firmly enforced.

(iv) Making the rules, and the point of the rules, as clear as possible to the pupils.

(v) Giving the pupils some degree of self-government, and establishing close communication in rule-making and rule-following.

(vi) Decentralizing the institution to produce psychologically viable groups (e.g. a house system): basing the groups on factors that genuinely unite (e.g., perhaps, eating together, entertaining other groups, and other group activities which are significant to the children), without producing an artificial or illiberal community.

(vii) Providing outlets for aggression, both in the 'letting off steam' sense (e.g. enough violent open-air activities) and in the 'challenging authority' sense (e.g. matches against the staff), that are unsophisticated enough to fit even the most primitive pupils (some kind of controlled fighting game, snowballing, battles in the swimming-bath, etc.).

(viii) Providing contexts which will significantly occupy the institution as a whole (e.g. some construction enterprise, mass camping or exploring, dancing, singing, etc.).

(ix) Arranging the criteria of success in the institution, insofar as some competition is inevitable (and perhaps desirable), so that everyone succeeds in something and acquires some prestige and self confidence thereby.

(x) Arranging that there is some one person (e.g. the headmaster) who acts as the ultimate authority (at least in a psychological sense, so far as the children are concerned); and who is actually on the premises, and visibly concerned with the day-to-day running of the school.

(xi) Making the significant teaching unit a small group, with the same 'teacher' or adult group-leader, perhaps over a period of years, with whom the pupils can form a close personal relationship: and fitting 'specialist' or subject-teaching as far as possible into this framework.

(xii) Compensating for the increased man-hours (necessitated by smaller groups) by giving the children more free time, by using mass communication (e.g. closed-circuit TV) for factual information, by providing other contexts in which large numbers can be handled together (e.g. large-scale games, gymnastics, etc.), and by making more use of older children to supervise and help the younger.

2. CONTENT

(i) Understanding of concepts and meaning: this (in an elementary form) involves the notion of 'philosophy' and is designed to produce awareness and mastery of different language uses.

(ii) Understanding of the general concepts, and of the basic facts, of psychology and the social sciences, perhaps particularly anthropology.

(iii) Mastery of other facts relevant to the prevailing morality of the child's society: e.g. the law, the system of government, the economic system, the 'professional ethics' attaching to certain jobs, etc.

(iv) The use of other subjects, perhaps particularly history and literature, designed to increase awareness of other people in society, to reinforce and correlate with (ii) and (iii) above.

(v) Activities designed to objectify moral or psychological problems: e.g. mime, drama, 'acting out' various roles (the bully, the cheat, the practical joker, and so forth), controlled 'group therapy sessions in which family and other problems are discussed overtly, discussions of particular case histories of other people (taken from books, films or elsewhere).

(vi) Using 'psychological documentary' films and tape-recordings, with subsequent discussion to objectify the pupil's own problems.

(vii) Teaching the child to talk clearly, describe, dispute and acquire other language-using skills.

(viii) Using music and the arts, as relevant to the way in which emotions are objectified.

(ix) 'Religious education' used as a method of obtaining insight and a sane outlook on life as a whole.

(x) Various kinds of games, designed to clarify the concept of rule-following, the point, purpose and mutability of rules, the notion of *contracting for* certain rules, etc.

(xi) The use of 'games', in the sense of microcosmic controlled social situations, acted out for special purposes under specific rules (e.g. the children act out a 'democracy', a 'dictatorship', etc.): the teaching of particular concepts by means of these games (equality, honesty, duty, justice and so on).

(xii) Teaching related to practical living, e.g. on sex, marriage, infant care, driving cars, dress and cosmetics, the use of money, etc.

(xiii) Opportunities to 'patronize' and feel needed, i.e. to be responsible for and of service to younger children, old people, the poor, the lonely, animals, etc.

(xiv) Use of practical 'order-and-command' contexts, to see the point of discipline relevant to particular situations (e.g. in sailing, mountaineering, building and other operations with highly specific goals).

The implications of this sort of approach for some other fields are tolerably obvious. Thus, it would suggest that the selection of teachers should be on the basis of personality-type rather than academic qualifications or social image: that they should be trained more in such fields as philosophy, psychology and the social sciences: that they should have some kind of personality-training in the form of group therapy, and in general be fitted to use the methods outlined in (1) and (2) above. Similarly, one might suggest also that the excessive *mobility* of teachers made it difficult for any effective or long-standing relationships to be formed with the children, and that there was a case for encouraging teachers to remain in one place for a tolerably long period (rather like house-masters at boarding schools having a longish tenure). There are other implications for the importance of parent-teacher relation-ships, the concept of teachers who are also social workers, the architecture and topographical arrangements and location of schools, and many other things.

A general question arises here about how far one can expect to formalize, or 'institutionalize', the desiderata which some of these suggestions aim to incorporate. For instance, we may talk about the importance of letting adolescents criticize their schools and teachers: we might hypothesize that, if they are not allowed to do this openly, they will tend to cause trouble in other ('worse') ways instead. So we might recommend, say, that criticisms of this kind should be allowed in school magazines. But now, suppose the teachers dutifully allow this, yet are psychologically unable to handle it: suppose they get very angry, break off communication with the adolescents who use the magazine in this way, and so on. Have we really achieved anything?

No doubt it would be ideally desirable first to select and train teachers who are psychologically adequate to handle this and other such suggestions, and only then to implement them: otherwise we may get no more than an empty form, or an institution which does not do the job it is supposed to do. Sometimes one might even think that premature institutionalization may make matters worse (rather like introducing full democracy into a very backward society). But, on the other side, it is also possible that the acceptance of the institution by teachers means that teachers will be able to learn, from the existence of the institution, how to handle it and react appropriately to it. A good deal of research and trial-and-error is required here.

This point shows, however, the crucial importance of the first stage of moral education: namely, that teachers, and others should understand the *general aims* which lie behind the suggestions. If they can understand and accept them, then there is some reason for hoping that they will at least try to handle them properly; and even if they fail, they will know that they have failed and that it is their fault (rather than blame someone else). What we require, there-fore, is *intelligent acceptance* on the part of teachers and other educators. This is a very different matter from insisting on a new selection and training process for teachers, which might itself take a great many years to formalize: and in any case, much of the training would be directed towards producing the kind of intelligent acceptance I am talking about.

Reginald D. Archambault · *Criteria for Success in Moral Instruction*

Reginald D. Archambault, 'Criteria for Success in Moral Instruction', *Harvard Educational Review*, 33, no.4 (Fall 1963), pp.474-481

It is thus that we arrive at the crucial question as to whether the responsibility of the school is to strive for success in the attainment of moral conduct on the part of its students. The answer to this, is, I believe, a qualified 'yes.' ... The more interesting question is the extent of this responsibility and precisely how this responsibility is to be fulfilled. Is it necessary to convert the school into a microcosm of society as the progressives would suggest, so that moral conduct in the school mirrors that in the 'world outside'? Must we have direct moral training such as we find in religious schools?

In order to answer these questions we must be clear as to what we mean by 'moral conduct', so that we can see what would be involved in achieving it. Moral conduct does not consist merely in acting in accordance with a norm. Such behavior may come about through compulsion or force, or may be performed automatically. To be properly considered moral, conduct must entail a 'reflective and impartial support of norms.'[12] This involves, then, four factors, jointly sufficient to entail moral conduct: (*a*) belief in a norm; (*b*) a tendency and capacity to offer a rationale supporting the norm; (*c*) a disinterested or impartial application of judgment concerning the norm; and (*d*) a tendency and capacity to act in accordance with the norm. As teachers engaged in moral instruction we may strive to achieve any of these objectives. The manner in which we attempt to achieve them would probably differ in each case because of what is entailed by the objective itself. Nevertheless, as I have already suggested, we would be properly considered to be engaged in moral instruction at any of the levels listed. The crucial point is that if we aim to achieve moral conduct (*d*) as a result of our instruction, *all* of the above objectives must be met. Can this be accomplished within the framework of the school? Should it be?

I have suggested that striving for moral conduct is a qualified aim of the school. The school's responsibility is not to insure moral conduct, for such insurance is impossible. The school hopes that the student will achieve various kinds and degrees of understanding, but it does not insure understanding. Rather, it makes available the means by which understanding can be acquired by presenting data, principles, and techniques to students, and testing for their success in learning these. It teaches for knowledge that promotes understanding. One of the conditions necessary for success in understanding rests with the pupil. We do not speak of failure in getting students to understand as a failure in teaching, unless our lesson has for some reason been incomplete. When we have offered a reasonable opportunity to the student to achieve understanding and he fails to do so, we attribute the failure to the pupil rather than to the instructor. Hence we say that we *promote* understanding rather than *teach* understanding. In this case we assume that understanding will be a by-product of our instruction. We try to make ourselves knowledgeable about those subsidiary learnings that are most conducive to the promotion of understanding and then proceed to teach and test for them. ... The final success in achieving understanding rests with the learner rather than the teacher. ... This, after all, is not surprising, for education, properly conceived, is concerned with the development of the freedom of the learner. It can be distinguished from training in that it involves unpredictable responses at the end of the teaching interval. In order to achieve this aim it is necessary to encourage independence in the learner, and with this independence, responsibility for final learning outcomes. This is what makes the process educative. We promote not only understanding, but freedom as well.

The promotion of moral conduct is analogous in some respects to the promotion of understanding. We cannot teach understanding. Nor can we 'teach' moral conduct if we construe it in sense (*d*) above. What we can do is to promote moral conduct by providing the means by which students can arrive at beliefs, defend them, demonstrate a commitment to them, and develop a method for criticizing them.

If we seriously set about to promote understanding in the pupil, we are reasonably specific about the types of understanding we wish to promote. We then choose a set of rules, techniques, and principles which will be most conducive to the promotion of that understanding, and teach directly for them. For the teacher this necessitates a ruthless process of choosing and specifying objectives of instruction, and then formulating means by which these objectives can be most efficiently attained. When testing for the attainment of them, our tests must be specific and must deal with the subject matter chosen for instruction. If our teaching has been successful, learning will have taken place. The knowledge derived will pertain not only to the specific subject matter used as a means of attaining knowledge, but to analogous situations as well. We assume that there will be a transfer of learning to other situations. If such transfer were not possible we would need to start afresh every time we taught anything.

In promoting moral conduct our task is similar. We aim at the acquisition of certain principles, skills and dispositions, but we are definitely limited, for example, in the number of rules and principles that can be taught, and in the scope of skills we can teach for specifically and directly. Here again we must assume a transfer in knowledge of principles, and skills, to wider areas of experience analogous to those taught for specifically in the teaching interval.

In promoting moral conduct, then, we are concerned with achieving objectives conducive to its attainment. Chiefly, these objectives are a knowledge of moral principles, a commitment to certain of them, and the ability and tendency reflectively to support moral convictions objectively arrived at. We have suggested that the true indicator of the objectives of moral instruction is the test that is given to determine its success or failure. How then would we test for the achievement of these objectives? We could do so by getting our students to present defensible moral positions and to indicate their convictions on ethical issues. We could teach for these objectives by presenting problems for apprehension and solution. Are we then not open to the charge that the attainment of these objectives, as measured by the tests we have designed, yields evidence only of intellectual apprehension of norms, and that we have not really striven for the attainment of those objectives that will promote moral conduct? We are presenting problems for intellectual apprehension and solution, but the *manner* in which these problems are studied and solved, and the manner in which norms are criticized, represent moral activity of a significant kind. If the student is involved in an active formulation, critique, and defense of norms, he is engaged in moral activity. Moral instruction thus construed aims at (*a*) intellectual commitment to norms; (*b*) reflection and criticism of norms held; (*c*) inculcation and promotion of a method of objective criticism and evaluation which in itself represents an important form of moral activity. Developing skill in scientific method involves the use of rules of evidence and procedure. Historical analysis involves considerable honesty in scholarship. The teacher of literature deals constantly with the understanding and resolution of moral problems.

These points suggest two implications. The first is that the process of reflecting on and criticizing norms is in itself moral activity, even though it takes place intellectually. The second is that in moral instruction, as in all other instruction, we assume that there will be a great deal of transfer (intellectual, to be sure) from the limited area of instruction to a wider range of situations in present and later life. In these important aspects moral instruction is analogous to instruction in other areas.

At this point we can postulate a notion of responsibility for the school in moral instruction. It should not aim directly for the attainment of moral conduct except insofar as the conduct can be taught for in the intellectual curriculum. (It is also necessary, of course, to *train* the child in practical moral matters.) But that curriculum is pregnant with possibilities for moral instruction. Indeed, it might be argued that the successful teaching of history, literature, and science necessitates the reflection on, discussion of, and criticism of moral issues in an objective and impartial fashion.

Thus we see that successful intellectual instruction often involves moral instruction, and that the successful attainment of the objectives of intellectual instruction entails the attainment of skills, attitudes, and commitments that are essential to the acquisition of moral conduct. Specifically, this entails getting the student to arrive at a position on issues that are moral, justifying that position, and demonstrating consistency in its application to other moral issues.

This indicates the manner in which moral instruction can take place, as well as the limits of the school's responsibility for it. The school should not directly strive to achieve aims that promote moral conduct except insofar as this is possible and feasible within the bounds of normal intellectual curriculum study. But as we have seen this gives a considerable responsibility to the school for developing habits, skills, and sensitivities that are conducive to moral conduct. If the student later fails to exercise these capacities in which success has been demonstrated, we must then attribute this to a failure of the will rather than a failure of instruction.

Perhaps the principal point to be made here is that the dichotomy suggested by the distinction between 'intellectual' and 'moral' instruction is not necessarily valid. As several recent writers have pointed out, the *manner* in which the process of instruction is carried out is a crucial factor in developing moral sensitivity, even in the supposedly 'morally neutral' field of science. Demonstrated success in the techniques and procedures of valid investigation and conclusion in these disciplines does represent a form of *moral* activity, behavior which will hopefully transfer to wider areas of moral experience. It is, in an important sense, a training of the *will*.

Notes

CHAPTER 1

1. F. H. Hilliard, *The Teacher and Religion*, James Clarke 1963, ch.1, makes this clear.

2. Schools Council Working Paper 36, *Religious Education in Secondary Schools*, Evans/Methuen 1971. The project materials are published by Rupert Hart-Davis. J. R. Hinnells, *Comparative Religion in Education*, Oriel Press 1969.

3. Ronald Goldman, *Religious Thinking from Childhood to Adolescence*, Routledge & Kegan Paul 1964; Harold Loukes, *Teenage Religion*, 1961 and *New Ground in Christian Education*, 1965, both SCM Press.

4. *Half our Future*, HMSO 1963.

5. This phase in American religious education receives brief treatment in Robert Ulich, *A History of Religious Education*, University of London Press 1968. A more extensive discussion is contained in J. D. Butler, *Religious Education*, Harper & Row, NY 1962.

6. OUP 1966.

7. Kenneth Hyde, *Religious Learning in Adolescence*, Oliver & Boyd 1965 and *Religion and Slow Learners*, SCM Press 1969; Colin Alves, *Religion and the Secondary School*, SCM Press 1968.

8. For instance, the accuracy of the description 'pluralist' frequently applied to the religious situation in Britain by writers on religious education, or the significance for religious education of 'residual religion'. On this latter phenomenon in a German context see J. Freytag and K. Osaki, *Nominal Christianity*, Lutterworth Press 1970.

9. Joseph A. Jungmann, *Handing on the Faith*, Burns & Oates 1957, is a seminal work on the catechetical movement. Luis Erdozain, 'The Evolution of Catechetics', *Lumen Vitae*, XXV, no.1, 1970, provides a useful survey of the international scene in catechetics. Erdozain discerns a 'political' phase, where the emphasis is upon contemporary political and social concerns, replacing earlier 'kerygmatic' and 'anthropological' phases of the movement. Gabriel Moran, *Design for Religion*, Search Press 1971, shows some signs of Erdozain's 'political' phase.

10. *The Recruitment, Employment and Training of Teachers of Religious Education*, British Council of Churches 1971.

11. For a Roman Catholic view see *Lumen Vitae*, XXV, no.4, 1970, on 'Catechesis as the Interpretation of Experience'.

12. Discussion of the inclusive/exclusive options in relation to the definitional problem in religion will be found in Roland Robertson, *The Sociological Interpretation of Religion*, Blackwell 1970, ch.3.

CHAPTER 2

1. M. Cruickshank, *Church and State in English Education*, Macmillan 1963, is the standard work. Two useful brief accounts which together cover the period 1870–1944 are to be found in the *British Journal of Educational Studies*: vol.XII, no.2, 1964, C. Channon, 'The Influence of Religion on Educational Policy 1902–1944', vol.XVIII, no.2, 1970, N. J. Richards, 'Religious Controversy and the School Boards 1870–1902'.

2. There is now a sizeable literature on 'indoctrination'. Apart from the appendix to the Durham Report to which reference is made in the text, other convenient points of entry are I. A. Snook, *Indoctrination and Education* and *Concepts of Indoctrination*, ed. I. A. Snook, both Routledge & Kegan Paul 1972.

3. *Realms of Meaning*, p.244.

4. Paul Hirst, 'Liberal Education and the Nature of Knowledge', *Philosophical Analysis and Education*, ed. R. D. Archambault, Routledge & Kegan Paul 1965.

5. For an application of Phenix's ideas in the construction of a specimen programme for secondary education see *Disciplines of the Curriculum*, ed. R. C. Whitfield, McGraw Hill 1971, chs 1 and 17. A different view (from a sociological perspective) of the integrative function of religion as a 'symbolic universe' will be found in P. L. Berger and T. Luckmann, *The Social Construction of Reality*, Penguin Books 1971.

6. G. W. Allport, *The Individual and his Religion*, Constable 1951, p.59.

7. Ibid., p.60.

8. Edwin Cox, *Changing Aims in Religious Education*, Routledge & Kegan Paul 1966, p.61.

9. D. J. O'Connor, *An Introduction to the Philosophy of Education*, Routledge & Kegan Paul 1957, p.125.

10. R. S. Peters in *Philosophical Analysis and Education*, ed. R. D. Archambault, Routledge & Kegan Paul 1965, p.107.

11. Ibid., p.110.

CHAPTER 3

1. T. S. Eliot, *The Idea of a Christian Society*, Faber 1939. Eliot's

thesis is examined and compared with the views of Coleridge and Maritain in H. J. Blackham, *Religion in a Modern Society*, Constable 1966, ch.4.

2. Spencer Leeson, *Christian Education*, Longman 1947, p.194.

3. Schools Council, *Enquiry 1: Young School Leavers*, HMSO 1968.

4. J. W. D. Smith, *Psychology and Religion in Early Childhood*, SCM Press 1936; revised edition 1953.

5. R. F. Dearden, ' "Needs" in Education', *British Journal of Educational Studies*, vol.XIV, no.3, 1966.

6. H. R. Hamilton, *The Religious Needs of Children in Care*, National Children's Home 1963; Douglas Hubery, *Teaching the Christian Faith Today*, Newgate Press 1965.

7. William Blake, *The Everlasting Gospel*.

8. In *Religion without Revelation*.

9. Quoted from Sten Rohde. See pp.68-74 of the present work.

10. Philip H. Phenix, *Religion and Public Order*, University of Chicago Press 1965, p.108.

11. J. F. Kerr, *Changing the Curriculum*, University of London Press 1968, p.22.

CHAPTER 4

1. Joan Dean, *Religious Education for Children*, Ward Lock Educational 1971, takes a broadly similar view of the primary stage and the Schools Council Working Paper 44, *Religious Education in Primary Schools*, Evans/Methuen 1972, is a useful survey of religious education in a sample of more than 200 county primary schools.

2. More extended treatments based upon these principles may be found in Dorothy M. Berridge, *Growing to Maturity*, Burns & Oates 1969, and (in relation to the secondary stage) Derek Lance, *Till Christ be Formed*, Darton Longman & Todd 1964.

3. Ed. Ian H. Birnie, SCM Press 1972.

4. Colin Alves, SCM Press 1968.

5. Now out of print. A revision is in preparation, for publication in 1974.

6. Paul Tillich, *Theology of Culture*, OUP, NY 1959, p.157.

7. Ronald Goldman, *Readiness for Religion*, Routledge & Kegan Paul 1965, p.65.

8. Ibid., p.69.

9. Ibid., p.140.

CHAPTER 5

1. H. F. Mathews drew attention to some interconnections in his *Revolution in Religious Education*, Religious Education Press 1966.

2. See, for example, the concluding pages of Ronald Goldman's *Readiness for Religion*, Routledge & Kegan Paul 1965; Elizabeth Kinniburgh, 'Religious Education – an attempt at a theological ap-

praisal', *Scottish Journal of Theology*, vol.23, no.2, 1970, offers some theological comments on the classroom materials which Goldman edited.

3. A restatement of this kind is offered in John Wren-Lewis, *What Shall We Tell The Children?*, Constable 1971.

4. Barth's essay on Schleiermacher (particularly section III) in his *Protestant Theology in the Nineteenth Century*, SCM Press 1972, is also relevant.

5. Colin Alves, *The Christian in Education*, SCM Press 1972. A brief consideration of this question will also be found in section XIII of the Working Paper 36.

6. Fr. Marie, 'El fin de la catequesis', in *Sinite*, II, 1961, pp.60-61.

7. Karl Rahner, 'The Prospects for Dogmatic Theology', in *Theological Investigations*, I, p.7.

8. Karl Rahner, 'Über die Wahrhaftigkeit', in *Katechetische Blätter*, LXXXV, September 1960, p.414.

CHAPTER 6

1. Harold Loukes draws attention to some examples of this assumption in ch. 2 of *New Ground in Christian Education*.

2. See, for example, P. R. May and O. R. Johnston, *Religion in Our Schools*, Hodder & Stoughton 1968, pp.40-42.

3. D. Tribe, *Religion and Ethics in Schools*, National Secular Society 1965.

4. Examples of joint work on the question by Christians and Humanists include: James Hemming and Howard Marratt, *Humanism and Christianity: the Common Ground of Moral Education*, published from Borough Road College, 1969, and *Moral and Religious Education in County Schools*, Social Morality Council 1970. See also *Prospects and Problems for Religious Education*, HMSO 1971, ch.2.

5. 'Declaration on Christian Education', *The Documents of Vatican II*, ed. W. M. Abbott, Geoffrey Chapman 1967, p.643.

6. The debate is to be seen very clearly and thoroughly in *Christian Ethics and Contemporary Philosophy*, ed. Ian T. Ramsey, SCM Press 1966. See also R. F. Atkinson, *Conduct: An Introduction to Moral Philosophy*, Macmillan 1969, ch.7.

7. P. H. Hirst, 'Morals, Religion and the Maintained Schools', first published in *British Journal of Educational Studies*, vol.XIV, no.1, 1965; reprinted in *Let's Teach Them Right*, ed. Christopher Macy, Pemberton Books 1969. For a critique of Hirst's views see D. Z. Phillips, 'Philosophy and Religious Education', *British Journal of Educational Studies*, vol.XVIII, no.1, 1970.

8. For a similar, but brief, discussion see Norman Bull, *Moral Education*, Routledge & Kegan Paul 1969, pp.137-139.

9. J. S. Mill, *Three Essays on Religion*, Longman 1874.

10. Reported in the *Durham Research Review*, March-April 1967. A

summary is given in P. R. May, 'Why Parents want Religion in School', *Learning for Living*, March 1967.

11. R. F. Atkinson, *Conduct: An Introduction to Moral Philosophy*, Macmillan 1969, p.107.

12. *Religious and Moral Education*, Blackfriars Press 1965, p.3.

13. In *Christian Ethics and Contemporary Philosophy*, ed. Ian T. Ramsey, SCM Press 1966.

14. G. E. Moore, *Principia Ethica*, CUP 1903, ch.1.

CHAPTER 7

1. W. K. C. Guthrie, *The Sophists*, CUP 1971, p.25 and ch.X.

2. Schools Council, *Enquiry 1: Young School Leavers*, HMSO 1968.

3. Jean Piaget, *The Moral Judgment of the Child*, Routledge & Kegan Paul 1932.

4. Much of this work is conveniently surveyed in William Kay, *Moral Development*, Allen & Unwin 1968, and in Derek Wright, *The Psychology of Moral Behaviour*, Penguin Books 1971.

5. Examples of the manuals we mean are: John MacCunn, *The Making of Character*, CUP 1903, and Edward Eyles, *Character Training*, Harrap 1912, an English version of the book of the same title by Ella Lyman Cabot of the USA.

6. The materials are published for the Schools Council by Longmans.

7. Those unfamiliar with this fascinating history might start with A. C. MacIntyre, *A Short History of Ethics*, Collier-Macmillan 1966.

CHAPTER 8

1. William Kay, *Moral Development*, Allen & Unwin 1968, p.241.

2. There is a full discussion of this in R. S. Downie and Elizabeth Telfer, *Respect for Persons*, Allen & Unwin 1969.

3. For an introduction to the moral philosophy of Kant see H. B. Acton, *Kant's Moral Philosophy*, Macmillan 1971.

4. J. A. Hadfield, *Psychology and Morals*, Methuen 1964.

CHAPTER 9

1. Peter McPhail, 'The Moral Education Curriculum Project', *Let's Teach Them Right*, ed. Christopher Macy, Pemberton Books 1969, p.135.

2. John Wilson has tried to show how this might be done in his book *Moral Education and the Curriculum*, Pergamon Press 1969.

3. For references to the literature on indoctrination see note 2 to ch.2.

4. 'Habit' has been an influential idea in moral education ever since

the time of Aristotle. For a discussion of this see R. S. Peters, 'Reason and Habit: the Paradox of Moral Education', *Moral Education in a Changing Society*, ed. W. R. Niblett, Faber 1963. The edition of Aristotle's *Ethics* mentioned in the Norman Bull extract is the translation by A. K. Thompson, Penguin Books 1953.

5. See R. S. Peters, 'Moral education and the psychology of character', *Philosophy*, vol.XXXVII, no.139, January 1962. See also the classic study of character in H. Hartshorne, M. A. May and J. B. Maller, *Studies in the Nature of Character*, The Macmillan Co., NY 1929-30 (3 vols.) and Derek Wright, *The Psychology of Moral Behaviour*, Penguin Books 1971, ch.9.

6. A convenient account of Freudian concepts and their development is to be found in J. A. C. Brown, *Freud and the Post Freudians*, Penguin Books 1961.

7. Erik H. Erikson, *Childhood and Society*, Penguin Books 1965 and W. W. Norton and Company, NY 1950.

8. Bruno Bettelheim, *Love is Not Enough*, The Free Press, Glencoe, Illinois 1950.

9. Fritz Redl and David Wineman, *Controls From Within*, The Free Press, Glencoe, Illinois 1952.

CHAPTER 10

1. See E. M. Eppel, 'Moral Beliefs of Young Workers', *British Journal of Sociology*, vol.14, 1963 and 'The Adolescent and Changing Moral Standards', *Moral Education in a Changing Society*, ed. W. R. Niblett, Faber 1963; Schools Council, *Enquiry 1: Young School Leavers*, HMSO 1968.

2. John Wilson, Norman Williams and Barry Sugarman, *Introduction to Moral Education*, Penguin Books 1967, p.311.

3. See, for example, the references given by Sugarman in *Introduction to Moral Education*; but see also papers by Sugarman and by Martin Shipman in early issues of *Moral Education*, a journal originally published by Pergamon Press, which has now been replaced by *The Journal of Moral Education* published by Pemberton Books.

4. Extensive reviews of recent research can be found in: Martin F. Hoffman, 'Moral Development', *Carmichael's Manual of Child Psychology*, ed. Paul H. Mussen, vol.2, John Wiley, 3rd ed., NY 1970; Lawrence Kohlberg, 'Moral Development and Identification', *Child Psychology*, ed. Harold W. Stevenson, University of Chicago Press 1963.

5. For Erikson see Erik H. Erikson, *Childhood and Society*, Penguin Books 1965 and *Insight and Responsibility*, Faber 1966. For Fromm see Erich Fromm, *The Sane Society*, Routledge & Kegan Paul 1956, especially ch. 3.

6. See, for example, 'Development of moral character and moral ideology', *Review of Child Development Research*, ed. M. L. Hoffman and L. W. Hoffman, vol.1, Russell Sage Foundation, NY 1964 and

'Moral Education and the Schools', *School Review*, 74, 1-30, 1966.

7. The views of H. J. Eysenck are developed in 'The development of moral values in children' and 'The contribution of learning theory', *British Journal of Educational Psychology*, vol.XXX, part 1, February 1960, and more fully in *Crime and Personality*, Routledge & Kegan Paul 1964. The views of B. F. Skinner are spelled out most fully in *Science and Human Behaviour*, Macmillan, NY 1953.

8. Actually, Piaget had previously made it a point to master the rules of this game, including all local variations, so as to spot any breaches in the rules as they occurred.

9. All references are to Jean Piaget, *The Moral Judgment of the Child*, Routledge & Kegan Paul 1932.

10. Piaget also sees an intrinsic connection between morality and thought *per se*, apart from the developmental parallelism, e.g., 'Logic is the morality of thought just as morality is the logic of action' (op. cit., p.404).

11. Omitted material is mainly illustrative.

12. W. McDougal, *An Introduction to Social Psychology*, Methuen 1905.

13. The means in figure 1 for age 7 are based on only 12 boys and a limited number of responses per child, compared to the older group.

14. The reference is to a story about a druggist who sold a rare cancer-curing drug at extortionate profit, and of a husband who stole the drug to save his dying wife.

15. Lawrence Kohlberg, art. cit. (see note 4).

16. It is historically true that all philosophic formulations of moral principles, such as those just mentioned, are variations of a basic prescription to take the role of all others involved in the moral situations.

17. B. Inhelder and J. Piaget, *The Growth of Logical Thinking*, Basic Books, NY 1958.

18. The fifth level of Peck and Havighurst's sequence, the Rational-Altruistic, is described in earlier extracts given in chapters 8 and 9.

CHAPTER 11

1. Emile Durkheim, *Moral Education*, The Free Press of Glencoe 1961.

2. Ibid., pp.147-148.

3. See the Schools Council *Enquiry One*, HMSO 1970. See also the enquiries described in Philip R. May, *Moral Education in School*, Methuen Educational 1971.

4. Peter McPhail, J. R. Ungoed-Thomas and Hilary Chapman, *Moral Education in the Secondary School*, Longmans 1972, and other materials published by Longmans in the 'Lifeline' series.

5. Schools Council/Nuffield Foundation, *The Humanities Project: An Introduction*, Heinemann Educational Books 1970.

6. John Wilson, *Practical Methods of Moral Education*, Heinemann Educational Books 1972.

7. A. J. Grainger, *The Bullring*, Pergamon Press 1970.

8. Peter McPhail et. al., op. cit., p.91.

9. John Wilson, op. cit., p.viii.

10. Ibid., pp.45-54.

11. W. R. Bion, *Experiences in Groups*, Tavistock Publications 1961.

12. I. Scheffler, *The Language of Education*, Blackwell 1960, pp.94-95.

Index of Subjects

Index of Names

N.E. pp. 1 à 14 pliée

ECHEANCE   DAT

I